The Bounce

ALSO BY G. RICHARD MCKELVEY
FROM MCFARLAND

*The MacPhails: Baseball's First
Family of the Front Office* (2000)

*Fisk's Homer, Willie's Catch and the
Shot Heard Round the World* (1998)

The Bounce

Baseball Teams' Great Falls and Comebacks

G. RICHARD McKELVEY

McFarland & Company, Inc., Publishers
Jefferson, North Carolina, and London

Library of Congress Cataloguing-in-Publication Data

McKelvey, G. Richard, 1935–
    The bounce : baseball teams' great falls and comebacks /
G. Richard McKelvey.
       p.   cm.
    Includes index.
    ISBN 0-7864-0955-X (softcover : 50# alkaline paper) ∞
    1. Baseball—United States—History.   2. Baseball teams—
United States—History. I. Title.
GV875.A1M33   2001
796.357'0973—dc21   2001030248

British Library Cataloguing data are available

Manufactured in the United States of America

*McFarland & Company, Inc., Publishers
  Box 611, Jefferson, North Carolina 28640
  www.mcfarlandpub.com*

Table of Contents

Table of Contents

Introduction

Baseball has given fans of the game many memorable moments. Some have come when a dramatic home run altered the course of a game or, on some occasions, the course of a season.

Defensive gems have accorded some players the special status of heroes; ghastly miscues have turned others into goats.

These events burn images of pleasant or painful memories in the minds of those who witnessed them. They become the objects wistfully recalled, the last, best answer to "Where were you when...?"

Other powerful and lasting memories came as a result of following a team for a season, a decade, or a lifetime. You climbed the peaks of the team's successes or sank to the depths of despair with the disappointments. There were those seasons when a team accomplished the unexpected and won, and there were many more when they failed, their play turning cool as October approached.

But even as their hopes flag, fans recall the 1914 Miracle Boston Braves or the 1969 Amazin' New York Mets, both clubs mounting thrilling late-season comebacks and capturing World Championships.

There were other teams that went the other way, of course. Fate rewarded the 1964 Phillies and 1969 Cubs, late-season leaders both, with only disappointment and pain. Their followers suffered through the precipitate declines and live with the emptiness of a near miss.

In three different decades, I have suffered along with others when three of my teams were each headed for glory and met defeat and disappointment along the way. On one of those occasions the fall was broken before bottom was reached; the other two times the teams dropped out of the race for the postseason and missed their quest for long-awaited world championships.

1

In 1950, as a youngster, I was living in Wilmington, Delaware, and rooting for the Phillies, who played their games in Shibe Park, about one hour north of my hometown. On a few occasions I made the special trip there to see the major leaguers play.

And though the lights of nearby Philadelphia glowed just beyond the outskirts of my hometown, my affection for the Phillies was no tepid fondness, born of regional loyalty. No, I belonged to the Whiz Kids much the same way that my elders belonged to Roosevelt—that is, altogether and without question. Wilmington was the home of the Blue Rocks, the Phillies' Class-B club in the Interstate League. Two of the Whiz Kids' prized pitchers had played their only season of minor league ball with the Blue Rocks— left-hander Curt Simmons in 1947 and right-hander Robin Roberts for a brief period in 1948. As they racked up wins for the parent Philadelphia team in 1950, I fondly remembered watching each of them go to the mound and star for my "Rocks" during their days in Wilmington Park. They had made it to the Bigs, and, in a sense, I had gone along with them.

The Phillies, who entered September with a seven-game lead over the Braves, suffered a brief decline and dropped to a 1½ length advantage. As I held my breath, they began to recover, and by September 19, they held what appeared to be a comfortable 7½ game cushion with two weeks remaining in the regular season.

But then, after hitting a stretch during which they went 3–9, some began to call the Whiz Kids the "Fizz Kids." While the Phils were losing ground, the Brooklyn Dodgers passed the Boston Braves to move into second place on the strength of a 13–3 streak.

The Phillies were one game ahead as they faced the Dodgers in Ebbets Field on the final afternoon of the season. A Philadelphia win would put them in the World Series against the New York Yankees; a loss would create a tie between the two clubs and necessitate a playoff for the National League crown.

I was relieved and overjoyed when Dick Sisler's home run in the 10th inning sent the Whiz Kids to the World Series. My team had done it!

By 1964, I had moved to a suburb outside Philadelphia. The Phillies were on a roll again and looked good enough to win not only the National League bunting for the third time in their long history but maybe—just maybe—good enough even to win the World Series for the first time since 1915, when Grover Cleveland Alexander pitched the team to glory. With any luck, Jim Bunning, Chris Short and others would now lead them to the promised land and accomplish what they had not been able to do 14 years earlier when the Yankees swept them in four well-played and hard-fought games.

As in 1950, I had my ties to the club. Dallas Green, one of the Phils' 1964 pitchers, had played varsity baseball and basketball with me in college. He had made it to the Bigs and I was pulling for him. I had taken the same field with Short, too. Years earlier, in 1952, Short was a 15-year-old ace pitching against my American Legion team in the Delaware state finals. We beat him that day. In 1964 I was following his successful major league career and cheering for him every time he took the mound.

But this Phillies team, too, would find itself skidding when it might have coasted. The difference: in 1950 the club had recovered just in time; in 1964 there was no recovery.

The Phillies broke quickly from the gate, winning 10 of their first 12 games, and that momentum had them at the top of the league or close to it through the first half of the campaign. On July 16 they took over first place, where they remained until September 27.

They had built a 6½ game lead over the St. Louis Cardinals and the Cincinnati Reds with only 12 games left to play. The postseason seemed all but assured.

The Phillies' fatal decline began on September 21 when the Reds' Chico Ruiz stole home for the game's only run. Each game thereafter seemed only a new frame in the team's slow motion free-fall: we dropped out of first, through second, and into third place coming to rest squarely— and with what seemed the weight of purpose—on the hopes of fans. At one point they went 0–7 during a homestand that set the scene for one of the game's greatest collapses.

After the season was over and the Cardinals had won the World Series, I invited Green to come and speak at a breakfast gathering for fathers and sons. Dallas was bombarded by questions from the disappointed audience, all of whom wanted to know what happened. He did not have the answer, but he obviously recognized the confusion and pain that all of us had brought to the table that morning.

In 1978 I was living in the western part of Massachusetts and had changed my primary allegiance to the Boston Red Sox, who were in need of almost as much support as the Phillies. The Red Sox had last won the World Series in 1918, and, after that the so-called "Curse of the Bambino" had prevented them from raising the championship flag again. In 1975 they had played in one of the most exciting Fall Classics of all time, but had ended up losing to the Reds, 4–3. Perhaps 1978 would be the year when the Old Towne Team would begin a new, winning tradition.

I didn't have a personal connection with any of the Boston players, but the Red Sox tradition—both good and bad—had become part of my baseball world.

In 1978 the Red Sox were on a roll which had me and other long-suffering fans dreaming of the postseason and a Fall Classic crown. Behind Dennis Eckersley's pitching and Jim Rice's jaw-dropping offensive production, the stars seemed aligned for wondrous things.

Near the end of June, Boston was 9½ games in front of the Yankees, who were bogged down by the clubhouse squabbles that had come to the surface the preceding year. Their fate would change later in the campaign when Bob Lemon replaced Billy Martin as the club's manager, and improved relations between the players replaced the challenges, innuendoes and accusations on the field and off of it.

By August, the Red Sox had lengthened their lead to 14 games. It was then, of course, that their famed swoon began. While the Yankees were putting together an impressive run, Boston was stumbling in almost every aspect of their game. Soon their lead had fallen to 6½ games, which was comfortable but far from secure—at least for the Bosox.

The [Second] Boston Massacre took place in early September in—of all places—Fenway Park. During that four-game series, the environs were friendly to only the Bronx Bombers, who blasted the Red Sox by scores of 15–3, 13–2, 7–0 and 7–4. Just when it looked like Boston was down for the count, they made a strong recovery and ended up catching the New Yorkers on the final day of the campaign to create a tie for the American League flag.

Hope was still alive. My spirits and those of many around me were buoyed. Perhaps the comeback Bosox would defeat the Yanks in a one-game playoff and be in the race for the long haul to the world championship.

But it was not to be, as any New England-variety stoic will glumly say. Bucky Dent's three-run homer in the seventh inning off Mike Torrez gave the Yankees a 3–2 lead which they went on to lengthen to 5–2 on their way to a 5–4 victory. All joy and expectation left me the moment Dent's high fly ball passed over Fenway Park's fabled Green Monster. Hope was defeated that day, and the horrible moment has been replayed in my mind and in the minds of others over and over again.

But this kind of comedown—and its ecstatic twin, the comeback—is unique to baseball. No other sport is as deliberate in disentangling the great from the near-great and the merely good. Over the six months of the regular season, teams that daily prove their mettle give us little reason to believe in surprises; they teach us that the difference between winning and losing lies in the habits you fall into. The steady set the pace, while the erratic—though they be brilliant—fall out of step.

And so surprise endings stay with us. Their improbability draws us back to the game, even while the players, and the stadiums, and the teams we love grow unfamiliar. They represent a kind of reasonable hope for even the most pragmatic or cynical among us, and they're what make baseball worth talking about.

1. 1903 New York Giants

Coming Back and Taking the
First Steps Toward a Dynasty

The 1902 New York Giants had three different managers during the season: John McGraw replaced George "Heinie" Smith, who earlier in the campaign had taken over for Horace Fogel. A long stay at skipper didn't seem likely. McGraw, however, hung on for 30 seasons in the Polo Grounds, and his Giants would finish first or second an astounding 21 times.

It was a strange set of circumstances which brought McGraw to New York. He had been the player-manager of the National League's Baltimore Orioles in 1899 and, when the team disbanded the following season, he went on to play third base for the St. Louis Cardinals. He was back in Baltimore in 1901, at the helm of the city's team during the American League's first season, and at the start of the 1902 campaign he seemed entrenched at the Orioles skipper.

Ban Johnson, the founder and president on the American League, admired McGraw and felt he was a good choice to lead the fledgling Orioles, but the two soon had a falling out when it became clear that on at least one issue they were diametrically opposed: Johnson was a staunch backer of the umpires in the league; McGraw had a tendency to fight them, both verbally and physically. The fiery McGraw, in fact, was known to instruct his pitchers to spit at an umpire when questionable calls went against the defense.

John T. Brush, owner of the National League's Cincinnati Reds, bought the Baltimore club during the 1902 season and then released McGraw and several key players, who signed with National League clubs.

McGraw had invested $7,000 of his own money to help defray Oriole debts. In exchange for the loan, he was granted his release from the Orioles, and he, too, returned to the Senior Circuit.

Five of the released players ended up with the Giants. Along with McGraw came third baseman Roger Bresnahan, first baseman Don McGann, and pitchers Jack Cronin and Joe McGinnity. McGinnity had been the first American Leaguer signed to a contract when he joined the Orioles in 1901.

Brush sold both the Reds and the Orioles following the season, as luck would have it, and he then purchased the Giants.

The versatile Bresnahan played outfield, catcher, first base, shortstop, and third base with New York after joining them during the 1902 campaign. He caught, played first base, and the outfield in 1903. McGann, a seven-year veteran, was hitting .316 when he left the Orioles and hit .300 during his partial season in the Polo Grounds. Cronin went 3–5 with Baltimore before his release and had a 5–6 mark with the Giants. McGinnity had put together 28–18, 28–8, and 26–20 records from 1899 to 1901, which were his first three major league seasons. He was with the Orioles in his rookie year and played for Brooklyn in 1900 when Baltimore was without a club. He went 13–10 with the Orioles in 1902 and then was 8–8 with the Giants to register his fourth consecutive 20-win season.

After joining the Polo Grounders in 1902, McGraw led his new club to 25 wins, 38 losses and two ties. The Giants finished with their worst-ever record, 48-88, and ended up an unfathomable 53½ games behind the pennant-winning Pittsburg Pirates.

That was New York's final year under the ownership of Tammany Hall politician Andrew Freeman. He had purchased the club after the 1894 season when the second-place Giants swept Baltimore in four games to capture their third National League championship. During the abrasive Freeman's eight years of inept leadership, the Giants averaged only 64 wins per season.

On April 15, rain washed out the 1903 National League openers in Philadelphia and St. Louis. A full schedule of games was on tap for the following afternoon, but rain was anticipated in the New York area and threatened to postpone the Giants' first game, a mid-afternoon contest against the Brooklyn Superbas in the Polo Grounds. According to the *New York Times*, elaborate plans had been made for the area's opener:

> The management of the local club has sent out an enormous number of invitations, and Gov. Odell is expected to be present to throw the ball from the grand stand. A band concert by the Seventh Regiment Band will begin at

2:30 o'clock, and the parade of the New York and Brooklyn teams will take place an hour later. The spectators will then be afforded an opportunity of getting a line on the respective merits of the rival teams in the warming-up practice, in which the players will indulge for half an hour, and at 4 o'clock Umpire [Henry] O'Day will start the teams in their long race for the pennant.[1]

Rain fell on the Polo Grounds, and the ceremonial first pitch was not delivered until the next day. Over 20,000 fans were in attendance as New York dropped its opener, 9–7. Their ace, Christy Mathewson, who had gone 20–17 and 13–18 for the beleaguered Giants the previous two seasons, was unusually wild, walking five Superbas and giving up nine hits.

Both teams scored four times in the opening frame. New York's George Browne dropped an easy fly ball during the Superbas' first at-bat, but he atoned for his error by slamming a home run as Brooklyn's lead-off hitter in the bottom of the inning. The Superbas' Jack Doyle and the Giants' Billy Lauder led the way, contributing three hits for his club.

McGinnity pitched the Polo Grounders to their first win in the club's second game. Doyle's single in the seventh inning was the only hit surrendered by the Giants' right-hander in New York's 6–1 victory.

After two regular-season games, the Giants had an exhibition on their schedule. New York law prohibited baseball games on Sundays, but they were allowed in New Jersey. The Polo Grounders traveled to the neighboring state and faced a team from Hoboken at St. George's Cricket Grounds. McGraw tested his ailing knee, injured during the pre-season, by inserting himself in the lineup as the third baseman. New York picked up an 11–9 win in front of a crowd of over 12,000 fans. The mass of people caused some problems on the field:

> It was a record-breaking attendance for the St. George's grounds, and the police and players had great difficulty in clearing a space sufficiently large to allow the game to be played. The managers of both teams agreed to restricted ground rules being enforced, so that a ball batted into or over the crowds of spectators was only good for one base, while any man on base or bases were advanced two bases.[2]

New York took the field against Brooklyn on April 20, and the two teams battled to a 5–5 tie, with the game called because of darkness after 11 innings. McGinnity was back in the pitcher's box after a day's rest, pitching two shutout innings of relief.

The club next moved to Brooklyn's Washington Park for a pair of games, which went to the Giants. In the opener, Mathewson topped the

Superbas, 2–1, on a three-hitter, and McGinnity handled the home club, 7–2, the next afternoon.

On May 1, New York was 8–3. Four of the victories belonged to McGinnity. In a couple of those wins Joe, a workhorse throughout his short career, had gone the distance after only two day's rest. In 1900 and 1901, McGinnity had led the league with 343 and 382 innings pitched. The durable right-hander had been discovered by a scout while pitching town ball in Rock Island, Illinois. He was 28-years-old by the time he made it to the majors with Baltimore in 1899.

Along with Mathewson and McGinnity, McGraw had sent pitchers Cronin, Roscoe Miller, and Dummy Taylor to the box as starters.

The month of May was exceptional for the rejuvenated Giants. They went 17–8 and even spent some time at the top of the Senior Circuit. Over a 31-day span, they won more than a third of the number of games they had taken during the entire 1902 season. At the end of May, they sat in second place with a 25–11 record. The Cubs were in first (28–11), and the world champion Pirates were in the third spot (25–16).

May was also "home time" for the Giants. From May 7 through the end of the month, they played all of their games in the friendly confines of the Polo Grounds.

Mathewson, who was a master of the "fadeaway," a pitch that broke in on right-handed batters, had an outstanding stretch, going 7–1 in May. He picked up the first of his seven victories on the first of the month, beating the Philadelphia Phillies, 11–3. Outfielder Sam Mertes aided the cause with three hits.

During May, the Polo Grounders went head-to-head with Pittsburg and Chicago and took three of four from the Pirates and two of three from the Cubs.

Mathewson was the winning pitcher in all three victories against Pittsburg. In the opening game, on May 16, he handled the Pirates, 7–3. He was in top form, and so were the excited fans:

> Mathewson, the idol of the local patrons, was never in better shape and the visitors could do nothing with his curves for seven innings, while New York batsmen located [William "Brickyard"] Kennedy's delivery for three runs in the third inning, and again in the fifth, seventh, and eighth innings for four more.
>
> There never was such a vast assemblage of men and women present at a baseball contest as that which gathered yesterday, the official count being 31,500. Long before the game began the entrances were blocked with a surging mass of struggling men and women, and when with the aid of policemen the management got the gate closed, there were fully 5,000 disappointed persons on the outside of the high fence clamoring for admission.[3]

Joe "Iron Man" McGinnity loosens up (National Baseball Hall of Fame Library).

After a Sunday off, McGinnity, who went 5–3 during the month, dropped the second game of the set, 3–2. The Pirates, for their part, were accused of rough play and unsportsmanlike conduct: Pittsburg pitcher Ed Doheny flung his bat high in the air after hitting an infield fly; shortstop Honus Wagner tagged McGinnity roughly while the latter was running to second base; and player-manager Fred Clarke, who was his club's final batter, interfered with Giants catcher Frank Bowerman on a routine pop fly. The Giants and their fans were incensed:

> At the conclusion of the game the occupants of the bleachers on both sides of the grounds jumped out on the field, and in order to prevent an attack on the visiting players, several policeman surrounded the Pittsburg men and guarded them until they had reached their dressing room. While there were many threats of violence no attempt was made to molest any of the three men who had caused all the disturbance.[4]

Mathewson relieved Taylor in the eighth inning of game three with the score tied, 3–3. The Giants' ace pitched the final two innings and picked up a win in New York's 4–3 victory. He was back in the box for the series finale, shutting out the world champs, 2–0, on a six-hitter.

During the month of May, New York also captured series from the Cardinals, Phillies, and Reds. Bresnahan and Mertes delivered a number of key hits in those games. Taylor, who was 4–1 in the month, picked up a win against each of the three teams. McGraw came in late in a couple of the games as an outfielder, infielder, or pinch hitter. His lengthy managerial career in the Polo Grounds was just beginning, but his playing career was near an end. He would appear in only 12 games in 1903.

None of the series was as important as the one which began on May 26 against the league-leading Cubs. New York was in second place at the start of the three-game set, and the Giants promptly beat Chicago twice to move to the top of the loop. Mathewson won game one, 4–3, and McGinnity stopped the Cubs, 5–4, the following day. In the second matchup, Browne was on base all afternoon and scored three of the Polo Grounders' runs. Chicago took the finale, 7–1, with Taylor taking the loss.

By June 1, Chicago had climbed back into first with a 28–11 mark. New York, which had played three fewer games than the leaders, was 25–11.

Mathewson and the Giants began the month with a 10–2 thrashing of third-place Pittsburg as the New Yorkers opened an extended road trip. The Pirates' loss turned out to be one of only four they would suffer in June while registering 16 wins. In the Giants' June 1 victory, Mertes banged a home run, and the "B-men"—Browne (three hits), rookie Charlie Babb (two hits) and Bowerman (two hits)—were the major offensive cogs.

Taylor and McGinnity lost games two and three in Pittsburg by scores of 7–0 and 5–0. It was the first time in the season that the Giants had dropped a series to an opponent.

Moving on to Chicago to face the league leaders, the Giants recovered their winning ways, sweeping a four-game series. Mathewson, backed up by another three-hit effort by Browne, won, 9–1. McGinnity, pitching with one day of rest, handled the Cubs, 5–2, in the second game.

The matchup in game three between the Senior Circuit's top two clubs, both of whom had played unexpectedly well to that point in the campaign, was an exciting affair:

> It was a great day for the game, and the patrons turned out in force. Every seat on the bleachers and grand stand was taken before the game started, and those who came late had to stand up. Fully 15,000 were present, and it was the largest crowd that has been to the West Side grounds on a Saturday for many a year.[5]

New York, with Taylor going the distance, took the contest, 7–4, when they scored three runs in the eighth inning to break a 4–4 tie.

The final game of the set was played on a Sunday—a day on which the New Yorks were not used to taking the field. McGinnity was back as the starter after having beaten Chicago two days earlier. He fashioned a 9–4 win, and McGann banged out three hits.

McGraw relied on a three-man rotation during the month, relying with but one exception on Mathewson, McGinnity, and Taylor. However, he wasn't tied to a *regular* rotation. As reported following the Giants' fourth win in Chicago,

> McGraw wisely selected McGinnity to pitch out of his turn, while Manager [Frank] Selee used up two of his staff, [Bob] Wicker and [Jock] Menefee, in a vain effort to save the home team from defeat.[6]

Heavy rains caused flooding in Illinois, and that kept the Giants from getting to St. Louis for their scheduled game the following afternoon. After arriving a day late, New York won the two games remaining in the series. The Giants' bats were alive, and the squad thumped the Cards, 11–2. Mertes had three-hits, two of them doubles, and with a sizable lead, McGraw brought Miller into the game in relief of Mathewson. Miller was the only pitcher besides the "big three" to see action that month.

The next day, Taylor handed St. Louis a 1–0 defeat, and helped his team tally the game's only run. In the third inning, Billy Gilbert was hit with a pitch before Bowerman followed with a single, which chased Gilbert to third. Taylor bounced into a double play, and Gilbert scored what proved to be the winning run.

Following Taylor's shutout of the Cardinals, McGinnity and Mathewson each whitewashed the Reds. In Joe's 2–0 win, Cincinnati turned a triple play in the ninth inning which kept the game scoreless. McGinnity was still in the box in the top of the 11th inning when the Reds' defense broke down. Each of the Reds' outfielders committed an error, and their horror show enabled Bresnahan and McGann to score.

Mathewson's 4–0 win was his second one-hit game of the season. Brooklyn's Doyle had ruined Christy's no-hit bid in April, and the Reds' Joe Kelley singled as the third Cincinnati batter in the first inning to bring the same fate to the Giants right-hander in June. Bresnahan's home run was the game's big blow.

In another Sunday affair, the Reds picked up the series finale, 7–6. Following the game, the Giants boarded a train and were off to Philadelphia's Huntington Grounds for a pair of games which would bring an end to their road trip.

McGinnity lost a 12-inning, 2–1 heart breaker in the opener, when Phillies pitcher Chick Fraser hit a ball into the left-field balcony for the winning run. The Giants' bats were more active the next afternoon, with Bresnahan delivering a trio of hits. New York and Taylor picked up a 7–4 victory.

The Giants' fans welcomed their heroes home after the lengthy 17-day road trip that saw the team go 10–4:

> Manager McGraw and his New York baseball team were accorded a royal welcome when they reappeared at the Polo Grounds yesterday after their successful trip through the Western circuit. Although the weather conditions were unfavorable, 5000 persons were present to greet the men, and the fact that so many were on hand was conclusive proof of the admiration which the local enthusiasts have for the team and its good work.[7]

It was not a pleasant home stay. Multiple rainy days and six losses in eight games dampened the locals' enthusiasm.

Chicago took the opener, 1–0, with Mathewson absorbing the loss. A rain out and a Sunday off set up a doubleheader the following afternoon. The Giants, behind McGinnity, stopped the Cubs, 5–4, in the first game, before a crowd of over 19,000. The winning run crossed the plate in the bottom of the 10th. Chicago won the nightcap, 10–6, battering Mathewson for six runs in the top of the ninth. The description of the inning did not paint a pretty picture:

[Jimmy] Slagle made a long fly ball to Browne in right field and retired. Mathewson was overconfident and [Doc] Casey hit him to left centre for a single. [Frank] Chance sent another in the same direction. [Davy] Jones bunted, but Mathewson slipped and fell as he tried to recover the ball and the bases were filled. This was the beginning of the end. [Joe] Tinker smashed the ball to right centre, sending Casey and Chance home and the score was tied. Mathewson was undone by this sudden change of affairs and he made bad worse by hitting [Johnny] Evers with the ball, again loading the bases. [Dick] Harley drove the ball over McGann's head, scoring Jones and Tinker and [Tommy] Raub's single brought Evers in. Harley tallied on [Jock] Menefee's out at first and Slagle came to bat for the second time, but he popped up a foul fly which Bowerman caught and the run-getting ended.[8]

On June 24, a day of rain washed out the scheduled game with Cincinnati and set up another doubleheader for the next afternoon. The Reds took both ends of the twin bill by scores of 5–0 and 11–2. McGinnity and Taylor took the losses as the Giants got only nine hits all day.

Mathewson got the Polo Grounders back on the winning track with an 8–2 victory in the opener of a two-game set against the front-running Pirates. Browne and Bresnahan joined the Giants in rapping out two hits each. McGinnity, going with a single day of rest, couldn't keep the winning going, and he lost 4–2, much to the disappointment of the 32,240 fans who stuffed New York's home park.

Things continued to deteriorate when the Giants took another Sunday trip to New Jersey for an exhibition game against Newark of the Eastern League. The minor leaguers took them, 2–0, as the Giants managed only three singles.

More rain caused the cancellation of Monday's contest, and the Cardinals brought a merciful end to June for the Giants by beating the home club, 4–2. New York had gone 2–6 on the home stand and, with a 37–21 record, were 2½ lengths behind Pittsburg at the end of the month.

The last 13 days of June were disappointing; the month of July was weird. A strange play, a player coming out of the stands to don a uniform, McGinnity going to the mound even more regularly than in the previous months, and the Giants dropping into third place were the oddities and the lowlights in July.

It began on the first day of the month in a game between the Giants and Cardinals in New York. McGinnity beat St. Louis, 5–2, but in the course of the game there was a curious baseball occurrence—a quadruple play. In the top of the sixth inning, the Cards' Jack Ryan hit a double, and he scored on a single by Clarence Currie. John Farrell, the next hitter, was safe on an error. Shortstop George Davis fumbled Patsy Donovan's grounder, loading the bases. Homer Smoot sent a fly ball to center. Bresnahan caught the ball and then rifled a throw to catcher John Warner, who put the tag on Currie. Warner then gunned the ball to Davis at second in time to get Donovan. Without hesitation, the shortstop fired the ball back to the catcher to nail a sliding Farrell. Four outs on one play—quite a feat, though only the first three went into the scorebook.

With rain still in the area, the finale with the Cardinals was postponed and the Giants headed to Chicago to open a series at the West Side Grounds.

On the fourth of July, McGinnity was back in the box in the first game of a doubleheader, relieving Taylor, who was shelled in the Cubs' 7-run first inning. The staff's workhorse struggled the rest of the way as Chicago administered a 16–9 beating to the New Yorks. The two ineffective Giants' pitchers gave up 19 hits. The morning affair was played on a bone dry field, but the rain came and turned the dust into mud and forced the postponement of the second game.

One day later it was McGinnity again. He handled the Cubs, 7–1, but the game was played under protest. Warner was behind the plate in Bowerman's absence. The Giants' regular backstop had suffered a serious spike wound in the exhibition game in Newark. Warner injured his finger, and the only remaining catcher was Bresnahan. The problem was that Bresnahan had been hurt the day before and was sitting in civilian clothes in the grand stand. Mertes was called in from left field to catch the rest of the inning while Bresnahan rushed to the locker room to pull on his uniform.

When Bresnahan entered the lineup, the umpire announced that Chicago was playing the game under protest. The basis for the protest was Rule 27, Section 1, which requires all players, including substitutes, to be on the field in uniform at the beginning of the game. The game continued, but with the outcome—in spite of the score—very much in doubt, as the *New York Times* reported:

> The condition of the protest is said to be unique in the history of National championship playing. Mr. Hart of the Chicago management said the game would probably be played over again rather [than] allow it to be given to Chicago.[9]

For the time being, at least, the win went into New York's column. They also picked up the series finale when Mathewson pitched the Giants to a 5–1 win.

The club was off to St. Louis for four games, which they split with the Cardinals. In the second contest, McGinnity went the distance in New

York's 10–5 victory, as Mertes played a brilliant game in the field and blasted a home run.

McGinnity relieved Mathewson in the bottom of the ninth inning the next afternoon and protected New York's 4–2 lead. He was out there again the following day with two innings of relief work after Miller went the first eight frames. This time he surrendered St. Louis' winning run in the tenth.

McGinnity had pitched before with two days rest, and even with a single day off, but on July 11 McGraw sent Joe to the box for the fourth day in a row—and this time he was back in the starting role. New York was in Cincinnati, and they built a 7–1 lead going into the seventh. When the Reds rallied for five runs, McGinnity was replaced by Mathewson. The Giants held on for an 8–6 victory.

After the Cincinnati series, in which they took three of four games, they traveled to meet the league-leading Pirates. New York took the opener, 6–3, behind Mathewson. He pitched 14 innings, and the Giants scored three times in the top of that frame to earn the 6–3 win.

After that game, the Polo Grounders began their July plunge. Beginning on July 16, when Pittsburg blasted New York, 16–4, driving McGinnity from the box in the fifth with an eight-run rally, until the end of the month, the Giants won only twice while losing 11 times, including three to the Pirates.

In the midst of their downward spiral, the Polo Grounders returned home. They still had their fans behind them, but that was not enough to stop the free fall as the Braves beat the Giants, 11–9:

> Although the New York National League players had not been successful during the latter part of their three weeks' absence from the Polo Grounds, a big Monday crowd gave them a warm greeting when they reappeared on the local diamond yesterday in the first game of the series with the Boston team. The weather was delightfully fine, and nearly 5,000 persons were on hand to welcome the team, but neither the auspicious surroundings nor the cheering encouragement of the local enthusiasts was sufficient to induce good luck to break in on the rather lengthy spell of defeats which the team has suffered.[10]

New York's extended slump dropped them into third place behind Pittsburg and Chicago with a 48–36 record at month's end. McGinnity made 12 appearances in July and went 6–3. Taylor had a horrendous month, going 0–6.

As the Giants entered the final two months of the season, they and their fans had enjoyed tremendous excitement after the deep despair of

1902, though at times they had also been overcome by a sense of foreboding during the team's occasional relapses. The last weeks of July had brought more gloom, but the first weeks of the new month would restore the Polo Grounders to good times.

New York entered August 7½ games behind Pittsburg, two in back of the Cubs. They went 12–2 through the first half of August to move back into second place.

It began with a gargantuan achievement and another first for McGinnity during his amazing season. On the first day of the month, he requested and received the go-ahead to pitch both ends of a doubleheader against the Braves, and he won them both. McGraw, hoping to end the Polo Grounders' swoon that Saturday afternoon, not only sent Joe to the box for the day but also inserted himself in the lineup as the Giants' third baseman in the first game. A post-game reported complimented the moves in Beantown:

> With the aid of McGraw himself, and the great pitching by McGinnity, the New York Nationals got out of their losing streak to-day, taking both games from Boston, the first 4 to 1 and the second 5 to 2. McGinnity requested McGraw to permit him to pitch both games, and his work was a revelation to the large crowd. In the two games Boston managed to get but 13 hits, 7 in the first and 6 in the second.[11]

McGinnity had accomplished an "Iron Man" feat. Although he had already been known by that name because of his work in a foundry in the 1890s, it now took on special baseball significance.

The Giants were off and running. Mathewson registered two wins in successive games, fortunate in having off days caused by scheduling and rain sandwiched between starts. Taylor also picked up a 6-2 victory over the cellar-dwelling Phillies.

A week after McGinnity's double-win day, he was back at it again, and with the same success! He pitched the Giants to a pair of wins over Brooklyn in front of the home folks in the Polo Grounds, as fans once again took hope. Helped along in the opener by a four-run first inning, Iron Man stopped the Superbas, 6–1. He followed with a 4–3 win in the nightcap. It was a close game all the way, and New York pulled it out with two runs in the bottom of the ninth. McGinnity helped himself with three hits in the double bill, and even stole a base in the nightcap.

It was an exciting time for the home folks, who were joined by their neighbors from Brooklyn:

> Never since the first baseball game was played on the Polo Grounds was there a larger or more enthusiastic gathering of local "rooters" on hand than that

which crowded every inch of vantage ground within the big enclosure yesterday. The official count of the multitude which passed through the turnstiles was 31,647. Of course all of this vast assemblage were not partisans of the local team. It was an interborough duel, and it is safe to say that at least a third of those present were from the Borough of Kings. Every bit of play, whether good or bad, was closely watched and criticized, and judging by the generous applause which greeted every brilliant play the spectators did not let their feelings get the better of their judgment, as no matter to which side the player belonged he received spontaneous and hearty cheers whenever they were deserved.[12]

New York split the next two games with the Superbas, with McGinnity dropping the second, 2–1. After the Giants took three straight from the Cardinals, they had edged ahead of the Cubs into second place.

While the teams in both major leagues were battling for superiority, the administrators of the clubs and the leagues were working toward an agreement which would allow them to cooperate for the good of the game. The combatants in the battle between the National League, which had begun operation in 1876, and the American League, which had come on the scene in 1901, had signed "The Cincinnati Peace Pact" in January. One part of the agreement allowed Davis, who had been with the Chicago White Stockings in 1902, to join the Giants in 1903. He became a pawn in the continued skirmishes between the two leagues and, after the White Stockings mounted a vigorous objection to the move, he ended up playing only four games for his new team. He was back in Chicago the following season.

A meeting in Buffalo during the third week in August resulted in a National Agreement which was approved by both circuits. The lengthy document attempted to address every important point regarding the governance of professional baseball, as outlined in four major objectives:

1. Perpetuation of baseball as the National pastime of America by surrounding it with such safeguards as will warrant absolute public confidence in its integrity and methods, and by maintaining a high standard of skill and sportsmanship in its players.

2. Protection of the property rights of those engaged in baseball as a business without sacrificing the spirit of competition in the conduct of their clubs.

3. Promotion of the welfare of ball players as a class by developing and perfecting them in their profession, and enabling them to secure adequate compensation for expertness.

4. Adoption of a uniform code of rules for playing baseball.[13]

The agreement also set guidelines for the relationship between the major and minor leagues. Major league farm systems were forbidden, and the rights of minor league clubs to their players were to be absolute. All major league acquisitions of players from minor league teams were to be governed by the procedures and guidelines spelled out in the agreement.

On August 21, the Giants completed a four-game set with the Pirates in which each club won twice. This was followed by an important matchup in the Polo Grounds between New York, in second place, and Chicago, half a game behind them in third.

The opener went to the Cubs, 8–5. Some were not impressed by the effort shown by the home team:

> Beaten by Chicago and forced back to third place in the National League pennant race was what happened to the New York baseball team in the Polo Grounds yesterday. It was the opening game of the series with Chicago, and over 16,000 persons were present, despite counter attractions on land and water, but there was a very significant absence of enthusiasm on the part of the spectators before and after the contest. New York had a lot to gain and a great deal to lose on the result of the game, but the local players did not seem to care which way the verdict went. They fielded loosely and were hissed frequently for their seeming indifference.[14]

That quality of play would have been almost expected a year earlier, but it was not acceptable in 1903.

Sunday was a day off from baseball in New York, and the club had an opportunity to reflect on Saturday's lapses and prepare to right itself. The day of rest did not help in the opener of a doubleheader on Monday, August 24, however, as McGinnity suffered a 7–3 loss at the hands of the Cubs, who moved back into second. The game was practically presented to Chicago in the opening inning through the porous fielding of Babb at shortstop, whose three errors enabled Chicago to score four times.

The Giants rebounded in game two, and Mathewson led them to an 8–1 win. Rain washed out the series finale and, when Chicago left town, the Giants held a tenuous half-game lead over the Cubs.

On the final day of August, McGinnity was in the box again for a pair of games against the Phillies. He won both contests, a feat he had performed three times in a single month. The scores of the double win were 4–1 and 9–2. McGinnity was also an offensive force, contributing four singles during his afternoon's work. Bresnahan, after getting one hit in the first contest, banged out four in the nightcap, including a pair of doubles.

After the wins, New York sat in second place with a 69–46 record, and Chicago was a game behind 67–46. McGinnity went 7–5 during

August, with one of the losses administered by his 1903 nemesis, the Pirates. He now stood 0–5 against the league leaders. While Iron Man was working his amazing feats, Mathewson was just chugging along, going 9–1 during the month.

It would take a September miracle for the Giants to catch the Pirates, who were 8½ lengths in front of them, but the race for the runner-up spot would be contested.

After beginning September with a 7–3 victory over Philadelphia, which was sparked by McGann's first-inning homer and Mertes' four hits, New York kicked off an extended interborough series with Brooklyn. The two teams played eight games in seven days against each other, with the site of the matchups moving back and forth between the Polo Grounds and Washington Park. On Monday, September 7, each club hosted a game in its own ball yard. In the morning, the Giants visited Brooklyn and, in the afternoon, the Superbas were in the Polo Grounds. The home fans of both clubs watched their teams suffer through a defeat at the hand of the visitors, as the Giants took the opener, 6–4, and Brooklyn captured the second game, 3–0.

The morning affair featured an angry moment for the visiting New Yorks:

> There was plenty of excitement during the game, and at one time a riot seemed imminent. This was during Brooklyn's half of the fifth inning, when [Jimmy] Sheckard palpably interfered with Bowerman when the latter attempted to throw the ball to second in order to head off [Sammy] Strang, who was stealing from first to second base. Strang had reached first on Gilbert's fumble, and Sheckard was at bat. Just at the moment Bowerman was throwing the ball to catch Strang, Sheckard raised his bat, and the ball hit and glanced off the bat, rolling back of first base. Strang kept on running, and the New York fielders, believing that Umpire [Timothy] Hurst would not allow the run, permitted Strang to get all the way home.[15]

Following Strang's run, McGraw, Bowerman, and a number of other Giants charged Hurst, bellowing at him. Bowerman, who was the most vociferous of the group, was ejected by the umpire. A loud and mixed chorus from the stands shouted their opinions. Some blasted the ump; others yelled their displeasure at the Giants.

New York captured four of the games in the prolonged series, with three going to the Superbas and the final matchup ending in a tie.

The Giants hit the road for the remainder of the season. After series in Philadelphia, St. Louis, and Cincinnati, New York was in position to decide its fate: the schedule had the Giants meeting first Chicago and then Pittsburgh.

Before opening a four-game set against the Cubs, New York had an 80–52 record and were 1½ games ahead of Chicago, who were 78–53.

McGraw called on his best to go to the box, which meant the duo of Mathewson and McGinnity would pitch the series. That would allow the pair of Giant workhorses a day off between starts.

Mathewson was in the box for game one. A day earlier, he had relieved Taylor in the sixth inning against the Reds and had gone on to register the victory in New York's 7–5 win. He had been ably aided by shortstop Babb, who had three hits, stole a base, and was part of a triple play pulled off with Lauder and Gilbert.

On September 19, Chicago took the opener, 3–0, on five timely hits to move within a half game of New York. The Giants rebounded the next day, scoring four runs in their first at-bat on the way to a 6–2 triumph. McGinnity was the beneficiary of his club's improved offense.

The following afternoon Mathewson was back in the box for the third time in four days and led New York to an impressive 8–3 victory. Browne banged out four hits, and Bresnahan slammed a home run and a single.

Chicago captured the final game of the season between the two dueling clubs, with McGinnity finishing on the short end of a 6–1 score.

New York's campaign-ending set was on tap in Pittsburg, with the Giants holding a 1½ game lead over Chicago. That would hold up as New York took two of three from the champion Pirates. Rookie right-hander Red Ames, making only his second major league start and seeking his second victory, shutout Pittsburg, 2–0, as the Giants eliminated the Cubs. The season ended on September 26, with McGinnity picking up his elusive first win over the Pirates, 4–1. He made short work of the pennant-winners, finishing them off in one hour and thirty-five minutes.

New York's comeback was remarkable. They hadn't achieved their last-to-first goal, but they had laid the foundation for the future. Their successful season was the result of a number of significant accomplishments by several of its players.

Mertes led the loop and tied for the major-league lead with 104 RBI. Browne was third in the National League in runs scored (105) and hits (185). Bresnahan, at .350, had the Senior Circuit's fourth highest batting average and was runner-up in on-base percentage at .435. None of the Giants had finished among the top five players in any offensive category in 1902.

McGinnity, with 31 wins (31–30), and Mathewson, with 30 (30–13), led the majors in victories. It was not surprising that the terrific tandem also led the way in complete games and innings pitched.

The following year, New York posted a 106–47 record to win the 1904 National League's pennant. They outdistanced the Cubs by 13 games.

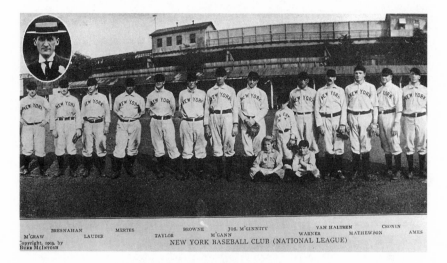

The 1903 New York Giants (NBL).

McGraw's Giants, who had been the National League's doormat two years earlier, had a ticket to the world's series, as it was known then.

A postseason meeting between the winners of the two leagues was first held in 1903 when the Boston Pilgrims beat Pittsburg, 5 games to 3. However, in 1904, McGraw refused to play Boston, the winners of the upstart American League, and the Series was canceled. McGraw believed that his players were the champions of the only real major league.

The New York Giants, it turned out, were more than an inspirational flash in the pan. During the decade beginning in 1904, they won a world championship (1905), took home five pennants, and finished second three times. They averaged an astounding 97 wins per season.

Notes

1. "Baseball Opening Delayed," *New York Times*, 16 April 1903, 7.

2. "New York's Close Game," *New York Times*, 20 April 1903, 5.

3. "31,500 Persons Saw New York Defeat Pittsburg Champions," *New York Times*, 17 May 1903, 10.

4. "Pittsburg's Unruly Players Protected by the Police at Polo Grounds," *New York Times*, 19 May 1903, 7.

5. "In a Late Rally the New Yorks Beat Chicago by Three Runs," *New York Times*, 7 June 1903, 10.

6. "New Yorks Again Beat Chicago—McGinnity Pitched in Good Form," *New York Times*, 8 June 1903, 8.

7. "Mathewson's Wild Pitching Lost New York Their First Game at Home on Return from the West," *New York Times*, 19 June 1903, 10.

8. "National League," *New York Times*, 23 June 1903, 8.

9. "New York Beats Chicago, but the Game May Be Played Over—Catcher Warner Injured," *New York Times*, 6 July 1903, 8.

10. "New Yorks Beaten by Boston in a Lively Batting Game," *New York Times*, 28 July 1903, 8.

11. "McGinnity Pitches in Two Games Against Boston, Which New York Won," *New York Times*, 2 August 1903, 12.

12. "McGinnity Pitched in the Two Games New York Won from Brooklyn," *New York Times*, 9 August 1903, 14.

13. "National Baseball Agreement," *New York Times*, 30 August 1903, 15.

14. "The New Yorks Played a Careless Game and Were Beaten by Chicago," *New York Times*, 23 August 1903, 15.

15. "New York and Brooklyn Quit Even on the Day—Rowdyism in Morning Game," *New York Times*, 8 September 1903, 10.

2. 1906 Chicago Cubs

All Those Wins and No Brass Ring

In 1906 the Chicago Cubs, who had won 92 games the year before and had finished the season in third place and 13 lengths behind the National League champion New York Giants, fashioned a remarkable 116–38 record and a .763 winning percentage that has yet to be surpassed.

However, when Chicago's two major league clubs met in the 1906 World Series, the White Sox from the Windy City's South Side knocked the West Siders from their lofty perch. The Series featured two player-managers, as Fielder Jones' "Hitless Wonders" beat Frank Chance's Cubs, four games to two.

An article in the *New York Times* on April 12, Opening Day, forecast a competitive race for the National League pennant:

> All indications point to an aggressive and well-contested campaign of the National League baseball clubs, the opening games being scheduled for to-day. It will be the thirty-first season for the league, and from the champion New Yorks down to the Brooklyn Tailenders, all the teams apparently have been materially strengthened....
>
> In the West, Chicago, Pittsburgh, and Cincinnati have made a number of changes in their teams, and all are regarded now as being very dangerous opponents. The Chicagos are reported to be in excellent condition for the opening, while the Pittsburgh players showed much strength in the Southern training campaign.[1]

In the Cubs' opener, right-hander Carl Lundgren, who had a 13–5 record the previous season, got Chicago off on its winning ways. Before 17,241 fans, on a perfect day for baseball, the Cubs beat the Reds, 7–2.

After capturing their second win the following day, Chicago dropped two close games to Cincinnati to split the series. Ed Reulbach was the losing pitcher in the club's first defeat, a tough 1–0 loss. Chicago's hard-luck hurler was coming off an outstanding rookie season in 1905, having gone 18–14 and led the league by limiting opposing hitters to a .203 average. Cincinnati's Cy Seymour scored the game's only run when Cubs right fielder Frank Schulte misjudged his long fly ball, allowing Seymour to round the bases for an inside-the-park home run.

Lundgren went to the box in the series finale and picked up his first loss in a 3–2 Cincinnati victory. Schulte led the way offensively for the losers, collecting a single, a double, and a triple.

Despite what the mixed results of the opening series might suggest, Chicago had a dominating pitching staff. In addition to Lundgren and Reulbach, Chance had Mordecai "Three Finger" Brown, who had been 18–12 in 1905, going to the box for his club. As the year progressed Jack Pfiester, who was 1–1 with Pittsburgh in 1904 but out of the majors the following season, played a major role for the Cubs.

The report about the Cubs' 5–2 victory over the St. Louis Cardinals on April 21 noted other key ingredients in Chicago's arsenal, saying, "Perfect fielding and good baserunning with an occasional hit gave Chicago an easy game to-day from St. Louis."[2] The infield defense featured shortstop Joe Tinker, second baseman Johnny Evers, and first baseman Chance. They had been together since 1902, and their legend was beginning to grow. Despite Franklin P. Adams' sense that Tinker, Evers, and Chance turned double plays with clocklike regularity—at least against Adams' beloved Giants—the trio turned an average of only one double play every three games during the 1906 season. Of course, playing behind a pitching staff that led the league with a microscopic 1.76 ERA, the celebrated trio seldom found itself with a runner on first and less than two out. Harry Steinfeldt was the third baseman and John Kling was behind the plate, filling out the infield. James Sheckard and John Slagle joined Schulte in the Cubs' "all S" outfield.

As the campaign unfolded, Chicago's offense also distinguished itself, with Chance, Schulte, Sheckard, and Steinfeldt leading the way.

On May 1, the Cubs were 10–6 and in third place, trailing the world champion New York Giants (12–3) and the Pittsburgh Pirates (9–5).

By the time the Cubs played the Giants in their initial meeting of the season, the Chicago club had climbed into first place with a 24–10 record. New York had fallen to second.

On May 20, the two teams met for their first game in the Windy City's West Side Grounds at Polk and Lincoln Streets. The ballpark had a double-decked grandstand that accommodated 16,000 fans and had small balcony boxes on top between first and third bases.

The home team picked up a 10–4 victory, which was reported in the following day's *New York Times*:

> The Giants and the Giant Killers, as Chicagoans now term their National League team, had their first clash of the season in the presence of a record-breaking crowd at Chicago yesterday, and the Giants, after being in the lead for four innings, were unable to hold the advantage, and were finally beaten 10–4. Red Ames' pitching was easily punished, while Lundgren's delivery, with the exception of one inning, was unusually effective.[3]

The second game of the set went to the New Yorks, 6–4, in a game which was far from a major league masterpiece:

> About 17,000 persons who went to the West Side grounds to-day saw New York trounce Chicago, 6–4, in one of the most tiresome and dragging games ever played by two teams. The victory went to [John] McGraw's men , who made six runs off four hits, two of which cut no figure in the result. Eleven bases on balls, two men hit by speedy curves, and four little singles yielded six runs for New York, while Chicago could get but three off ten nice hits and three bases on balls.[4]

The Giants took game three, 8–2, behind Joe "Iron Man" McGinnity. Then, with New York within one victory of retaking first place, the rains came and the final game was washed out.

Chicago maintained first place into the month of June. While the thrill of success continued to grow in the Windy City, the New York press focused on the growing excitement about baseball elsewhere:

> England's favorite pastime is threatened, and baseball bids fair to supplant cricket with the sport-loving Britishers. Repeated attempts have been made to introduce America's National game in Albion, but the conservatism of the Englishmen stood in the way of such a radical departure, and the rupture and smashing of traditions, which have stood the test for over two centuries. The entering wedge has been driven in and several meetings have recently been held for the purpose of effecting a permanent organization, the objects of which is the encouragement and development of the National sport of America. At the last meeting of the promoters of the sport, held at the Charterhouse Hotel, in London, the Chairman prophesied that before the end of the Summer a twenty-club baseball league would be formed, and Englishmen will be playing ball as it is played in the United States, though not the same quality.[5]

In early June the next meeting between the Senior Circuit's top two teams took place in the Polo Grounds in New York. The Cubs throttled the Giants, 6–0, in the opener, and followed with an 11–3 rout the following afternoon. But the worst was yet to come to the New Yorks: The third game went to Chicago, too, and by a lopsided score of 19–0. The Giants' ace, Christy Mathewson, who had led the majors with a 31–6 record in 1905 and had gone on to shutout the Philadelphia Athletics three times in the World Series, lasted only one third of an inning against the red-hot Cubs, who scored eleven times in the opening frame. The report about the game documented the Giants' struggles:

> The champion New Yorks suffered another crushing defeat yesterday at the hands of the Chicago team, the beating being one of worst that a New York major league team ever sustained. The Chicagoans rolled up a total of nineteen runs to nothing for the champions, and the unusual spectacle was presented, in not only one instance, but in several, of the visiting players deliberately giving the Giants an opportunity to retire them. That was plainly in evidence in the fourth inning, when with a big lead and an overcast sky, they desired to complete the five innings necessary to constitute a game.[6]

The embarrassed champs rebounded and won the final matchup in the Polo Grounds, 7–3. As the Cubs moved to Brooklyn to play three games against the sixth-place Superbas, they were 34–16 and 2½ games in front of the Pirates, who had taken over the runner-up spot.

Chicago captured two of the games played in Brooklyn's Washington Park, which was so named because its location was in the area where George Washington's Continental Army had fought the Battle of Long Island. In the pair of Cubs' victories, Orval Overall and Fred Beebe went the distance.

On the fourth of July, the Cubs were in first place, having continued to build their lead over their closest National League pursuers. In the American League, three clubs had been battling for the top spot. The Greater New Yorks (the Highlanders, who became the Yankees in 1913), the Cleveland Naps [named for player-manager Nap Lajoie, they became the Indians in 1915), and the Athletics had been moving up and down the top three places in the Junior Circuit. The White Sox were in fourth place.

The second-place Giants returned to Chicago for a July 17 confrontation with the front-running Cubs. Their goal was clear:

> When the champion New Yorks marched into Chicago's ball yard to-day they acted as though they expected to see Manager Chance and his men climbing the fences to escape annihilation. Two hours later, when "Chicago,

6, New York, 2" was hung up as the result they left by the side door. They were completely outclassed, and Mathewson was no match to-day for Mordecai Brown.[7]

The following day the two teams played to a twelve-inning, 3–3 tie, which was called because of darkness. Each club put together a three-run inning with only one hit.

Chicago and New York split the final pair of games in their head-to-head series. In the Cubs' win, they "worsted" the Giants, 6–3.[8] The big blow was delivered in the eighth inning:

> Harry Steinfeldt, with one swing of the bat, turned the West Side baseball grounds from a damp, funereal place, fit for a Coroner's inquest, into a shrieking madhouse of wildly dancing maniacs to-day just before the close of the final battle between Chicago and New York. The swing turned the score from 3–2 in New York's favor to 4–3 in Chicago's, and before the Giants recovered from the awful blow it was 6 to 8.[9]

Chicago had captured their third consecutive series from the Polo Grounders, and the world champions left the Windy City on a down note. Then they lost a golden opportunity to close the gap on the Cubs, who dropped three of the four games they played against the visiting Superbas. Pittsburgh took all three games in their set with New York, and slid past the Giants into second place. The Windy City club was 61–27 and 4½ games in front of the Pirates.

An article in the *New York Times* on July 28 was a reminder of another gap between baseball in Chicago, Pittsburgh, and New York:

> The Sunday baseball question will be decided by Justice Blanchard in the Supreme Court next Monday, when the case against "Jack" Hart, "Joe" Woods, "Jack" Pepper, Harry Wonder, and John Henning, members of the Cedar and Emerald baseball teams, who were arrested on Sunday, July 1, and who have been held by Magistrate Walsh on the charge of violating the Sabbath enactments, will be finally disposed of. Judge Blanchard made this ruling yesterday.[10]

The group of players involved in the court case were not major leaguers, but they were under the same Sabbath rules as were the Giants, Superbas, and Yankees. Games were played on Sundays in some other American and National League cities, but never in New York.

On Saturday, August 4, the Cubs returned to the Polo Grounds and were part of a raucous scene involving a record crowd of more than 25,000 enthusiastic fans. When every seat in the house was taken before game time, the late arrivals crowded on the field:

> While the policemen were busy with the crowd on the field the boys in the twenty-five cent stand clamored over the seats and joined the throng on the field and in the stands. Several times the carriage gates were forced open, and several hundred men, women, and boys secured free admission before the police could gather in sufficient force to drive them back.[11]

The Giants, behind Mathewson, registered a 7–4 victory. Following New York's Sabbath holiday, the Cubs, in front of another large crowd, evened the series with a 3–1 victory. Brown limited the Giants, who committed four errors, to six singles. McGraw and third baseman Art Devlin, who argued bitterly with umpire James Johnstone, were tossed out of the game.

The ejections set the scene for another volatile disagreement before the next day's contest. The Giants' club officials refused to allow Johnstone to enter the Polo Grounds to umpire the contest. From outside the park, the rejected official awarded a 9–0 forfeit to the visiting Cubs. The Giants' rationale for refusing to admit Johnstone was that they were protecting him from a possibly riotous situation created by fans still incensed about his ejecting McGraw and Devlin the day before.

The home team, refusing to heed Johnstone's ruling, appointed utility infielder Sammy Strang to assist umpire Robert Emslie, who was scheduled to officiate the contest. A second umpire was not essential since many of the regular season games had only one arbiter assigned for them.

Emslie refused to umpire the game because of the Giants' actions against Johnstone, and Chance refused to send his team on the field with Strang there. National League president Harry C. Pulliam sharply disagreed with the Giants' actions and upheld the forfeit. He was certain of his position, stating:

> I uphold the action of the umpires absolutely, and if I am not sustained by the National League Board of Directors I will not only resign my position as President of the National League, but I will quit professional baseball forever. I am a National League man through and through and will never serve another organization.[12]

Johnstone was back on the field, umpiring the bases, for the series' finale, which went to the Cubs, 3–2.

The Giants protested the forfeit, and on August 21, Pulliam denied the appeal and Chicago's victory stood.

M. BROWN.   J.PFEISTER   A.HOFMAN   C.G.WILLIAMS   O.OVERALL.   E.REULBACH.   J.KLING.
H.GESSLER. J.TAYLOR.   H.STEINFELDT. J.M℠CORMICK. F.CHANCE.   J.SHECKARD.   P.MORAN.   F.SCHULTE
C.LUNDGREN.   T.WALSH.   J. EVERS.   J.SLAGLE.   J.TINKER.

CHICAGO NATIONAL LEAGUE BALL CLUB 1906

The National League Champion Chicago Cubs (NBL).

Following the set with the Cubs, New York took five straight from Pittsburgh, but they did not gain any significant ground on the Cubs, who were winning a series with Brooklyn.

On September 1, the Chicago Nationals were 92–31 and opened a 13-game lead over the second place Pirates, who were 77–42. They continued their determined march to the league championship and gained their ticket to the world's series.

In the American League the surprising White Sox had taken the lead and were three games in front of the Yankees as the clubs entered the home stretch. The Chicago Americans had waged a nip-and-tuck battle with the Greater New Yorks until the Sox captured the Junior Circuit pennant on October 3. The Cubs had won 116 times, the White Sox 93.

A glance at the season's statistics showed some of the reasons the Cubs were heavy favorites to capture the world championship. Their .262 team batting average, for instance, was the best in the league. The Pirates' Honus Wagner captured the batting title at .339, but Steinfeldt's .327 and Chance's .319 placed them among the league leaders. Chance led the circuit in on-base percentage [.406], and he was tied for the top spot in runs scored (103). Steinfeldt led the league with 176 hits and was tied for the RBI lead with Pittsburgh's Jim Nealon with 83.

On the other hand, the White Sox, who had been dubbed the "Hitless

Wonders," brought a team batting average of .230 to the series. The club's six home runs represented the major league's most paltry output. Only one of the Chicago White Sox hitters, George Davis, appeared on the lists of the top offensive performers, and his 80 RBIs placed him only third in the league.

The Chicago Cubs pitchers had performed admirably. Brown's 26 wins [26–6] was one less than the Giants' McGinnity [27–12]. Reulbach [19–4], who put together a 12-game winning streak during the campaign, had the league's best winning percentage [.826], and Brown was right behind him at .813. Reulbach had limited opponents to a .175 batting average, and Brown and Pfiester [20–8] both allowed a stingy .204. Brown led the loop with a 1.04 ERA. The other two of the big three, Pfiester and Reulbach, registered 1.56 and 1.65 ERAs respectively.

If the White Sox were going to be competitive in the Series, their impressive pitching staff would have to play a major role. Their combined 2.13 ERA was higher than the Cubs' 1.76, but Frank Owen was 22–13, and Guy White [18–6], who had held his opponents to a .207 batting average, brought a .750 winning percentage into the postseason. Big Ed Walsh had thrown 10 shutouts to lead the majors, and White led the led the league with a 1.52 ERA.

It had been a great year for the two clubs who were set to battle for the world championship. It had also been an economically profitable season for 15 of the 16 major league clubs, with only the Detroit Tigers finishing in the red. The Tigers and the Naps were the only teams other than the three from New York who did not benefit from having fans in the stands on Sunday afternoons.

Most baseball people favored the Cubs, even the writers at that most prominent of rival-run papers, the *New York Times*:

> The world's record of victories which they established during the recent campaign and their splendid team work made Chance's men 2 to 1 favorites, and while it was conceded that the Americans had annexed the championship of the league after a gallant and prolonged struggle old patrons of the game could not see where there was a possibility of the team owned by the "Grand Old Man" Comiskey winning.[13]

The Series opened on October 9 in West Side Grounds, under a light rain, which at times became flakes of snow. A crowd of 12,603 hardy enthusiasts attended, despite the inhospitable conditions, and saw the White Sox make their inaugural appearance in the postseason—the first game of the first-ever intra-city World Series.

In a surprise move, Jones, the White Sox's manager, sent left-hander

Nick Altrock [20–13] to the box to face the Cubs' Brown. The American Leaguers scored single runs in the fifth and sixth innings while Altrock limited the Nationals to a run in the bottom of the sixth in the 2–1 victory. The first run of the game resulted from some on-the-field barriers and Mother Nature's intervention:

> In the first half of the fifth ... [George] Rohe electrified the crowd by sending a stinging hit down the third-base line and under the temporary benches in Sheckard's territory, reaching third base on the hit. [John] Donohue struck out attempting to bunt, but "Pat" Dougherty was more fortunate. He laid down an easy one half-way between the pitcher and catcher. Brown scooped up the ball in beautiful fashion and tossed it to Kling. Rohe was tearing wildly for the plate, and he got there, for Kling's frost-bitten fingers refused to close around the ball.[14]

Years later, Reulbach commented on Jones' maneuver, which helped get the White Sox off to an impressive start:

> Miner Brown was going at a wonderful clip. It was certain that Chance (Frank Chance, the Cub manager) would pitch him in the opening contest. Fielder Jones attacked the problem somewhat in this light: "If I pitch Walsh, who is my best pitcher, I will probably lose, for Walsh is certainly not as good as Brown. Then I will have opened the Series with a defeat and temporarily used up my best man. On the other hand, if I use another pitcher and he loses, I am no worse off and I can bring Walsh into the second (or third) contest and probably win."
> So he chose Altrock to pitch the opening game feeling that if Altrock won (which he did) it would be a tremendous moral victory, while if he lost it would not be such a serious affair, since no one expected him to win. Jones felt that Altrock might as well lose a game 15 to 1 as to let Walsh lose by a score of, say, 2–1. A defeat was a defeat.[15]

The teams moved to South Side Park for game two. The cold weather, which had kept the temperature near the freezing mark the previous afternoon, was still there, but the Cubs' offense, which had also been cold in game one, heated up. The West Siders picked up a 7–1 win behind Reulbach, who limited the White Sox to a pair of hits. Steinfeldt's three singles led the Cubs to the win over White.

The third game of the series, with Walsh hurling a two-hitter, went to the White Sox, 3–0. Rohe's hit down the left-field line in the bottom of the sixth, which went under the benches that had been friendly to him in the first game, allowed Lee Tannehill, Walsh, and Bill O'Neill to score. Along with Walsh, Rohe, who had batted .258 in 77 games during the regular season, had become an instant hero. The game report offered an account of the splendid pitching:

> To-day's game between the Chicago teams of the National and American Leagues was a battle royal between Pitchers Walsh and Pfiester, and the American League won, 3–0. This places the Americans ahead in the series by two games to one.
>
> Twenty-one batsmen struck out, twelve of these go to the credit of Walsh. In addition he gave only one base on called balls, and allowed only two safe hits, in the first inning. Thereafter the Nationals, until the ninth inning, never had any sort of a chance to score....
>
> It took a large force of policemen to protect Walsh and Rohe from their frenzied admirers who thronged onto the field after the game, but they finally reached their carriages without being hoisted on anybody's shoulders.[16]

The next afternoon, Brown came back with two day's rest to throw a two-hit shutout at the Americans, who lost, 1–0, before 18,385 fans. Evers drove in Chance with the game's only run, after the Cubs manager started the top of the seventh with a single to short right field. Sacrifices by Tinker and Steinfeldt moved him to third base, setting up Evers' run-scoring single. With the series tied at two games apiece, each team had won in their opponent's ballpark.

In the fifth matchup, on a warm afternoon and in front of 25,000 fans at the West Side Grounds, the White Sox forged ahead again in the back-and-forth series. Their 8–6 victory moved them to within a single game of pulling off a whopping upset.

The pitchers on both teams had rough going. Reulbach, who had handled the White Sox hitters in the second game, surrendered five hits in 2⅓ innings. Pfiester followed him to the box and gave up a single and a pair of doubles in one frame, and Overall finished the game. Walsh went 6⅓ innings for the South Siders to pick up the win. Big Ed also had a tough outing, giving up six hits and walking five. The Americans collected eight two-base hits, four of them by second baseman Bill Isbell. Schulte's double and two singles led the Nationals.

As reported, it was not a pretty game, but the Americans were willing to take the win:

> Out of a bedlam of errors, long hits, vanquished pitchers, and the vociferations of half-frenzied spectators, the Chicago American League team emerged victorious over the Nationals to-day 8 to 6. The Americans won in spite of five bad errors, which were accountable for nearly all the runs made by the Nationals.[17]

"Three Finger" Brown follows through (NBL).

On October 14, game six was played in South Side Park, and for the first time in the 1906 World Series, the home team won. The White Sox became world champions. In front of 19,000 fans, the victors topped their victims, 8–3, behind White, who bested Brown. White went the distance after having lost the second game and pitching 2⅔ innings in relief the previous afternoon.

Manager Chance had led his club to 118 victories up to that point in the season. His decision to bring Brown back after only one day's rest didn't produced the desired results. Mordecai gave up eight hits during his 1⅓ innings of work as the White Sox built a 7–0 lead after two frames. The Chicago Nationals wouldn't recover as "The Hitless Wonders," who had been one-hit and two-hit in their losing efforts, banged out 14 hits in the clincher, and the Cubs exciting season's ride came to a crashing halt.

Following the disappointing loss, a gracious Cubs president, Charles W. Murphy, said,

> The best team won. They won because they played the better ball. Too much praise cannot be given to President Comiskey and Capt. Jones and the team which by unprecedented pluck climbed in midseason from seventh place to the top of their own league and then topped off that great accomplishment by winning the world's championship from the team that made a runaway race of the National League contest. I call for three cheers for Comiskey and his great team.[18]

The world champions carried away $25,051.53 from the gate receipts to divide among their players. The Cubs finished a distant second in the payoff, receiving a total of $8,350.17 to be dispersed among the members of their club.

Nearly a decade later, Evers was playing for the Boston Braves. Writing before the start of the 1914 World Series, which involved his Miracle Braves, who had climbed from nowhere to a postseason appearance, and the mighty Athletics, he commented about the 1906 experience:

> The Cubs went into the world's series of 1906 4½ to 1 favorites in the betting over the White Sox. There was hardly a man on the Chicago Americans who had hit his weight that season. I think we had just a great ball club then as the Athletics are today. Three or four years after that the Cubs were not as great a club, I'll admit, but in 1906, 1907, and 1908 I figure that they were as strong as the Athletics. Yet the Cubs got a drubbing from the White Sox.[19]

The 1906 series holds a special place in the lore of Chicago's rich sport's history. In a 1998 article in the *Sports Collectors Digest*, it was cited as the twelfth greatest moment in the Windy City's sporting life:

> The Elevated World Series. It was a World Series that had everything. An unknown hero, five Hall of Famers, a decided underdog, great pitching duels—and two teams from Chicago. Yes, in 1906 the Cubs and White Sox met for the only time in the World Series. The 1906 Cubs were 116–36 and had the famed infield of Joe Tinker, John Evers and player/manager Frank Chance. Their pitching corps included Mordecai "Three Finger" Brown (26 wins, 1.04 ERA) and Ed Reulbach (19–4, 1.65). The Sox? They were called the "Hitless Wonders," with their .230 team batting average.
>
> But the South Siders got the last laugh, winning the Series in six games. Game six was played before 25,000 fans who squeezed into South Side Park on a chilly autumn Sunday. Unknown hero George Rohe batted .333 for the

"Hitless Wonders" in the Series. The next season? He batted .213. and was sold to a minor league team in New Orleans. But Sox fans will never forget him.[20]

Notes

1. "First Baseball Games for the Championship," New York Times, 12 April 1906, 7.

2. "Chicago, 5; St. Louis, 2." New York Times, 22 April 1906, 10.

3. "Giants Easily Beaten by Chicago Leaders," New York Times, 21 May 1906, 10.

4. "Chicago's Weird Pitching," New York Times, 22 May 1906, 10.

5. "Baseball in England; Leagues Being Formed," New York Times, 3 June 1906, 10.

6. "Giant Badly Beaten," New York Times, 8 June 1906, 7.

7. "Too Much for the Giants," New York Times, 18 July 1906, 8.

8. "Giants Are Worsted Again," New York Times, 21 July 1906, 4.

9. "Steinfeldt's Long Hit," New York Times, 21 July 1906, 4.

10. "Sunday Baseball Decision," New York Times, 28 July 1906, 4.

11. "Record Baseball Crowd at the Polo Grounds," New York Times, 5 August 1906, 5.

12. "Giants Play Chicago and Lose Game, 3 to 2," New York Times, 9 August 1906, 4.

13. "Americans First for World's Championship," New York Times, 10 October 1906, 6.

14. "Americans First...," 6.

15. John Devaney and Burt Goldblatt with Barbara Devaney, The World Series (Chicago: Rand McNally, 1981) 23.

16. "Americans in Lead for World's Honors," New York Times, 12 October 1906, 11.

17. "Americans One Shy of World's Pennant," New York Times, 14 October 1906, 12.

18. World's Championship Goes to Americans," New York Times, 15 October 1906, 6.

19. Johnny Evers, "Braves Do Not Fear Athletics—Evers," New York Times, 7 October 1914, 10.

20. Mark Mandernach, "The 15 Greatest Moments in Chicago Sports History," Sports Collectors Digest, 21 August 1998, 101.

3. 1914 Boston Braves
The Miracle Comeback

The headlines and the articles on the front page of the *New York Times* on October 9, 1914, the opening day of the world's series, were focused on the expanding war being waged on European soil. Austria-Hungary had declared war on Serbia on July 28, about one month after the double assassinations of Archduke Francis Ferdinand, heir to the throne of Austria-Hungary, and his wife, the Duchess of Hohenberg. On August 1, Germany had declared war on Russia and two days later against France. On the opening day of the series, the newspaper gave details about the destructive bombardment of Antwerp, Belgium, from the land by ground troops and from the sky by zeppelins.

One article suggested a quick end to the war:

> A belief that the war will be far shorter than the present situation indicates is gradually gaining ground in diplomatic circles here. The Secretary of the embassy of one of the involved powers has made a large wager that the war will be over within three months and he is known to be a careful bettor, not anxious to lose money.[1]

On this side of the Atlantic, there were predictions of a short world's series, and the good money was on the Philadelphia Athletics. Manager Connie Mack, "The Tall Tactician," had led his club through another successful campaign. They had captured the series the previous season, and were ready for game one in Shibe Park against the Boston Braves, who had pieced together one of the most miraculous comebacks in major league history.

The Athletics, a dynasty, were clear favorites to capture their second straight crown and their fourth in the last five years. In 1914 they had won 99 games and had beaten out their closest American League rival, the Boston Red Sox, by 8½ games.

After toiling in the cellar until July 19, the Braves found strength, climbing into a first-place tie on August 23. Then they dropped down a bit but climbed right back, taking over the top spot alone on September 8. Once in control, manager George Stallings and his squad zoomed to a 10½ length finish ahead of the New York Giants, who had captured the National League pennant the preceding three years.

Although Boston's wild second-half dash had enthralled baseball fans, the Braves were not expected to be much of an opponent for the veteran, series-tested Mackmen. It would be a short series indeed, and the Athletics were expected to be crowned world's champions.

The major leagues had their own opponent in 1914. The Federal League was in its initial year of operation. Discontent on the part of American and National leaguers swirled around the reserve clause, salaries, the draft system, black-listing, and other manipulative practices. The reserve clause, which was thought to be the bulwark of organized professional baseball, had come into being in 1880, when the National League adopted a by-law declaring that the club with which a player signed a contract retained his services indefinitely.

Lured by the promise of increased salaries and welcoming the opportunity to get out from under the control of the reserve clause, 81 American and National leaguers and 140 minor leaguers jumped to the Federal League, which opened operation in eight cities. Four of the cities also had clubs in the majors—Brooklyn, Chicago, Pittsburgh and St. Louis.

In 1914 the Braves played their games in 11,000-seat South End Grounds as they awaited the 1915 opening of their new ballpark on Commonwealth Avenue. Two years earlier, James Gaffney had acquired the team, which had previously been known as the Boston Beaneaters, the Doves, and the Rustlers. Gaffney, a Tammany Hall "Brave," renamed the club.

Boston took up regular residency in the league's basement from 1909 through 1912. In 1913, Stallings, in his first year at the helm of the Braves, after having managed the Philadelphia Phillies, the Detroit Tigers, and the New York Highlanders, led the club to a fifth-place finish.

The peppery Stallings, who had reclaimed a number of his players from baseball's scrap heap, looked for even better results in his second year as the Braves' manager:

The Boston Nationals aspire to first division honors this year. With a team that has been practically made over since he took charge last season, Manager Stallings predicts that Boston will finish at least fourth, and possibly third....

The accession of Johnny Evers, crack second baseman and manager of the 1913 Chicago Cubs, and the resultant loss of Bill Sweeney [to the Cubs], was probably the most notable change in the team. Much is expected by local fans from the combination mid-infield play of Evers and young [Walter "Rabbit"] Maranville, the diminutive shortstop of last year. Recruits will cover the other infield positions, [Charles "Butcher Boy"] Schmidt, at first, replacing Hap Meyers, and [Charlie] Deal, at third, filling a position uncertainly occupied for several years. Both are from the International League.[2]

Evers had been tapped to be the Braves' captain, and, with his managerial background, would be counted on to help Stallings lead the club. The former member of the Cubs' famous double-play combo of Tinker, Evers, and Chance was teamed with the young Maranville, who was playing his second full season with Boston.

The celebrated Chicago trio, who first played together in 1902, were with the Cubs until after the 1912 season, when Frank Chance, who had been the Cubs' player-manager for eight years, left to become the skipper of the Yankees. Joe Tinker also departed that year to take over at the helm of the 1913 Cincinnati Reds. In 1914 he jumped to the renegade Federal League and was the player-manager of the new loop's Chicago entry. Tinker and Evers, who, according to tradition, would not speak to each other off the field during their playing days, had good reason to be enemies in 1914.

The Braves opened the season on April 14 against the Brooklyn Superbas in Ebbets Field. A crowd of 12,000 half-filled the ballpark on a cold afternoon in Flatbush. Brooklyn built an early 8–0 lead and the outcome was never in question as the Superbas went on to an 8–2 win. George "Lefty" Tyler, who had gone 16–17 the previous season and had led the league with 28 complete games, gave up 11 hits in a short five-inning stint and took the loss for Boston.

Although the weather warmed up, the Braves didn't. On May 1, after having a number of rainouts, they were in the basement with a 2–7 record. On May 15, their 3–14 record was the worst in the National, the American, and the Federal leagues. Their most recent loss was to the Cincinnati Reds, 6–0. Under the headline, "Reds Easily Outclass Braves," the account mentioned that Tyler had pitched fairly well, but an error by Evers and two by Maranville had led to several of the Reds' runs.[3]

As Boston entered June, they were 10–22, still in the cellar, and 11 games behind the front-running Giants, who were being carried by the strong right arm of veteran Christy Mathewson. The Brooklyn club's president, Charles H. Ebbets, Sr., had shown his business acumen by scheduling a doubleheader as the first direct scheduling confrontation with the rival Brooklyn Federals of the new league. On June 1, Boston dropped two games to the Superbas, 6–2 and 4–2, and fell farther behind New York. Brooklyn picked up wins in four of the five games played in the series against the Braves, with a sixth contest being rained out.

At that point in the campaign, Boston showed a bit of life and put together a 7–6 streak. For the season to date, Schmidt was the leading hitter at .291, and Evers was next in line with a .277 average. The Braves' top pitchers were specializing in "threes," with Bill James at 3–4, Tyler at 3–5, and Dick Rudolph at 3–6.

On July 4, the traditional mid-point in the season, Boston rested comfortably in eighth place, with a 26–38 mark. The Giants sat at the top of the league with a 38–24 record. Thirteen games separated the first place Polo Grounders and the cellar-dwelling Beantowners. That day, Boston played the perfect host at South End Grounds, dropping the morning game to Brooklyn, 7–5, in eleven innings, and losing the afternoon contest, 4–3. James and Tyler each went the distance and became holiday losers. Evers had a 5-for-10 day in the hitting department, offset by Maranville's five errors in the fielding department.

July 11 was the day that the Braves took their first small step on their long march to the pennant. The Braves, who owned a 30–41 record, beat the second-place Cubs, 5–2, in Wrigley Field. Perhaps the game was an omen: Chicago committed four errors, the usually bumbling Braves none. After a day for travel to St. Louis, Boston nipped the Cardinals, 8–7, in 11 innings. James and Rudolph divided the pitching chores, and Maranville went 3-for-6 at the plate. St. Louis won the next two days, and Stallings' men wondered if they were back to their losing ways.

A glance at the National League's batting averages and pitching statistics showed that Josh Devore, who had come from the Phillies during the season, was the only Brave hitting over .300 at .317. Outfielders Larry Gilbert and Joe Connolly were at .295 and .287, respectively. Evers was at .288, and Schmidt had dropped to .276. James led the boxmen with an 8–6 mark, Rudolph was 7–7, and Tyler was 6–8.

On July 17, James went the distance in a series-opening, 1–0 Boston win over the Reds. Two days later, after completing a three-game sweep of Cincinnati, Boston moved out of the cellar for the first time. They were still 10½ games behind New York, but things were looking up.

The National League's teams in the middle of the pack were tightly bunched. Following a 1–0 win over Pittsburgh behind Tyler on July 20 and a 6–0 defeat of the Bucs the next afternoon, the Braves found themselves in fourth place. The Giants were winning also, and their lead remained at what must have seemed to Boston an insurmountable 10½ games.

The Braves posted 1–0 and 2–0 shutouts over Pittsburgh, with an 8–4 Pirate win in between. Stallings' pitchers had thrown four games of goose eggs at Pittsburgh in the five-game set. Early in July, the manager had decided to go most of the rest of the way with a three-man pitching rotation featuring 6'4" right-hander Big Bill James, 5'9" righty "Baldy" Rudolph, and Lefty Tyler. James and Rudolph were both in their second full major league seasons. It was a risky decision for the manager with almost three months remaining in the season.

The Braves had posted an eye-opening 9–3 record on the road since July 11, and on July 24, they headed back home to open a series with the Cubs. The surging Braves dropped the first contest, but came back to take the next two from Chicago, 5–3 and 8–3. In the final game, the top three in the Beantowners' lineup—Devore, George "Possum" Whitted, and Connolly—each had two hits.

Manager Gene Stallings flanked by Bill James (left) and Dick Rudolph (NBL).

A pair of well-pitched games by Tyler and Rudolph brought the Braves 2–1 and 2–0 wins over the Cardinals to close out July. They had gone 14–4 since their momentum-starting victory on the eleventh. At the end of the month, Boston was in fourth place, nine games behind New York.

On the first day of August, Boston beat St. Louis again, with James going 10 innings. Whitted's single scored Evers in the 10th for the margin of victory. That afternoon, Cincinnati finished giving the Giants a three-game beating in their series, and the Polo Grounders' lead dropped to eight.

During the next week, Boston moved to within 6½ games of the top spot. The players' personal stats were climbing as well. Connolly had reached .306, Evers was at .296, and Gilbert stood at .290. Stallings' pitching maneuver was working: Rudolph's record had risen to 14–7, James stood at 13–6, and Tyler was 11–9. Rudolph was riding the crest of a seven-game winning streak and James had put together five wins in a row.

The Braves went head-to-head with the Giants in New York in a three-game set in mid–August, and the Braves made the most of their opportunities. The final game of the series sweep, which cut the Giants' lead to 3½ games, was a 2–0, 10-inning win for the Braves. In the top of the final frame, catcher Hank Gowdy, the raw-boned Texas red-head, drove in Red Smith with a triple and then scored on a wild pitch. The following report caught some of the flavor of the hard-fought contest, which was played in front of the Giants' largest crowd of the campaign:

> Through nine tense innings, in which a great crowd of 33,000 people saw one of the most brilliant struggles ever staged at the historic Polo Grounds, George Tyler, the little pitcher of the Boston Braves, and Christy Mathewson, the wonderful Giant veteran, battled yesterday without advantage on either side. Then, in the tenth inning, came the break which swept "Big Six" and his mates down to their third straight defeat at the hands of the Boston team by a 2–0 score.
>
> Pitcher after pitcher of the Giants staff had been swept before the Boston avalanche in previous games of the series, until only Mathewson remained to stem the tide. Even Matty, however, proved unequal to the task, and in that last great rally was hurled down to a bitter defeat.[4]

On August 20, Rudolph rang up his eleventh win in a row, with a 6–3 victory in Pittsburgh. The surging Braves were only 2 games behind New York. Two-base hits by Rudolph and Schmidt along with triples by Les Mann and Smith helped deliver the victory.

While Boston was taking two-of-three from Pittsburgh, the struggling Giants were dropping three to the Reds. On August 23, the two clubs sat deadlocked at the top of the National League with identical 50–48 records.

Boston had arrived. It had been a struggle getting there, it would not be easy staying there, and they didn't.

The next afternoon, Chicago beat the Beantowners, 9–5. Stallings used two of his three-man rotation in an attempt to halt the Cubs, calling on Rudolph to relieve Tyler. The Giants were rained out, and the Braves dropped half a game back.

During the remainder of the month, Boston suffered some tough losses, spending time in second place and even dropping to the third spot. The rival New Yorkers benefited from a couple of rainouts:

> John McGraw and his wearied athletes rested again today [August 26] when a continued downpour of rain prevented the scheduled game double-header with the Cardinals. This means a double-header tomorrow, but it prevents the third game of the series from being played, as the Giants will not return to St. Louis again this season.
>
> The Giants' leader was by no means averse to the postponement. It gives his hard-worked twirling staff a much-needed rest, and he feels more confident of holding his own tomorrow when he will be able to use Mathewson and [Charles] Tesreau in better shape than they have been for weeks.[5]

The Giants and the Cards split their games the following afternoon. In Chicago, the Cubs nipped Boston, 1–0, in a pitchers' duel. The well-pitched game lost some of its glamour, however, when fisticuffs broke out at second base. After a sliding Heinie Zimmerman was tagged out by Evers, the Cubs' baserunner came up swinging. The battling Evers, who had been Chicago's second baseman in 1913, stood his ground, took Zimmerman to the mat, and the two men had to be pried apart by teammates.

Boston saw a bright spot on August 30, when Tyler threw a one-hit shutout at the Cards in a 2–0 win. Sherry Magee's single was the only hit off the Braves' lefty.

After an early September doubleheader win against the Phillies in Philadelphia, the Braves climbed back for a brief stay at the top. The contests hadn't been much of a battle:

> Boston did not meet with much opposition from the lowly Phillies, who threw away the first game and were unmercifully trounced in the second. The opening half of the bargain day session somewhat resembled a ball game, and the Phillies should have won it. They outbattled Boston, obtaining thirteen hits for a total of twenty bases. The second was a burlesque on the great national pastime, and ["Red"] Dooin's withering Daisies never had a look-in.[6]

The following day, the Phillies bounced back and downed the Braves, 7–4, while the Giants were administering a pair of defeats to Brooklyn.

Boston was back in second. They Braves moved back into a tie for first place the next afternoon with a 7–1 win over Philadelphia, which was coupled with a Giants' split with the Superbas in Ebbets Field.

Both of the front-runners boarded trains for Boston for the September 7 opener of a crucial series. Because of the interest in the games, they were played in Boston's largest baseball field, the Boston Red Sox's new home, Fenway Park, which had opened in 1912. The largest number of fans ever to see one day of baseball in Boston took in the morning-afternoon twinbill. In the morning game, over 34,000 saw Mathewson surrender two runs in the bottom of the ninth as the Beantowners came back from a 4–3 deficit to pick up a 5–4 victory. In the afternoon "nightcap," the Giants battered Tyler and shellacked the Braves, 10–1. The morning crowd had been a happy one, but most of the over 39,000 fans for the second game went home upset. However, before they left they let their feelings be known:

> In the afternoon, however, trouble was narrowly averted. [Fred] Snodgrass, midway through the game, twinkled his fingers at Tyler, forgetting to remove his thumb from his nose. The Boston pitcher then came back with a pantomime reproduction of Snodgrass' muff in a recent world's series. Then, when the Giants took the field, the pop bottles began to fly. There was a real fusillade of them directed at Snodgrass by the crowd along the centre field ropes. Mayor Curley of Boston rushed out of the stands, and with a force of policemen stopped the embryo riot. Snodgrass continued to play, but in the ninth McGraw put [Bob] Bescher in centre field so that Snodgrass might not be the victim of a possible rush at the finish.[7]

The Boston fans' had seen their dream of leaving the ballpark two games ahead of the Polo Grounders reduced to another tie.

The next day, the Braves topped the Giants, 8–3, and they had first place all to themselves again. They would not give it up. They added to their lead the following afternoon when New York dropped a 9–3 decision to Brooklyn and the Beantowners split with the Phillies. After dropping the opener 10–3, Boston's "youngest boxman, George Davis, formerly of Williams College and now a student at the Harvard Law School," not only shutout the Phillies, 7–0, but also no-hit them.[8] Because of the large number of double bills, Stallings had been forced to supplement his three-man rotation, and the 23-year-old right-hander, a Yankee castoff, brought magic to the ballpark. A day later, Rudolph and James beat Philadelphia twice, 3–0 and 7–2, and the Braves were off to the races.

Boston ended the season at 94–59, the Giants 84–70. The Braves finished with a miraculous 10½ game lead.

On September 30, the National Baseball Commission decided that

The Miracle Braves (NBL).

the first two games of the series would be played in Philadelphia's Shibe Park on October 9 and 10. The series would then shift to Fenway Park in Boston for the October 12 and 13 contests. Game five was scheduled back in Philadelphia on October 14, and the sixth game would take place in Boston the next afternoon. A coin toss would determine the site of the seventh game, if it was necessary. In both cities, fans began to line up to buy tickets, though many of the Braves' fans may have lined up quite a bit earlier, since only 500 of them were at the ballpark for Boston's final home game on September 28.

When one looked at the clubs' final statistics, it was clear that the Athletics brought the stronger hitters to the postseason. Mackmen Eddie Collins [.342], Stuffy McInnis [.321], and Frank "Home Run" Baker [.316 and nine homers] led the club at the plate. The top three Boston hitters were Connolly [.318 with seven home runs], Schmidt [.281], and Evers [.275]. Stallings' use of his pitchers during the second-half of the campaign had produced outstanding results for his staff, as James finished at 26–7, Rudolph at 26–9, and Tyler at 18–13. Philadelphia's top hurlers were Eddie Plank, solid as always with an 18–6 record; Chief Bender, who had the league's best winning percentage with a 17–3 mark; and Bob Shawkey, who finished at 16–8.

An assessment of the two teams, position by position, appeared in the *New York Times*, beginning on October 1. The *Times* writers introduced the series of articles, saying:

> The situation which confronts the prophets in this year's world's series is
> difficult and uncertain, inasmuch as the Athletics of the American League
> outclass the Bostons of the National League very decisively as far as com-
> parison of past performances is concerned. The angle which increases the
> uncertainty is that Stallings's sensational Braves are an unknown, untried
> proposition as far as world's series play is concerned. Their shortcomings as
> far as facts and figures are concerned will probably not be borne out in actual
> play.[9]

The first article focused on the first basemen, and the nod went to
McInnis over Schmidt. McInnis, a member of the Athletic's famed $100,000
infield, had much to recommend him:

> The Bostonian [Schmidt] is not as quick a thinker as the alert McInnis. He
> is not as speedy a fielder and cannot run bases with the Athletics first sacker.
> Schmidt is big and clumsy, while McInnis moves around and covers ground
> with the quickness of a fox.[10]

At second base, Collins was a narrow choice over Evers. The two stars
had already been declared winners of the 1914 Chalmers Automobile Company trophy which went annually to the most valuable members of the pennant-winning clubs. Each would also receive a brand new Chalmers to drive
home. Collins, who had outstanding world's series in 1911 and 1913, brought
recent postseason experience to the Fall Classic:

> If one should come right down to the question: Has Evers been more valu-
> able to the Braves this season than Collins has been to the Athletics in the
> past few world's series, the best of judges would confront a problem which
> would be hard to answer. On paper the only way to judge these two stars is
> on their performances. On this basis Collins stands above Evers....
> As great a record as Evers has in baseball, Collins has a greater one.[11]

Philadelphia also was given the edge at third base. Baker's postseason
exploits were a factor in the choice of him over Smith:

> The figure of John Franklin Baker looms up so largely in the history of the
> world's series that he overshadows J. Carlisle Smith, the Boston third base-
> man. As far as actual mechanical play goes, Smith has shown, since he joined
> the Braves, that he is a far better player than he was when he played for the
> Superbas.... It is Baker's great resourcefulness as a timely batsman which
> gives him the edge over Smith. Few players have acquired a nickname in the
> sensational manner in which Baker was branded with his "Home Run" title
> in the world's series of 1911....
> Baker is a free, hard swinger. His eye is true, and his disposition is the
> kind that never gets ruffled. He's always cool and calculating.[12]

The Braves' situation became even more worrisome when Smith broke his right ankle and was in a Brooklyn hospital on the opening day of the series. Boston's hot-corner was manned by Charlie Deal.

The one position which was put in the Braves' column was shortstop. Maranville was chosen over the Athletics' Jack Barry:

> Walter Maranville, the diminutive short fielder of the Braves, has done such phenomenal work this season, that he is favored in the baseball classic above the reliable Jack Barry, the fourth member of the famous Mackian infield.
>
> Maranville has played in a dozen more games this season than Barry and tops him in every way.[13]

When it came to the catching corps, it was all the Athletics. The pair of Philadelphia backstops far outdistanced their counterparts with the Beantowners:

> Right at the start, probably no one but a deep-dyed partisan will deny the fact that Gowdy is no Li Hung Schang and that Bert Whaling is no Jack Lapp. On the face of a comparison, the Athletics' backstops are much superior to Boston's.[14]

The evaluation of the outfields was also one-sided in favor of the Mackmen:

> It is difficult to recall a major league championship club which has had such a makeshift outfield as the Boston Braves. Someone has aptly said of the Braves that they have no outfield: they just have outfielders. There is only one player in Stallings's outfield who is more than an ordinary outfielder, and that one is Joe Connolly.[15]

Stallings' Braves had made it through the season by stationing Connolly in left field and platooning Ted Cather, Mann, Herbie Moran, and Whitted with him. It had worked during the season, and, perhaps, it would work the rest of the way. The Athletics outfielders weren't the power of their lineup, nor were they household names, but Eddie Murphy, Rube Oldring, Amos Strunk, and Jimmy Walsh had provided strong defense.

Philadelphia had its stable of veteran boxmen; Boston had three young pitchers. Which would carry the day in the world's series? That was the question on most fans' minds and it was a question the *Times*' prophets addressed:

> The pitching problem in the world's series presents the interesting situation of age and experience pitted against youth and ambition....

Manager Stallings has used the "triple alliance" since early in July in turn, and has knocked sky high the theory, which has been followed in the major leagues for many seasons, that a pitcher could not work every third day and retain his best form. Boston's trio has done it and won a pennant, and now the Athletics are asking themselves the question, "Can these three pitchers still maintain the phenomenal pace they have set through the season's grueling fight?"

Stalling answers, "Yes."

Mack shakes his head, "No."[16]

Evers, the ex-manager of the Cubs and the Braves' captain and second baseman, became an author during the series, penning a newspaper column. In an article before the opening game, Evers wrote about his belief that pitching amounted to 50 percent of the strength of a team, and he thought that the Braves had the strongest staff. He went on to talk about two of the pitchers that the Athletics would face:

On the Boston staff is one of the best pitchers in baseball—"Big Bill" James, a kid in years, but a veteran for steadiness and nerve...Don't let anybody tell you that James depends on his speed and lets it go at that. He studies batters. He is a smart pitcher.

But one of the brainiest pitchers I ever saw go into the box is little Rudolph. He has everything that a pitcher needs except size, and his head and heart make up for this. He has courage. He won't care whether he is pitching against the Philadelphia Athletics or the Cleveland Indians.[17]

Evers' optimism was clear:

If paper statistics amounted to anything, our ball club would be beaten now before it ever started in the series, but they don't, especially not in a world's series.... If anyone is interested enough to take the trouble I wish he would cut this out and paste it in his hat:

The Boston Club has a very good chance to beat the Athletics.

Take off your hat and look at the prediction when the series is over. See how near I am to being right.[18]

Regardless of the captain's optimism, many of the fans in Boston feared the worst. The odds in the miracle-team's city were 100 to 40, with the Mackmen the favorites.

The world's series opened on Friday, October 9, at 2:00 P.M., in Philadelphia's Shibe Park. It was not the only major league game going at the time. City series were being played in New York, Chicago, and St. Louis, where the two teams in each city were facing each other for the area's bragging rights.

The series in New York was their first since 1910. (The Giants, of course, had been busy playing in a more important set of games the previous three Octobers.) An article in the *New York Times* indicated the degree of the excitement about the contests in that city:

> Experts who have followed both clubs all season do not hesitate to make the following predictions about the coming series. In the opening game ——— will pitch for the Giants and ——— for the Yankees. The series will probably be won by ———.[19]

There were other options for those New Yorkers who didn't care to go out to the Polo Grounds, where both teams had played for two years. (In 1913, the Yankees [née, Highlanders] had accepted an invitation to play there, after leaving Hilltop Park, which was located on Broadway between 165th and 168th streets.) An advertisement presented the opportunity for fans "to be at" the world's series:

> World's Series—World's Series
> BASEBALL
> At 71st Regiment Armory, 34th Street and Park Avenue
> Beginning Today and Every Day During Series at 2 P.M.
> Direct Wire to Ball Grounds
> Every play reproduced instantly by the celebrated
> "COLEMAN LIFE-LIKE BASEBALL PLAYERS"
> acknowledged by the Press and Public where shown to be the greatest Baseball invention in the world. You see every play as it is made on the field, with life-like pictures of players that hit the ball, run the bases, get put out or slide to safety. The ball sails through the air, actually players run, catch or pick up the ball and make the play. Umpires give decision. You see errors, fumbles, wild throws. In fact, it is just like being at the game
> NOTHING LIKE IT OR NEAR IT IN THE WORLD
> Don't forget—this wonderful invention in New York City ONLY at the
> 71st Regiment Armory, 34th Street and Park Avenue
> BRING THE LADIES   ADMISSION 25 and 50 cents[20]

Another advertisement announced the "Nokes Wizard Scoreboard," which would be "transferring games" to Madison Square Garden. There was only one price to attend this event—a quarter.[21] But, only in the City of Brotherly Love would fans see the *real* first game.

Mack tapped Bender to be his opening-game pitcher, and he was matched up against Boston's Rudolph. On a bright, Indian summer afternoon, the Chief was peppered by the Braves' booming bats in their 7–1 romp before 20,562 patrons in the Athletics' sold-out home park. Gowdy delivered a triple, double, single, and walk in five trips to the plate, and Schmidt smacked a pair of singles. Baker's double was the only hit produced by Philadelphia's best three batters. Boston displayed its exciting style of play when their final run crossed the place on a well-executed double steal.

After Bender was blasted from the box in the sixth inning, manager Mack, always attired in a suit, tie, and starched collar, and called all of his players "Mr." and expected to be addressed in like manner by them, had some not-so-kind words for Mr. Bender. They were not precipitated by the pitcher's sorry performance that day, but by something that had happened a few days earlier. Before the start of the series, Connie told the Chief to go to Boston to scout the Braves. The next day, when the manager saw the pitcher, he asked him why he hadn't made the trip. Bender replied,

> "What's the good of looking over a bush league outfit?" ... During the first game of the series, Mack looked up at the crestfallen Chief as he came into the dugout after being batted out of the box and rasped, "Pretty good hitting, isn't it, for a bush league team?"[22]

Stallings, ever-alert in the dugout, had been active during game one, keeping a wary eye on "the Mackmen and even Connie Mack himself for he well knew how foxy were his opponents who were looking for Rudolph's signs for the next game."[23]

Evers, in his daily column, had some things to say about the contest:

> If the Athletics thought before the series that we were not a bunch of fighters, if they thought that we were a joke ball club, I guess they have a different view of things tonight. We beat the team today, and we beat their best bet, Chief Bender.[24]

Maranville, speaking from his experience as a fielder, added, "The fielding on both sides was, I thought, very good, but when a pitcher is being hit hard, the men behind him do not show up so well as those who are playing with a pitcher who is not letting his opponents hit the ball much."[24]

The second game in Philadelphia was an exciting pitchers' duel between James and Plank. The nod went to the Boston right-hander, who faced only 28 batters, as the Braves picked up their second series win, 1–0. Before another full house, Deal, the Beantowners' substitute third baseman, scored the game's only run in the top of the ninth inning. After doubling, he pulled off a daring steal of third, and he scored on Mann's line-drive single to right. James held the powerful Mackmen to two hits, a single by Collins and a double by Schang.

Stallings was ecstatic, saying, "Today's game was unquestionably the greatest world's series game ever played. Both clubs were keyed up to the highest pitch of determination, and the gamest club won."[26] The manager's son revealed just how thrilled his father was, adding, "I am willing to state that there is not a better pleased man in the United States tonight than my father. His smile in the main event betters that of yesterday, when the broad grin appeared on his face, to remain throughout the series."[27]

The teams traveled north to Boston for games three and four. Fenway Park, which had been the site of the Boston Red Sox's first championship season in 1912, was ready to welcome the National League pennant-winning Braves. After the gates were flung open at 9:00 A.M. on October 12—and many entered at that time—35,520 spirited fans crowded into the park, and thousands more meandered on the sidewalks and in the streets outside the park. On newspaper row in South Boston, 25,000 additional fans gathered outside, receiving bulletins about the game and following its progress on a make-shift scoreboard.

Those who were inside the park witnessed a nerve-racking, twelve-inning battle which finally went into the Braves' column, 5–4. Philadelphia's starter was Lester Ambrose Bush, a youngster on the Athletics' veteran staff, who had gone 15–12 during the regular season. He went the distance that afternoon, surrendering nine hits. For Boston, Tyler pitched 10 frames, and James picked up his second series win with two innings of effective relief.

It was a see-saw affair, which was tied, 2–2, after nine innings. In the 10th, both clubs scored twice as Baker drove in two runs for the Athletics with a single and the Braves scored on a run-scoring sacrifice and Gowdy homer. The score stood at 4–4.

In the bottom of the 12th, Gowdy started a Boston rally with a double, which was his third hit of the day. Managerial wheels began to roll. Stallings sent Mann to run for the Braves' catcher. Mack ordered an intentional pass to Gilbert, a pinch hitter, setting up a force at second and third. With no one out, Moran dropped a bunt down the third-base line. Bush scampered over to field it, wheeled, and threw wildly to Baker, who was on the third-base bag. Mann raced home with the winning run. Amazingly, the Braves had win number three.

While Boston celebrated, something else was happening in another part of the park. The 21-year-old Philadelphia pitcher who later in his career would be dubbed "Bullet Joe" was suffering the pain of his errant toss:

A heart-broken youth, his eyes blurred with tears, slunk away under the big stands as the paeans of victory rang in his ears. His had been a great responsibility. His team mates, the fading world champions, had played masterful ball behind him, and they were all fighting shoulder to shoulder to try to stem the relentless onslaught of an all-powerful enemy.

Then, by one tragic throw, he had knocked the foundation from under the Mackian machine and it came tumbling down in ruins.[28]

The newspaper report about the game captured the special nature of the contest:

It was fully as interesting as, and perhaps more fiercely contested than, any ever played for the honors. The immense crowd—one of the largest that ever watched one of these games—became intensely enthusiastic as the Braves hung to the Athletics, who kept continually in the lead, forcing the home team to follow by dint of nerve and to hustle for everything in sight.[29]

In game four, under a chilly, gray sky, Rudolph went back to the box for Boston, and Shawkey was the starter for the visitors from Philadelphia. The key moment occurred in the fifth inning:

Johnny Evers, nervous and irritable, faced Bob Shawkey in the momentous fifth inning at Fenway Park this afternoon. Rudolph and Moran were crouched on the dusty base paths ready to dash for home. The score was tied, 1–1.

Crash! Evers's bat smacked the ball solidly and it whistled its way to centre field. Two Braves flashed across the plate with the baseball championship of the world.[30]

In reality, it would be four more innings before the miracle Braves could claim the 3–1 victory and the world's series crown. Rudolph held the Athletics' power in check the rest of the way, and he chalked up his second series win. He and James ended their amazing seasons with 28 victories apiece.

Captain Evers commented about the Braves' plan of attack:

Throughout this series we have played desperate ball and have talked to the Philadelphia players incessantly in an effort to take their hearts out. The bunch on the bench have helped out. They took after Baker whenever he went to bat today and "rode" him hard.

"Who is that at bat now?" was the chorus he got from the bench. "He swings like a busher."[31]

Following the game, Mack sent his assistant, Ira Thomas, to lead the procession of humbled Athletics to shake Stallings' hand and those of the surprising victors. Mack wouldn't make the journey. He was too angry. He thought that too many of his players had their minds more on the potentially large checks that the Federal League was waving at them than on the job at hand.

Still, the defeated and ever-humble Athletics manager was effusive in his praise of the champion Braves. "The Boston Braves are the best team that has ever played baseball," he said. "We lost fair and square and in saying that the Braves are the best team that has ever played the game, nothing more remains to be said."[32]

Indeed, Boston's batters had put together a phenomenal series. Gowdy banged the ball at a .545 clip and had the club's only home run. Evers came away with a .438 average, Maranville was at .308, and Schmidt hit .294. Only Connolly struggled at the plate, hitting .111. The awesome Athletics' hitters, on the other hand, were awful. Baker led the way for them with a homerless series and a .250 average. Collins was .214, Murphy .188, Schang .167, McInnis .143, Barry .071, and Oldring .067.

During the off-season, Mack purged Philadelphia. Pitcher Herb Pennock was traded to the Red Sox and Shawkey was sent to the Yankees. Contract disputes caused Bender and Plank to defect to the Federal League, which folded after the 1915 campaign. Baker was a holdout all season long and then was traded by Mack to the Yankees in the winter of 1916. The dynasty had ended.

Once Boston's 1914 mad march began, it was slowed down once or twice, but no team was able to stop it. The goal was total victory, and Stallings' men, who had come from obscurity to celebrity, climbed to the peak of major league baseball. It was the game's first memorable miracle, and perhaps it remains baseball's most outstanding meteoric rise.

Notes

1. "Envoys Now Look for Shorter War," *New York Times*, 9 October 1914, 1.
2. "New York's Three Teams All Stronger," *New York Times*, 14 April 1914, 9.
3. "Reds Easily Outclass Braves," *New York Times*, 15 May 1914, 13.
4. "'Big Six' Fall Before Braves," *New York Times*, 16 August 1914, sec. 3, 2.
5. "Rest May Help Giants," *New York Times*, 26 August 1914, 7.
6. "Braves Rush Past Giants in Race," *New York Times*, 3 September 1914, 8.
7. "Giants Unable to Oust Braves," *New York Times*, 8 September 1914, 8.
8. "No-Hit Game for Yankee Castoff," *New York Times*, 10 September 1914, 10.
9. "How Boston Rates with Athletics," *New York Times*, 1 October 1914, 9.
10. "How Boston Rates," 9.
11. "Collins Superior to Johnny Evers," *New York Times*, 2 October 1914, 9.
12. "Baker Bats Hard in the World's Series," *New York Times*, 3 October 1944, 9.

13. "Maranville One of Boston's Stars," *New York Times*, 4 October 1914, sec. 9, 2.

14. "Athletics Have Two Best Catchers," *New York Times*, 6 October 1914, 12.

15. "Braves' Outfield Below the Average," *New York Times*, 5 October 1914, 9.

16. "Will Old Pitchers Down Youngsters?" *New York Times*, 7 October 1914, 10.

17. John J. Evers, "Stallings Depends Upon Rudolph, James and Tyler to Beat Bender and Plank," *New York Times*, 8 October 1914, 12.

18. "Braves Do Not Fear Athletics—Evers," *New York Times*, 7 October 1914, 10.

19. "This Is the Series!!" *New York Times*, 30 Sept. 1914, 8.

20. *New York Times* advertisement, 9 October 1914, 10.

21. *New York Times* advertisement, 10.

22. John Devaney and Burt Goldblatt with Barbara Devaney, *The World Series* (Chicago: Rand McNally, 1981) 61.

23. T.H. Murnane, "Said Hitting at Right Time by Boston Champions Gave Them an Easy Triumph," *Boston Daily Globe*, 10 October 1914, 7.

24. John J. Evers, "Bender Now Out of Series—Evers," *New York Times*, 10 October 1914, 8.

25. Walter J. Maranville, "Glad to Win First Game," *Boston Evening Globe*, 10 October 1914, 7.

26. George T. Stallings, "Greatest of All World's Series Games—Stallings," *Boston Sunday Globe*, 11 October 1914, 9.

27. George T. Stallings, Jr., "Braves' Hitting Is Surprise to Macks," *Boston Sunday Globe*, 11 October 1914, 9.

28. "Boston Takes Third Game, 5–4, in 12th Inning" *New York Times*, 13 October 1914, 1.

29. T.H. Murnane, "Crowd of 35,520 Has Thrills Aplenty in Three-Hour Battle at Fenway Park," *Boston Daily Globe*, 13 October 1914, 1.

30. "Braves Capture World's Series in Four Straight," *New York Times*, 14 October 1914, 9.

31. John J. Evers, "Stallings's Genius Proved, Says Evers," *New York Times*, 14 October 1914, 9.

32. "Calls Braves Best Team Yet," *Boston Daily Globe*, 14 October 1914, 1.

4. 1934 Detroit Tigers

Rising from the Second Division

In 1934, after six consecutive finishes in the second division of the American League, the Detroit Tigers clawed their way to the top of the Junior Circuit. Detroit's most dismal season during the disappointing stretch was 1931 when they ended in seventh place with a 61–93 record and a franchise-worst 47 games behind the front-running Philadelphia Athletics. Although the Tigers held the distinction of being the only major league club never to have finished in last place, that was a hollow honor.

Prior to 1934, Detroit had not won a pennant since they accomplished the feat three seasons in a row from 1907 to 1909 during the heyday of fiery Ty Cobb.

During the six frustrating seasons leading up to 1934, few Tigers were listed near the top of the league's leaders in offensive and pitching statistics. Second baseman Charlie Gehringer appeared regularly among the American League's best in doubles, and in 1932, he finished second with 204 hits, right behind Washington's Heinie Manush, who had 221. Outfielders Roy Johnson and Gee Walker were occasionally listed among the stolen base leaders.

Right-handed pitchers Vic Sorrell and George Ulhe and lefty Earl Whitehill appeared in a couple of categories on the lists of the loop's top pitchers. But those appearances were few and far between. In 1932, a new name was there. Tommy Bridges received mention for a number of accomplishments, and, a year later, he and Fredrick "Firpo" Marberry were listed among the American League's best hurlers.

Detroit's 1934 comeback from mediocrity began months before the start of the new season when on December 12, 1933, the Tigers bought 30-year-old Gordon "Mickey" Cochrane from the Athletics. An outstanding catcher, Cochrane, who had hit .322 in his final year with the A's, was named Detroit's player-manager.

Detroit fans were hoping that manager Cochrane, a windfall from Connie Mack's second historic fire sale, would restore the franchise to the glory it knew in the Hughie Jennings era. He had led the Tigers to their three consecutive pennants nearly three decades earlier.

A newspaper account of Cochrane's appointment as Detroit's manager noted one of the club's shortcomings:

> Cochrane succeeds Stanley R. (Bucky) Harris, who resigned last Fall near the end of his fifth year at the Tiger helm. During his regime Detroit finished in the first division but once. Criticism had flared up last Summer, the loudest complaint of the fans being that Harris was unable to instill the fighting spirit in the players.[1]

One day after acquiring Cochrane, the club made a deal for another player who would prove to be a valuable asset. Detroit sent outfielder John Stone to Washington in a trade for 33-year-old, power-hitting outfielder Goose Goslin, who had had a sub-par season with the pennant-winning Senators.

Cochrane brought a winning attitude to the organization. He had been on the pennant-winning A's in 1929, 1930, and 1931. Those squads went on to become the world champions the first two seasons, and Mickey would settle for nothing less from the Tigers.

Hank Greenberg was excited about Cochrane's arrival. However, he had a personal battle to settle before starting to work with Detroit's new skipper. In 1933, Greenberg had hit .301 in 117 games as a rookie, and he was now holding out for a $5,500 contract. He had earned $3,300 his first year with Detroit. Detroit owner Frank Navin countered with an offer which would raise Greenberg's salary to $4,500. Hank continued to hold out for $5,500, and, as spring training rapidly approached, he and Navin agreed on $5,000 with a $500 bonus if the Tigers finished among the top three teams in the league.

Greenberg commented about his new manager's approach to the game:

> In 1934, the first year we trained in Lakeland, the first thing Cochrane told us was, "Listen, we're going to win. We're not going to lose." He also showed us how to get a man on first, move him over to third, and then get him in. And we would use what he told us during the entire season. We needed somebody to take charge and show us how to win and that's what Mickey did.

We didn't always drive a runner in with hits; there was the strategy of winning ball games with sacrifice flies and ground balls. Cochrane was the one who taught us how to do it. He was an inspirational leader.[2]

The Tigers began to show some spark during spring training. On April 1, the club received a scare when Cochrane, who had displayed outstanding catching and hitting skills along with dynamic leadership during the early exhibition games, was admitted to a hospital in Lakeland, Florida. Cochrane had been suffering recurring pain in his right side. He faced surgery which would keep him out of action for eight weeks if tests indicated that appendicitis was the cause of the discomfort. Happily, Cochrane escaped surgery and was back behind the plate five days later.

As the clubs prepared to open the new campaign, American League president William Harridge envisioned a tight race in the Junior Circuit and noted Cochrane's addition to the Tigers: "Everyone will endorse my statement that Frank Navin of Detroit made a master stroke when he purchased Gordon Cochrane from the Athletics, for he not only acquired a wonderful handler of pitchers but a batsman with punch."[3]

Detroit's opening day lineup featured only two new faces among the previous season's starters—Cochrane and Goslin. First baseman Hank Greenberg was preparing to play his first full season in the majors. Veterans Gehringer and Billy Rogell were at second and shortstop with Marv Owen, in his third year, at third base. Frank Doljack and Walker manned the outfield along with Goslin. Pete Fox and Jo-Jo White would become regulars in place of Doljack and Walker as the season progressed.

Cochrane was behind the plate, and he had six starting pitchers from the 1933 club to send to the mound. Bridges, Carl Fischer, Marberry, and Sorrell had more experience than Elden Auker and Lynwood "Schoolboy" Rowe, who were beginning their second big league campaigns. Chief Hogsett once again was designated to be the club's main relief pitcher.

Detroit went to Chicago for their April 17 opener, and the Tigers, behind Marberry, beat the White Sox, 8–3, making Cochrane a winner in his major league managerial debut.

They also won the second game of the season against the White Sox, 6–5, on home runs by Goslin and Walker. Bridges went the distance to register the victory. The visiting Tigers dropped the series finale, 9–8. Chicago pounded Rowe for seven hits in 2⅓ innings to take a commanding lead. Detroit battled back but couldn't catch the White Sox. Goslin blasted a pair of doubles and a triple, and Gehringer went 3-for-4, including a round-tripper.

The Tigers traveled to Cleveland's League Park where Fischer, a left-

Mickey Cochrane in spring training (Corbis).

hander, shutout the home club, 4–0, in the first of a scheduled three-game set. Detroit scored all of their runs in the top of the ninth inning. Oven's three-run double off the right-field wall highlighted the rally. The final two games in Cleveland were postponed because of rain and cold weather.

On April 24, Detroit faced the White Sox in their home opener in Navin Field. The fast-starting Tigers improved their record to 4–1 with a 7–3 decision over the visitors from the Windy City. Marberry hurled a complete game and his club scored six times in the sixth inning. Following the win, the Tigers sat alone in first place.

Detroit went 2–3 during the remainder of the month of April. Even though they hadn't maintained the pace they had established out of the gate, Cochrane and his club were beginning to generate fan excitement. On April 29, 30,500 spectators—the largest Sunday home crowd in two years—watched the Tigers lose to Chicago, 7–1.

On May 3, Detroit was scheduled to begin an eastern swing, but the first game against New York in Yankee Stadium was rained out. The following afternoon, Vernon "Lefty" Gomez shut out the Tigers, 3–0, and Babe Ruth hit his fourth home run of the season to lead the Bronx

Bombers. Ruth powered two more four-baggers the following day as the Yanks picked up their second win of the series, 10–6. Fischer surrendered six hits in 1⅓ innings and was followed to the mound by Auker and Rowe. Rowe, Walker, and White each collected a pair of hits for the losing Detroiters.

The Tigers next headed to Fenway Park in Boston and were shell-shocked after the opening game. In the bottom of the fourth inning, the Red Sox slammed four triples off Marberry to begin the frame. Before Tiger relievers Hogsett and Steve Larkin could register the third out, Boston had scored 12 times. The final score of the rout was 14–4.

Detroit showed some life the next afternoon, battling back to score three runs in the top of the ninth to tie the game, 6–6. Two innings later, Rowe, who had come out of the bullpen, blasted a two-run homer to bring the Tigers an 8–6 win, their first of the road trip.

Detroit split the final two games of the series, winning 5–1 behind Bridges and then dropping the finale to the Beantowners, 5–4. Goslin's two costly errors in the outfield were critical in the loss and offset Rogell's 4-for-4 afternoon.

The Tigers took two of the three games played in Philadelphia against the Athletics. In the second contest, which Detroit won, 10–5, the Tigers' bats came alive as Cochrane and Gehringer homered and Walker had a four-hit day.

Detroit traveled to Washington where they split a pair of games. Bridges had a shutout into the bottom of the seventh in the opener but ran into a streak of wildness, and the Senators rallied to win, 3–1. Sorrell threw a two-hitter the next day and the Tigers ended their road travels with a 5–0 victory. Cochrane and Goslin led the way with a pair of hits apiece.

On May 17, the New York Yankees came to Navin Field to open the Tigers' homestand. Detroit picked up wins in the first two games against the league leaders to climb into second place, a bit of rarefied air for the local club. They dropped the series finale, however, as Gomez registered his sixth straight win of the campaign.

Detroit ended up 15–14 during the month of May. At that point in the season, Marberry led the staff with a 4–2 record. The bats of most of the players had not yet warmed up. Gehringer was banging the ball at a .371 clip, but Doljack, with a .300 average, was the Tigers' next best hitter.

June was a much better month for the club, which put together a solid 19–8 record. By the end of June, the batting averages were much more impressive. Gehringer had risen to .391. A number of players had cracked the .300-mark, with Goslin at .328, Rogell and Owen at .307, Walker at .302, and Greenberg joining the group at .300. Cochrane had also climbed significantly, and was holding steady at .289. Marberry had shot to a 10–3 record and Bridges was 8–5. Auker and Rowe were behind them at 6–2 and 6–4.

The Tigers maintained their impressive pace during July, going 20–11 for the month. People were beginning to believe that the 1934 version of the usual second-place finishers was for real.

Three members of the club were selected to the All-Star team for the game played on July 10 before 48,363 in the Polo Grounds. Gehringer was the starting second baseman and played the entire game, going 2-for-3. Cochrane went behind the plate late in the contest, replacing the Yankees' Bill Dickey. Bridges wasn't called to go to the mound.

The second annual game went to the American Leaguers, 9–7, as they improved their record in the Mid-Summer Classic to 2–0. The highlight of the game belonged to a National Leaguer. In the first two innings, Carl Hubbell, the New York Giants' left-hander with a disarming screwball, struck out Ruth, Lou Gehrig, Jimmie Foxx, Al Simmons, and Joe Cronin in order. That would rank as one of the All-Star Games' memorable accomplishments.

The Tigers played a crucial home series against the Yankees to open the second half of the campaign. New York came to Detroit holding a slim lead over the Tigers. After Detroit took the opener on July 12, 4–2, they moved into first place by one percentage point. Rowe collected the win in the postseason setting:

> With bands blaring and seat cushions and straw hats making a veritable shower on the field, more than 20,000 Detroit fans celebrated in world series style today after the Detroit Tigers had set the Yankees down, 4–2, and dislodged the McCarthymen as leaders in the scramble for the American League pennant.
>
> The crowd constituted one of the greatest midweek gatherings in a decade at Navin Field.[4]

The second game of the set went to the Yankees, 4–2, and they climbed back to the top of the circuit. In the midst of the excitement about the Tigers, Detroit fans watched as Ruth reached a milestone. In the top of the third inning with a runner on base, the Babe slammed his seven-hundredth home run to give the New Yorkers a lead they would not relinquish. It was, declared the *New York Times*, a record for the ages:

> It promises to live, first, because few players of history have enjoyed the longevity on the diamond of the immortal Bambino, and, second, because only two other players in the history of baseball have hit more than 300 home runs.[5]

The Tigers and the Yankees staged a barn-burner the following after-noon. The Bronx Bombers blasted Sorrell from the mound after one-third of an inning and then slammed Auker as they took a commanding 9–1 lead into the bottom of the fourth frame. The Tigers would not go quietly, though, and they battled back fiercely. They would not catch the Yanks until the final inning, when they scored four times to capture the game, 12–11.

There was a new ground rule in effect because of the special seats which had been placed in the outfield. Any ball hit in them was ruled a double. Goslin and Fox each deposited three balls in the area, accounting for six of the ten hit there by the Tigers. The Yankees added three "spe-cial" doubles to the day's output.

Detroit took the series finale, 8–3. Greenberg, who had grown up in the Bronx and had gone to high school there, broke a 2–2 tie in the sixth with a bases-loaded double which scored a pair of runs. He added another RBI on a single later in the game. The Tigers had won three of the four games and had put some distance between themselves and the Yanks.

As the month progressed, however, New York put on a spurt and reclaimed the lead.

The Tigers closed out July with a 4–2 win in the second game of a doubleheader in Cleveland against the Indians. On August 1, Detroit finished a road trip, beating Cleveland, 10–7. The Tigers amassed 17 hits in the onslaught, with White's three singles and Owen's double and home run leading the way. Detroit climbed into first place as the Yankees were dropping a 7–4 decision to the Red Sox.

August proved to be an outstanding month for the roaring Tigers. They put together a 23–6 mark and took a firm hold on the American League's top spot.

Upon their return home, they proceeded to win all seven games played in Navin Field. On August 2, Auker tossed a 3–0 shutout at the White Sox in the series opener. Cochrane had changed his pitching rotation, a switch the *New York Times* called "a pretty piece of strategy," and the maneuver paid off.[6]

The following afternoon both the batting and the pitching were on fire in Detroit's 14–0 romp over Chicago. Goslin and White each banged out three hits, and Greenberg added a double and a homer to the attack. On the mound, Rowe held the White Sox to one hit—Jimmie Dykes' sin-gle in the top of the seventh inning. Schoolboy raised his record to 15–4 and was in the midst of a lengthy winning streak.

Detroit amassed 19 hits the next day in a 10–4 win over the Pale Hose. Cochrane had a three-hit game, and Greenberg continued his torrid pace, banging out a single, double, and home run.

Greenberg, who had struggled at the plate early in the season, was carrying the offense. At the end of July, Harry Salsinger of the *Detroit News* wrote:

> The development of Greenberg is one of the most amazing features of an amazing baseball season. He was a good hitter last year and a long one, but today he is one of the most powerful sluggers who has come along in years. All at once he gained confidence.... The unusual feature of Greenberg's development is that Greenberg's fielding has improved with his hitting. He was probably the weakest fielder among the first basemen of the American League last season but today his defensive work is as good as you will see.[7]

Bridges' six-hitter highlighted the Tigers' fourth win in the sweep of Chicago. The final tally was 7–0.

The St. Louis Browns didn't fare any better when they came to town on August 7 as the red-hot Tigers took a three-game set from them by the scores of 12–3, 7–6, and 13–2. The home club's second win took 10 innings to secure. After tying the game, 6–6, in the bottom of the ninth, Cochrane hit a single in the tenth to score Rogell with the winning run.

Cleveland suffered the same fate at the hands of the Tigers as they dropped all three of the games they played in Detroit. Rowe pitched the series opener and was around in the 11th inning when his sacrifice fly scored the winning run in the 6–5 victory. Auker's six-hit shutout paced the Tigers in the second game as the home club scored all seven of their runs in the first two innings. Cochrane's three hits led the way.

Game three on August 12 was another nail-biter, which went for 10 innings before Detroit pulled it out, 6–5, before 30,000 believing Tiger fans. Owen doubled in the winning run and started Detroit's second triple play of the season in the seventh inning. Right-hander Luke "Hot Potato" Hamlin got a rare start for Cochrane's club, and Marberry picked up the win in relief.

The first-place Tigers boarded a train for New York to face Joe McCarthy's Yankees, who were 4½ lengths behind them in the pennant race. Prognosticators in New York were predicting a full house in Yankee Stadium on August 14 for the doubleheader which would open the five-game set. There was also mention that the Yanks were the favorites in the matchup:

> Although the Tigers have been mopping up their opponents in the West, the White Sox, Browns and Indians, and the Yankees have been performing in rather an in-and-out fashion against the Athletics, Senators and Red Sox in the East, the betting last night favored the Yankees.[8]

Only one of the predictions came true. The stadium was jammed as 79,000 came to witness the double bill. An additional 20,000 fans roamed around outside the stadium, unable to get into the ballpark.

The betting line, however, was out of whack as the Tigers swept the Bronx Bombers, 9–5 and 7–3. In the first game, Detroit trailed, 5–0, but they bombed Gomez, the Yanks' ace, for five runs in the top of the sixth and added four more an inning later. Ray Hayworth, who was giving Cochrane a break behind the plate in the opener, had a 3-for-3 afternoon. Rowe pitched the second win with Gehringer, who had homered in game one, adding another blast in the nightcap as he knocked in four of the Tigers' seven runs. Detroit's amazing win streak had reached 14 games.

New York ended it the next afternoon, winning, 8–2. It rained the following day, and the two clubs were forced to play another doubleheader on August 17. Gomez was back in form, shutting out the Tigers, 5–0, in game one. Rowe was equally as effective as he picked up a 2–0 win in the second game. Schoolboy surrendered only three hits and fanned 11 Yankees.

Detroit had won three of the five important confrontations and had extended its lead to 5½ games.

The Tigers were standing 12–2 for the month of August and were off to meet the third-place Red Sox in Beantown. Boston opened the series with an 8–7 win, but the Tigers came back the next day to take both ends of a doubleheader. The Fenway fans had also caught the spirit as over 50,000 made it to the ball yard for the double bill with 46,995 paying to get in. The turnout represented the largest crowd in Boston's baseball history.

Greenberg banged out four hits in the pair of games, including three doubles. Gehringer, though he was hitting .367, went hitless.

After a day off, Detroit took the series finale, 8–4, with Rowe chalking up his 15th consecutive win.

On August 22, Washington was the next city to welcome the American League's most exciting team. The Senators handed the Tigers two setbacks in the first two games, a rarity for the motoring Detroiters. However, the league leaders came back to take the final two contests. In the first, Cochrane's double and single in the fifth inning helped the Tigers to a seven-run frame which led to a 12–8 win.

The following afternoon, Rowe was back on the hill, and he picked up his sixteenth straight win and his twentieth of the campaign. The victory tied the American League record for consecutive games won. The 22 year old found himself listed among some outstanding pitchers—Grove, Walter Johnson, and Joe Wood.

Shibe Park, Philadelphia, was the Tigers' next stop in their lengthy road swing. They remained on the winning track, topping the Mackmen, 7–6, in 10 innings. Greenberg's mighty home run in the upper left-field stands kept Detroit in the game early, and Gehringer's double scored Cochrane in the top of the tenth with the deciding run.

There was no suspense the next day as Bridges led the roaring Tigers to a 11–0 romp. After a day of rain, Detroit took the opening game of a double bill, 12–7. In the nightcap, the Athletics pounded Rowe and ended his streak with a 13–5 win. He would not stand alone at the top of the American League for consecutive wins: Tim Keefe in 1888 and Rube Marquard in 1912, both members of the Giants, had won 19 in a row to set the major league mark.

Detroit finished the month by picking up a 6–1 win in Cleveland. They began September with a 6–4 victory the next afternoon. It was the Tigers tenth extra-inning win of the season as they extended their lead over the second-place Yankees to 5½ lengths.

For Detroit, the early part of September was marked by doubleheader rainouts, a struggling offense, and effective pitching.

On September 2, Mel Harder of the Indians beat the Tigers, 1–0. Auker, who gave up only two hits, took the heartbreaking defeat. Two consecutive rainouts against the White Sox in Chicago washed out the entire series there.

Detroit returned home and beat the Athletics behind Rowe, 4–2. The next day, a doubleheader fell victim to the rain. When play was resumed on September 7, Philadelphia took a pair of games from the league leaders by identical scores of 5–4. Another twin bill was played a day later, and the A's took their third straight from the Tigers in the opener, 4–3. Detroit captured the second game, 2–1. Bridges and Philadelphia's Merritt "Sugar" Cain hooked up in an outstanding pitchers' duel. Greenberg's single off Cain in the first inning scored White and Walker with both of the Tigers' runs. Detroit managed only one more hit the rest of the way.

The Tigers won another extra-inning affair on September 9, dropping the Red Sox, 5–4, in 10 innings. Rowe picked up his 22nd win, and Greenberg's single scored Gehringer to nail down the victory.

Greenberg was on another tear. A day later, he stroked a pair of homers to account for all of Detroit's runs in a 2–1 victory over Boston.

The Red Sox followed with wins on successive days. Detroit suffered a rare extra-inning defeat, losing 4–3, in 11 innings. Then they dropped a 1–0 decision to the Beantowners and their lead was down to 3½ games.

Earlier in the month, John Kieran, in the *New York Times*, mentioned an often overlooked characteristic of the Tigers' club:

What they have mainly is speed. They have power, too, but it's their speed that has so often given them the winning edge in tight games. ... They have no [Bill] Werber in a Detroit uniform, but they have a well-rounded track squad. All the regulars are fairly fast afoot except Goslin and Marvin Owen. White, Fox, Walker, Cochrane, Gehringer, Greenberg and Rogell have the speed and inclination to dig in and get going with the pitcher's motion. They use their speed to get an extra base here and the on the longer hits, too.[9]

Following the series with Boston, Washington came to town, and on September 14, Detroit beat the Senators in 12 innings, 6–4. The Tigers came from behind three times, including in the bottom of the 11th and 12th innings, to pick up the win on Gehringer's two-run shot.

Detroit's offense came alive in a 12–2 win over the Senators the next day, but managed only three hits in a 2–1 victory the following afternoon.

On September 17, the Yankees, who were 5½ games behind the front-running Tigers, came to Detroit for a showdown:

Pennant hysteria, which has swept this city in a rather virulent form since Mickey Cochrane's Tigers went on the rampage a few weeks back and climbed to the American League leadership, reached a new high at Navin Field this afternoon. ... The populace turned out in such numbers that the fans overflowed the stands and bleachers and stood several deep in a continuous rim behind the outfielders.[10]

Right-hander Alvin "General" Crowder, in front of 36,211 screaming fans, throttled the Yankees, 3–0, in the series opener on September 17. Crowder had come from Washington by the waiver rout on August 4. He had been struggling with the Senators and brought a 4–10 record with him to Detroit. However, he had been a key member of Washington's staff for a number of years, going 26–13 in 1932 and 24–15 the next season.

Rowe repeated the shutout trend in the second game of the set, stopping New York, 2–0. The home team was getting ready for a rare postseason appearance. While Rowe was doing his pitching, workmen behind the left-field fence were busy building new bleachers for the expected crowds who would come to Navin Field to watch the American League pennant winners go against their National League counterpart.

The Yanks took the next two games, 5–3 and 11–7, to close out the series, but the Tigers had maintained their 5½-length lead. There was a rarity in the first contest. Greenberg was not at first base. Hank, a member of the Jewish faith, was observing Yom Kippur. It was the only game that season that Detroit's starting infield would not be intact.

After a day of rain in St. Louis, Detroit returned to the field and took two from the Browns, 8–3 and 15–1. Bridges won his twentieth game in the opener. After the doubleheader sweep, the Tigers' magic number to clinch the pennant was down to two.

Figuring that his club was in the World Series, Cochrane took the opportunity to announce that Rowe would be his pitcher in the opener of the Fall Classic regardless of whether the St. Louis Cardinals or the Giants, who were still battling for the National League flag, made it to the series.

Detroit continued to brace itself for the excitement. A newspaper report said:

> The old Tiger town has gone baseball crazy.
>
> It doesn't happen very often; about once in a generation. But when it hits, the ground shakes, fires glow, bands blare and the roar of thousands echoes across the city from Dearborn to Belle Isle, and from Cadillac Square to Royal Oak.
>
> When baseball pennants come to Detroit only once every quarter of a century, there is nothing blasé about the sporting spirit of this town for all its big city trappings. The first Roosevelt was in the White House and horse-drawn carriages were still in vogue when old Detroit turned out in 1907 to celebrate its first pennant winner of the twentieth century.[11]

In a doubleheader against St. Louis on September 23, Detroit had the opportunity to nail down the league championship. The Browns refused to follow the script, however, and took the opener, 4–3. The Tigers came back and took game two, 2–1, reducing their magic number to one.

Detroit was idle the next afternoon, but the Yankees were not. When New York dropped a 5–0 decision to the Red Sox, the Tigers could finally claim another league championship. The celebrating began on Monday, September 24.

Detroit played out the remaining five games of the season, winning four and losing one. With a 101–53 record, the Tigers were seven games ahead of the Yankees. They posted a .300 team batting average, with Gehringer, "The Mechanical Man," leading the way with a .356 mark. He finished right behind the Yankees' Gehrig, who led the loop with a .363 average. The Tigers' second baseman led the majors with 134 runs scored and was tops in the Junior Circuit with 214 hits to go along with 127 RBIs. Greenberg, the 23-year-old future great, batted .339 and banged 26 homers, 139 RBIs, and a league-leading 26 doubles. Cochrane finished the regular season at .320, White at .313. and Goslin at .305 with 100 RBIs. Rogell [.296] and Owen [.317] each enjoyed his finest season at the plate. Altogether, Greenberg, Gehringer, Rogell, and Owen accounted for 462 RBIs,

AMERICAN LEAGUE PENNANT WINNERS, 1934
Front Row—Lynwood "Schoolboy" Rowe—Herman Clifton—Coach Baker—Joyner White—Mickey Cochrane—Cy Perkins, Coach—Ervin Fox
Second Row—York—Elden Auker—Marvin Owen—Ray Hayworth—Bill Rogell—Vic Sorrell—Tom Bridges—Henry "Hank" Greenberg
Third Row—Hank Schuble—Frank Doljack—Charley Gehringer—Luke Hamlin—Elon Hogsett—Fred Marberry—Goose Goslin
Fourth Row—Trainer Carroll—Bat Boy Willis—Charley Fischer—Alvin Crowder—Gerald Walker

The 1934 American League Champs, the Detroit Tigers (NBL).

which set a major league record for an infield. In addition to Greenberg's 139 and Gehringer's 127, Rogell finished with 100 RBIs, Rogell with 96.

Cochrane had demonstrated his ability to improve the effectiveness of the pitching staff. Rowe [24–8] and Bridges [22–11] were the Tigers' big winners. Auker and Marberry each chipped in with 15 victories.

Detroit was also a big winner at the gate. For the first time in the history of the franchise, which stretched back some sixty years, the club drew over a million fans to the ballpark.

Detroit faced St. Louis in the World Series. Because of their fiery and daring style of play, the 1934 Cardinals would come to be known as the "The Gashouse Gang." The Cards, under manager Frankie Frisch, claimed the National League pennant on the final day of the campaign. They had made a late–September run at the Giants, winning 20 of their final 25 games and finishing two lengths in front of player-manager Bill Terry's Polo Grounders.

The Dean brothers, Jay Hanna "Dizzy" and Paul "Daffy," won seven games in the final 10 days of the regular season to lead the Cardinals to the flag. During the campaign, Dizzy went an astounding 30–7 with a 2.66 ERA and Daffy was 19–11.

A new dimension had been added to Series: The Ford Motor Company in Detroit had put up $100,000 for the broadcasting rights. Commissioner Kenesaw Mountain Landis assigned the unexpected income to the players' pool. The games were on the air for the first time.

Cochrane, who was only the twelfth manager to win a pennant in his first season at the helm since the birth of organized major league baseball in 1876, commented on the philosophy he employed during the season— one he planned to stick to in the series:

> Your first five batters in your line-up are your heavy hitters. Why waste them with sacrifices and leave the lower end of the batting order to bring in the runs? We stuck to our system of playing for a big opening in one inning and cleaning up, and we have won a pennant as the result of it.[12]

On October 3, Dizzy won the Fall Classic's opener in Detroit, 8–3. Cochrane changed his mind about starting Rowe in the first game and sent the veteran Crowder to the hill. Crowder, who had gone 5–1 with the Tigers after coming from Washington, suffered the loss. Outfielder Joe Medwick smacked four hits, including a home run, for St. Louis, and Greenberg homered for Detroit.

Navin Field welcomed 43,451 excited fans for game two, and they watched Rowe pitch the Tigers to a 3–2, 12-inning win over the National League champs. The hurler gave up single runs in the second and third innings, but allowed only one baserunner the rest of the way. Detroit tied the game, 2–2, in the bottom of the ninth. They continued their extra-inning magic and won it three innings later on a pair of walks and Goslin's RBI single.

On October 5, the series moved to St. Louis's Sportsman's Park for game three. Paul Dean pitched the Cards to a 4–1 victory, with Bridges taking the loss. A Detroit run in the top of the ninth ruined Daffy's shutout.

Detroit rebounded the following afternoon, pounding the Cardinals, 10–4, behind Auker, to knot the Fall Classic, 2–2. The Tigers also captured Game Five, 3–1, to take the Series lead. Gehringer, who was enjoying an outstanding postseason, banged a homer as Bridges went the route, surrendering seven hits. Dizzy Dean, who had ended up in the hospital a day earlier after being beaned as a pinch-runner in a would-be double play attempt, was the losing pitcher. At the time of the beaning, some feared that the Cards' top pitcher was done for the Series. However, a newspaper headline the following day passed on both good and interesting news, saying, "X-Ray of Dean's Head Reveals Nothing."[13]

The Tigers held a one-game advantage as the clubs left St. Louis for Detroit to conclude the Fall Classic. Detroit could almost taste the club's first-ever world championship.

Game Six was won by the Cardinals, 4–3, as Daffy bested Schoolboy in front of an expectant throng of 44,551 in the Tigers' home park. Shortstop Leo Durocher slid across the plate on Dean's single with what proved to be the winning run.

The season's two best teams had stretched the World Series to seven games. October 9 was the critical day. Detroit's fans still hoped for a victorious conclusion to their club's exciting comeback season.

It was not to be in 1934. Before the final game, Dizzy, the Cardinals' starter, shouted to Cochrane after watching Auker warm up, saying, "He won't do, Mickey."[14]

Dean, who went back to the mound after only a day's rest, was on his game as were the Cardinals' hitters. In the top of the third, St. Louis bombarded Auker. Before the inning was over, Rowe, Hogsett, and Bridges had been called into the game to pitch, and seven runs had crossed the plate. Dizzy contributed a single and a double during the uprising.

In the sixth inning, Medwick, who was having an exceptional series, hit a triple and slid hard into Owen at third base. The collision stirred up the Tigers' fans, who were growing irritable. Frisch spoke about what followed:

> As Medwick went out to left field, the Tigers fans met him with cushions, bottles, lemons, and some of them took off their shoes and tried to beat him. They tried to climb the 18-foot wire fence to murder him. For 15 minutes the game was stopped and finally Commissioner Landis told Cochrane and me to bring Owen and Medwick up to his box. He asked Medwick, "Did you kick him?" and Joe said, "You're darn right, I did." They wouldn't shake hands and the noise got worse. Cochrane would run out and beg the bleachers to be good, but they would have none of his advice. So Landis put both Medwick and Owen out of the game and we went on to finish it.[15]

Medwick's banishment was the only victory the Tigers fans had that day. Dizzy and the Cards went on to thrash Detroit, 11–0 in a 17-hit uprising. The Cardinals became the world champions.

Though Detroit's exciting comeback had fallen a game short, the Tigers completed their quest in 1935 after winning the American League title for the second year in a row. From there, they went on to the world championship, defeating the Chicago Cubs, four games to two, in the Fall Classic.

Notes

1. "New Tiger Pilot Is 10th Since 1900," New York Times, 13 December 1933, 32.

2. Ira Berkow, Hank Greenberg: The Story of My Life (New York: Times Books, 1989), 51.

3. Will Harridge, "Harridge Outlines His Views on Race," *New York Times*, 15 April 1934, Sec. 3, 5.

4. James P. Dawson, "Yankees Bow, 4–2, Drop League Lead," *New York Times*, 13 July 1934, 20.

5. "Ruth's Record of 700 Home Runs Likely to Stand for All Time in Major Leagues," *New York Times*, 14 July 1934, 8.

6. "Tigers Blank Indians," *New York Times*, 3 August 1934, 21.

7. Berkow, 55.

8. "Tigers Invade Yankee Stadium Today," *New York Times*, 14 August 1934, 24.

9. John Kieran, "On the Trail of the Tiger," *New York Times*, 10 September 1934, 24.

10. "Crowder, Tigers, Blank Yanks, 3–0," *New York Times*, 18 September 1934, 29.

11. "Detroit Is Tense with Pennant Near," *New York Times*, 23 September 1934, Sec. 3, 4.

12. "Governor and Detroit City Council Honor Tigers as Fans Shower Players with Gifts," *New York Times*, 26 September 1934, 27.

13. John Thorn, Pete Palmer, Michael Gershman, and David Pietrusza, *Total Baseball, Sixth Edition* (New York: Total Sports, 1999), 141.

14. John Devaney and Burt Goldblatt with Barbara Devaney, *The World Series* (Chicago: Rand McNally, 1981) 145.

15. Charles Einstein, Editor, *The Baseball Reader* (New York: Lippincott & Crowell, 1980), 132.

5. 1946 Boston Red Sox

The Premier Post-War Comeback

In 1946 major league baseball welcomed back many of the players who had, over four wartime seasons, taken off their baseball uniforms and gone to serve their country's military in the various battle theaters during World War II. In January 1945 it had been reported that 5400 of the 5800 professional players at the time of Pearl Harbor were or had been in the military. Since a significant number of them were returning in 1946, teams faced the challenge of providing places for them to play. Most of the clubs were rebuilding their farm systems so that there would be additional teams for the returning heroes. Early in the season, many major league teams carried more than 40 players. Later, the limit became 30, which was five more than previous seasons.

There was excitement about the upcoming campaign. Some of the stars of the game had in fact made it back during 1945: Hank Greenberg rejoined the Detroit Tigers in July and sparked them to the world championship; Bob Feller had gone to the mound for the Cleveland Indians in August; and Virgil "Fire" Trucks, back on the mound in the Motor City, worked five innings in a late-season game and then pitched the second game of the Fall Classic, beating the Chicago Cubs, 4–1.

Not all the ex-soldiers were heading for baseball in the States, however. The Mexican League had launched a raid on major league players, offering them fabulous opportunities to play ball south of the border. When there was an attempt to block the Mexican raid, Bernardo Pasquel, brother of the Mexican Baseball League's president, reacted, saying that his organization would fight the U.S. leagues all the way to the Supreme Court:

"We have offered players better salaries, improved working conditions and reduced working hours to play in Mexico and we have no apologies for these actions."[1]

Vern Stephens, who had played for the St. Louis Browns during the war years, was one of the first to jump at the offer to play for more money. After playing briefly with Veracruz, however, he reconsidered the move and returned to the Browns for the 1946 season. Mickey Owen, who had played for Brooklyn before entering the Navy, and Luis Olmo, who had been in the majors from 1937 until 1945, first with the St. Louis Cardinals and then with the Dodgers, went to Mexico to continue their careers.

Returning stars and record-setting attendances during the exhibition season set the stage for an exciting regular campaign. The major league teams promised to be much improved with the return of players who had served in the war. Before the start of the season, one estimate predicted that "all teams would be strengthened by 50 to 75 percent."[2]

In anticipation of the openers, Arthur Daley of the *New York Times* saw 1946 as the beginning of a new era for the great American pastime:

> This is it. The long-awaited first post-war baseball season is about to begin, and no campaign in the entire history of the diamond game ever received the brisk attention that this one has drawn. All the pent-up yearnings of the fans and all the hemmed-in desires of the players will erupt in full fury today. To the hills, men. The dam has burst. It's almost as violent as all that.[3]

In the American League, the world champion Tigers were scheduled to meet the Browns in Detroit, and the Indians and the Chicago White Sox would play in the Windy City. The star-studded New York Yankees were prepared to go into action in Philadelphia against the Athletics.

Boston, with Joe Cronin in his twelfth year as the club's manager, opened its season on April 16 in Washington's Griffith Stadium. Harry S Truman, the first presidential southpaw to throw out an opening pitch, got the game going shortly before 3 P.M. Truman's toss was the renewal of a long-standing baseball tradition stopped by Franklin Delano Roosevelt after the start of the war.

The Red Sox fielded a very different team from the one which had finished the 1945 campaign in seventh place with a 71–83 record and 17½ games behind Detroit. Only first baseman–outfielder George "Catfish" Metkovich, third baseman–outfielder Leon Culberson, and second-year starter Dave "Boo" Ferriss had been with the '45 club.

The opening day infield featured second baseman Bobby Doerr and shortstop Johnny Pesky, both war returnees. First baseman Rudy York had come from Detroit and Culberson was at third. The outfield was Metkovich, and two returning stars: Dom DiMaggio and Ted Williams. Another war veteran, Frankie Pytlak, was behind the plate. As the season progressed, Hal Wagner and Roy Partee, both of whom had missed the 1945 season, would do the bulk of the Bosox's catching. Also, war veteran Rip Russell and ex–Tiger Pinky Higgins would spend time at third base.

Besides Ferriss, the pitching staff featured Tex Hughson, who had also been away from the game the previous season, and Joe Dobson and Mickey Harris, each of whom had spent a lengthy stint in the military. Jim Bagby had joined the staff, coming from the Indians. The bullpen featured two ex-servicemen, Earl Johnson and Bob Klinger.

The Red Sox, behind Hughson, got their season off on a winning note, 6–3, before 30,373 fans. With the exception of Hughson, every Boston starter got at least one hit. The big blow was Williams' 430-foot blast into the center-field bleachers, the longest home run seen in Washington in 15 years. The prodigious drive by Williams, who had served as a pilot-instructor in the Marines through 1945, brought the crowd, including Truman, to its feet:

> The President was an enthusiastic if outwardly restrained spectator throughout the contest as he carried out his accustomed role of unofficial umpire. Twice, when home runs went sailing into the center-field bleachers or over the right-field wall, the President left his seat along with the other fans to watch the ball disappear beyond the playing field.
>
> Then as each of the batters of the circuit clouts crossed home plate the President doffed his hat in a smiling "well done."[4]

The next afternoon, Boston stopped Washington, 13–6. Ferriss, who had won 21 games in 1945 as a rookie, was shelled from the mound in the fourth inning after surrendering five runs. Johnson, a left-hander who had won a battlefield commission for showing bravery under fire during the war, controlled the Senators the rest of the way. DiMaggio hit a three-run, inside-the-park home run, and Williams went 3-for-3 and had three walks during his perfect day at the plate.

The Red Sox captured the series finale, 3–1, behind Harris. Pesky was 3-for-3 with two RBIs, and Williams ended his outstanding series with a 2-for-2 afternoon, driving in the Bosox's other run.

The curtain was raised in Fenway Park on April 20. An opening day crowd of 30,446, the largest in the famous ball yard's history, watched the Bosox beat the Athletics, 2–1. Pesky's game-winning homer in the eighth inning helped Hughson pick up his second win of the season.

The following afternoon, in the first game of a doubleheader, Boston won its fifth consecutive game, beating Philadelphia, 12–11, in extra innings.

Down 7–0, the Beantowners battled back and the outcome was finally decided when Williams singled with the bases loaded in the bottom of the 10th. For the second time in a row, Ferriss was battered, but did not pick up the loss. He gave up six hits in 2⅔ innings of work.

The winning streak came to an end when the A's beat the Red Sox, 3–0, in the second game. Bobo Newsom, who was pitching for his seventh club in a lengthy major league career, kept Boston's hitters at bay until the game was called after five innings because of the Sunday curfew. Williams had his first hitless game of the campaign.

On April 22, Washington came to town and the Bosox topped them, 5–4. It was a scary afternoon for the Fenway fans. They gasped when Pesky got hit on the head by a fast ball from right-hander Sid Hudson. He had to leave the game, but fortunately it did not prove to be a serious injury. Rookie Eddie Pellagrini, making his first major league appearance, ran for Pesky and then took over at shortstop. In the seventh inning, with the score 4–4, Pellagrini slammed a game-winning homer for the Sox. Doerr and York had connected for home runs earlier in the game.

Washington won for the first time in five meetings with Boston, beating the Sox, 8–2, the next day. With the game tied, 2–2, they exploded for six runs in the top of the 11th inning. Veteran Mike Ryba, who was nearing the end of a ten-year career in the majors, was the victim of the attack.

Beantown was prepped for the Yankees' first visit. Beyond the battle between the American League's most ferocious adversaries, who were tied for the top spot at 6–2, the two-game set offered the first matchup of Williams, "the Splendid Splinter," and Joe DiMaggio, "the Yankee Clipper," since 1942. In 1941, their exploits had thrilled the baseball world when Williams hit an astounding .406 and DiMaggio put together an unbelievable 56-game hitting streak.

On April 24, neither slugger thrilled anyone as the New Yorkers blasted the Bosox and Hughson, 12–5. During the slugfest, Williams banged a triple but that was the only hit among the two luminaries in 11 official at-bats. "The home fans were especially upset; Williams, to their dismay, broke the back of two Red Sox rallies by hitting into double plays and then ... terminated a miserable afternoon by bouncing into his third twin killing on the final play of the game."[5]

A day later, Boston did the blasting, beating the Bronx Bombers, 12–5. Pesky had recovered from the beaning and returned to shortstop, moving Pellagrini to third base. The twosome ignited the Red Sox, with Pesky contributing two doubles and a pair of singles while Pellagrini added a double, a triple, and a home run.

Pellagrini though he might have preferred to play shortstop, was determined to contribute to the team. As he recalled, "Cronin asked me if I could play third base. I said, 'I can play any place.' I was a little reluctant to play third, but I gave it a go."[6]

And the ex-soldier gave more than his on-field cooperation to his club; he devoted himself to the men he considered close friends. "We were also the best dressed team in the league," he remembered. "I loved clothes. Culberson, Wagner, Partee, DiMaggio and Pesky all loved clothes. My father, Eddie Pellagrini, was a real good custom tailor and he took care of us."[7] Such is the stuff of team chemistry.

Boston traveled to Philadelphia, where they took three straight games. In the opener, Ferriss had his first effective outing of the season, shutting down Connie Mack's club, 7–0, on six hits. Hughson and Harris kept things going the next day, picking up 2–1 and 5–1 wins over the Athletics. The double victory moved the Bosox into first place, one game ahead of the Yanks.

After an open date, the Red Sox closed out April with a 4–0 victory over the Tigers in Boston. Dobson's three-hitter, York's two-run double, and Doerr's homer were the highlights of the win.

Boston had an auspicious start to May, thumping Detroit, 13–1, and batting around in each of the first two innings. The club was on a roll.

The Red Sox met the Yankees in the Bronx on May 10 to begin a three-game series. The Beantowners beat the Yanks, 5–4, scoring two runs in the top of the seventh. Trailing 3–0 in the fifth, Joltin Joe DiMaggio hit a grand slam off Dobson to give the Bronx Bombers the lead. Cronin took the shell-shocked Dobson out of the game and replaced him with Johnson, who held New York scoreless the rest of the way. Left-hander Joe Page, who had relieved 42-year-old Red Ruffing, took the loss.

The victory was special for the Olde Town Team, as it was their 15th in a row and represented the longest winning streak in its history. It was also the longest in the American League since 1931.

The loss did not please Yankees' president Larry MacPhail, but the turnout did. A special Ladies Day crowd of 64,138 filled the stadium. One of MacPhail's many innovations was to schedule special occasions to introduce women to baseball and get them into the ballpark. They were there in full force on that May day.

Boston's lengthy streak came to an end the next afternoon when Ernie Bonham whitewashed the Red Sox, 2–0. Tommy Henrich's double and homer accounted for both New York runs. Hughson took the loss. In a futile attempt to keep the streak alive, Cronin used Ferriss in relief late in the game.

As reported in the *New York Times*:

A train stops. An elevator stops. Even a radio stops—sometimes. So it was only natural that the Red Sox, for all their power, reached the end of their skein of uninterrupted victories. Sooner or later it was bound to happen, and happen it did yesterday at the Stadium.[7]

Boston took the finale, before 69,401 rejuvenated New York fans. Yankee ace Spud Chandler, going for his sixth straight win, didn't get it. Harris went the distance for the Bosox in their 3–1 victory. Each club garnered only three hits, but Boston's offensive efforts were helped by key Yankee errors. Only one of the winner's runs was earned.

There were a couple of firsts that day. It was the first time during the season that Chandler failed to go the distance, and the Yanks dropped their first series of the campaign.

Boston left town with a 22–4 record and a 5½ game lead on the second-place Yankees.

Later in the month, the two clubs met in Boston, and the outcome was the same. The Red Sox took two of the three games.

New York came to town with a new manager. Bill Dickey had taken over the night before for Joe McCarthy, who had given his resignation to MacPhail. The previous July, McCarthy had tried to resign, but the president had not accepted it. On May 24 of the '46 campaign, however, he did.

Arthur Daley described the dynamics between the two men:

Both men like fiercely to win. But there their similarity ends. Marse Joe is an ultra-conservative man, who hates change, emotionalism, gloss or glitter. Larry is a radical who relishes change, flash, color, excitement and argument. Temperamentally they are as far apart as the poles. That they'd some day come to a parting of the ways was absolutely inevitable.[8]

Boston won the series opener, 7–4. Ferriss pitched into the seventh inning, but he was shelled at that point, and Johnson came in from the bullpen to save the game.

It was only May, but the doubleheader in Fenway the next day brought an exuberant World Series atmosphere. Fans waited in line overnight outside Fenway Park for tickets, and thousands were unable to get into the ballpark after the gates were opened.

The Beantowners took game one, 1–0. Hughson went the distance and scored the only run in the bottom of the seventh. He opened the inning with a single and later, with the bases loaded, Floyd Clifford "Bill" Bevens walked Williams to force Tex home.

Manager Dickey shook up the lineup for the nightcap, including taking himself out from behind the plate. His maneuvers worked, and New

York stopped Boston, 4–1. Page went the distance in the rain-shortened, seven-inning game. Joe DiMaggio and Phil Rizzuto hit home runs for the Bronx Bombers.

The Yankees left town after their second series in May against the Bosox, trailing the league-leaders by six lengths.

By the first of June, Boston had put together outstanding offensive and pitching statistics. Williams was banging the ball at a .349-clip, and DiMaggio and Pesky were not far behind at .336 and .333, respectively. The staff had three undefeated pitchers: Ferriss, who had righted himself after his early-season struggles, was 8–0; Johnson had a 3–0 mark; and lefty Clem Dreisewerd was 2–0. Harris had built an 8–1 record, and Dobson had gone 5–1. Only Hughson, at 4–4, was absent from the list of the league's top hurlers.

On June 15, Boston was nine games ahead of the Bronx Bombers. The Red Sox went 9–8 the rest of the month, but only lost one-half game of their lead.

The Bosox were in New York on July 2 to begin a two-game series. A crowd of 69,107 poured into Yankee Stadium for the opener, setting a record for the largest number of people ever to attend a night game. Chandler had a no-hitter going through 7⅓ innings before Doerr ended his masterpiece. It was a strange evening for Spud, who ended with 2–1 win and a two-hitter. Usually a control pitcher, Chandler was uncharacteristically wild, and walks led to a Boston run in the fourth without benefit of a hit. Harris suffered the loss, giving up five safeties.

The following afternoon, Hughson lost, 3–2. Page, in relief of Bevens, picked up the win when New York struck for two runs in the bottom of the ninth. It was an important victory for the Yankees:

> The Red Sox are leading the American League pennant race as the traditional Fourth of July point is reached, the date which historians claim foreshadows a similar position at the season's end. The Yankees had just ripped two victories from their grasp and were beginning to breathe most disconcertingly on the backs of their necks.
> The Bronx Bombers had to win these two to stay in the pennant fight. So they did—yesterday's coming in Frank Merriwell style as Aaron Robinson, a stolid gent who never before had been accused of being a Merriwell, bashed out a double in the ninth to give the Yanks a totally unexpected but highly appreciated 3–2 triumph.[10]

In a Sunday doubleheader right before the All-Star break, the Red Sox bombed the Senators, 11–1 and 9–4, to build a 7½ game bulge over the Yanks. Boston banged out 30 hits to go with the 20 runs. DiMaggio,

Williams, and York each had five hits. Williams, who was leading the league in bases on balls, drew a couple more free passes and scored seven times in the double bill.

The July 9 All-Star Game was the next bit of excitement on Boston's platter. Fenway Park was hosting its first-ever midsummer dream game. Eight Red Sox players, including DiMaggio, Doerr, Ferriss, Harris, Pesky, Wagner, Williams, and York, were on the American League's squad. DiMaggio and Williams came into the game as two of the league's top three hitters. Dom's .349 average was two points higher than Ted's, and they were right behind the Senators' Mickey Vernon, who led the circuit with a .364 mark.

Williams thrilled the home crowd and the baseball world with an incredible performance as the Americans shocked the Nationals, 12–0. He collected four hits, scored four runs, and hit two homers. One of the home runs came off Rip Sewell's "Eephus Ball," a pitch with a 20-foot-high arc.

After the game, Pittsburgh's Sewell talked about what Williams had done with his special pitch:

> I've been using it since 1941 and the longest previous hit was a triple by Stan Musial.... That one was high and windblown, too. Don't tell me the American League ball isn't much livelier than ours.[11]

On July 24, Williams experienced a first in his career. After the Red Sox topped the Indians, 11–10, in the opener of a Sunday doubleheader at Fenway, Cleveland manager Lou Boudreau, who had a home run and four doubles in game one, came back in the second matchup with a new approach to handling Williams. "The Splendid Splinter" had smashed three homers and a single and had driven in eight runs during Boston's victory. When Williams came to bat in game two, he stared at the new defense which greeted him:

> The Cleveland manager [shortstop Boudreau] played back on the grass midway between first and second. Jimmy Wasdell, the first sacker, posted himself on the grass near the foul line.
>   The third baseman was on the grass on the right side of second base and the right and centerfielders patrolled as deep as possible in that sector.[12]

Left fielder George Case was stationed just behind the shortstop's position.

Ted, hitting into the teeth of the "Cleveland Shift," which would soon be known as the "Williams Shift," lined a shot down the right-field foul line over Wasdell's outstretched glove for a double in his first at-bat. He also drew his 95th and 96th walks in his first confrontation with Boudreau's strategy. The Indians retired Williams in one of his plate appearances as the Red Sox went on to win, 9–4.

Boston entered August with a 12½-game lead over the Yankees and the world champion Tigers, who had joined New York in second place. Williams, meanwhile, had moved closer to Vernon in the batting race, his .353 average only four points behind the Washington first baseman. Williams [94], York [87], and Doerr [81] were the top three RBI-leaders in the majors.

Yankee Stadium was the site for the next Boston–New York series, which began on Friday, August 9. It was the Red Sox's final trip to the Bronx during the 1946 season. Before the opener, MacPhail, who always had his sight on the attendance figures and never could stand being second-best, took the opportunity to challenge Cleveland's claim that the 74,529 who had come to Municipal Stadium for the Indians-Yankees doubleheader the previous Sunday was the largest crowd in the history of the major leagues. MacPhail insisted that the record was 81,841. That was the number who had seen the Yankees and the Red Sox play at the Stadium on May 30, 1938.

Although the present-day Yankees were not making much headway toward catching the Bosox, their fans were still coming to the stadium in large numbers. The first game of the series drew 63,040, and they watched as York hit a three-run homer in the top of the sixth to wipe out a 3–1 New York lead and give Boston a 4–3 win. Ferriss registered his seventh consecutive victory to improve his record to 19–4.

New York took game two on Saturday, 7–5 in 12 innings. In the top of the seventh, with the game tied, 1–1, Williams blasted a three-run homer to give the Bosox a 4–1 lead. In the bottom half of the inning, the Bronx Bombers' Aaron Robinson hit a home run to ignite a three-run rally which tied the game at 4–4. In the 12th, Williams connected again to give Boston a 5–4 advantage. In the bottom of the frame, Robinson trumped Thumpin Theodore, driving a pitch from Dreisewerd into the stands for a game-winning, three-run homer.

The two teams split a Sunday double bill before 72,320 fans. Boston took the opener, 7–5, and New York, behind Page's two-hitter, captured the nightcap, 9–1.

By the time the Yankees came to Fenway in mid–August, Eddie Collins, the Red Sox's general manager, was making plans to try to handle the many requests the team expected for World Series tickets. Since Fenway had a capacity of approximately 34,000, Collins knew that many more Beantowners and others in the vicinity would want to come to the ballpark for the Fall Classic. On August 18, he announced that fans would be restricted to two tickets for no more than one of the games played in Boston.

In the middle of their World Series dreams, Boston took the series from New York, three games to one, thereby extending their lead to 14 games.

In September a streak was ended and a pennant was clinched. On September 7, Ferriss finally lost. He had gone from the Fourth of July, when he suffered his fourth defeat, until five days after Labor Day before he lost his fifth. During the two-month period, he had won 12 times in a row. Ferriss' 4–2 loss, interestingly enough, came at the hands of the cellar-dwelling Athletics.

The Red Sox struggled a bit before they wrapped up the American League pennant, dropping six straight before winning the clincher in Cleveland on Friday, September 13. The Bosox beat the Indians, 1–0, on Williams' first-inning home run. Unlike the other 37 homers he had hit to that point in the season, long drives powered by his smooth upswing, this one was an inside-the-park variety. Facing Boudreau's Cleveland Shift, Ted belted a 3–1 pitch from Red Embree deep to left field. It went far beyond left fielder Pat Seerey, who was posted just behind shortstop. The ball rolled to the fence, and Williams circled the bases and slid across the plate before Seerey could retrieve the ball and get it to catcher Jim Hegan to make the tag.

Having dominated the American League in 1946, finishing with a 12-game cushion, Boston was the prohibitive favorite to win the 1946 World Series. Still, it was strange, unfamiliar territory for the Sox and their fans: They had not been in or won a Fall Classic since 1918. Although the Cardinals had captured the pennant the previous three seasons and had been the world champions twice, Eddie Dyer's Cards were thought to be overmatched.

Boston's mound corps was led by two 20-game winners. Ferriss finished 25–6, and Hughson ended 20–11. Williams' accomplishments were staggering. Leading the majors in runs scored (142) and walks (156), he also finished number one in total bases (343). He trailed only Vernon in the batting race, finishing at .342, and he added 38 home runs and 132 RBIs to his impressive list of statistics. He also picked up the American League's Most Valuable Player Award.

The Cardinals featured first baseman Stan Musial, who had hit a league-leading .365 and served, like Williams, as his league's greatest all-around hitter for the era. Musial—again like Williams—returned from the service in 1946. It was expected that the National Leaguers, who relied on speed and experience, would finish second best to the power and pitching

Dave "Boo" Ferriss and Rudy York celebrate a 4–0 win over the St. Louis Cardinals in Game Three of the World Series (Corbis).

of their rivals from Boston. Under rookie manager Dyer, the Cards had ended the season in a first-place tie with Brooklyn. They went on to beat the Dodgers two straight games in baseball's first post-season play-off.

The opener took place in Sportsman's Park on October 6. York was the hero for the victorious Red Sox in games one and three. His 10th inning home run in the opening game provided the winning margin in the 3–2 triumph. In the third contest, which was played in crowded Fenway Park, York's first-inning blast with two teammates on base staked Ferriss to a lead. The season's leading winning-percentage pitcher held the Cards in check, 4–0.

York had rejuvenated his career with the Red Sox in 1946, hitting .276, slamming 17 homers and driving in 119 runs. He had been hounded out of Detroit by writers and fans for failing to adequately fill Greenberg's huge shoes both offensively and defensively while the Tigers' All-Star first baseman was in the military. In 1944, Rudy had hit 18 home runs and driven in 98 runs. The following year his numbers were 18 homers and 87 RBIs. York was a streak hitter who could carry a team when his bat was hot. Earlier in his career, in fact, he had set the record for home runs in a month with 18.

Although York had ended the 1943 season leading the majors in homers with 34 and RBIs with 118, those numbers didn't put him up there with Greenberg, who was tops in the major leagues with 183 RBIs in 1937 and had led the majors with 58 homers a year later.

Doerr, commenting about some of the major factors which contributed to the Bosox's amazing season, said, "Rudy York was a great help to us that year."[13]

St. Louis tied the series with victories in games two and four. Harry "The Cat" Brecheen tossed a 3–0 shutout at the Bosox in St. Louis, picking up the Cards' first win. In Boston, the fourth game had an altogether different script from the three preceding it: The Cardinals offense broke out, amassing 20 hits and crushing the helpless Red Sox, 12–3. Every Cardinal in the lineup hit safely, with the middle of the order—Enos Slaughter, Whitey Kurowski and Joe Garagiola—leading the way with four hits apiece.

Boston recovered and captured game five in Fenway Park with a 6–3 victory behind the four-hit pitching of Dobson. The Red Sox held a 3–2 lead, and the Series appeared to be moving toward its anticipated outcome.

Williams, who had been expected to power Boston to the World Championship, was having a mighty struggle at the plate. The magic bat of the Splendid Splinter was nearly silent as Ted managed only five singles in the Series. Suffering with a sore elbow, he was also facing the Dyer Shift, a modification of the defense Boudreau had sprung on him in July.

Williams described what happened when he came to bat for the first time:

> Eddie Dyer was the Cardinal manager and he had been quoted before the game as saying he planned no changes for me, but when I got up to lead off the second inning the Cardinals started moving around. They were going into a shift, all right, but they were waiting until the last second to show it,

I suppose to give me a little psychological jolt. I can't say I was surprised. By this time shifts were nothing new to me.[14]

Dyer's shift was a bit different from Boudreau's. The Cardinals manager had Marty Marion cover his regular shortstop area, moved third baseman Kurowski behind second, and positioned the other infielders and outfielders a little toward the right-field line.

In the third game, Williams went against the shift and bunted down the third-base line for one of the five hits he would get. The bunt, seldom-seen when Williams was at the plate, sparked a front page headline in a Boston newspaper. Williams, carried his anger about the report for some time and commented in *My Turn at Bat*: "Williams Bunts," not the score, not the result of the damn game, just "Williams Bunts."[15]

Ted's decision to challenge the shift forced Dyer to modify his defense. Williams, however, struggled throughout the Series.

Williams was possibly distracted by trade rumors swirling around the events taking place on the field. Reports in Boston had Ted going elsewhere for 1947—perhaps, to the Yankees for Joe DiMaggio. The picture of an intense organizational struggle among Red Sox decision-makers was painted in the press for Beantown readers. Manager Cronin appeared to be pushing for a trade, but club owner Tom Yawkey was adamant about retaining the left-handed superstar. All the while, the Boston slugger's hitting was highlighted in a special box in the *Boston Evening Globe* entitled, "What Williams Did."[16] The daily reports were very discouraging.

As the teams took the field at Sportsman's Park for the sixth game, the favored Red Sox were one game away from the 1946 world championship.

Brecheen went to the mound for the Cardinals. When the power-packed Bosox finally scored in the top of the seventh, it was the first run they had chalked up against the "Cat" in 16 innings. That run would not be enough, as St. Louis went on to win, 4–1, evening the Series. Slaughter, who had been hit on the elbow by a pitch in the final game in Boston, was barely able to hold the bat. He did, however, manage a key single in the third inning, when the Cards broke on top, 3–0.

On October 15, the stage was set for the finale. For only the third time in World Series history, the teams had alternated wins in the process of arriving at the final contest.

In the top of the eighth, with Boston trailing 3–1, the Red Sox bounced back to tie the game. Dom hit a solid double that drove in the two runs. On the play, Slaughter hustled to retrieve the ball at the base of the fence and made a relay throw to Terry Moore. DiMaggio pulled up lame as he reached second base. Unable to return to his position when the Cards came to bat in the bottom half of the eighth inning, Culberson replaced the flawlessly fielding "Little Professor" in center field.

Going into the bottom of the eighth inning, with the games tied at 3–3 and the score tied at 3–3, the hometown Cardinals came to bat.

The decisive moment was near. Slaughter led off with a single to center field. The next two batters were retired, and Enos was unable to advance. With Harry Walker at the plate, Slaughter broke for second base on a 3–2 pitch. Walker lined the ball over shortstop into left-center field. Culberson, who had just replaced an injured DiMaggio, chased the ball down, fumbled it momentarily, and then threw it to Pesky, who was out beyond shortstop. Pesky appeared to hesitate briefly before throwing the ball to the plate. Slaughter, having rounded third, headed for home. As the determined Cardinal flew toward the plate, Partee, the Bosox's catcher, took Pesky's throw on a short hop. Slaughter slid across the plate and scored what proved to be the winning run.

Boston, dazed by the dash, battled back and had runners on first and third with one out in the top of the ninth. But Brecheen, who had relieved Murray Dickson in the eighth, retired the next two Red Sox hitters to pick up his third victory and end the series.

The Red Sox had not captured the world championship, but during the regular season they had forged one of baseball's greatest comebacks. They had improved dramatically on their 71–83 record and seventh-place finish in 1945 to end up with a 104–50 mark and a pennant just one year later. It had been quite a run for the Bosox and their Fenway fans—though it ended in a fashion Boston fans have since grown accustomed to.

The Fall Classic was finished, but powerful memories about the campaign still remain. Doerr, despite the October defeat, counted 1946 his favorite season, saying, "We all had come back from being in the service and that year [we] only lost 16 games at Fenway Park. We had the best pitching staff that year in all the time I was at Boston."[17]

Ferriss, too, was pleased with the club's accomplishments:

> A memorable season, our club getting off to a fantastic 41–9 start and going on to win 104 games. We had a great group of fellows and a fine manager...
>
> [We] had some funny guys who were good for the club, lots of laughs— Klinger, [Bill] Zuber, Harris, Pellagrini, Bagby, Wagner....
>
> I feel fortunate to have been a member of this outstanding team and to play with two Hall of Famers, Williams and Doerr. What a thrill to watch Ted go to the plate every day. [I am] thankful to have played in the World Series.[18]

Notes

1. Joseph M. Sheehan, "Hearing on Yankees' Application to Restrain Pasquels Postponed," *New York Times*, 8 May 1946, 30.

2. John Drebinger, "Big League Season Starts on Tuesday,' *New York Times*, 14 April 1946, Sec. 5, 2.

3. Arthur Daley, "Play Ball," *New York Times*, 16 April 1946, 35.

4. "Truman Watches Senators Bow, 6–3," *New York Times*, 17 April 1946, 36.

5. "Yankees Vanquish Red Sox by 12–5 to Take Undisputed Hold on Lead," *New York Times*, 25 April 1946, 27.

6. Eddie Pellagrini, Telephone Conversation, 9 December 1998.

7. *Ibid.*

8. Louis Effrat, "Assault Beats Lord Boswell in Preakness; Yanks Win, 2–0, End Red Sox Streak; Dodgers Triumph," *New York Times*, 12 May 1946, Sec. 5, 1.

9. Arthur Daley, "Exit for Marse Joe," *New York Times*, 26 May 1946, Sec. 5, 2.

10. Daley, "An Afternoon at the Stadium," *New York Times*, 4 July 1946, 14.

11. "Williams Called Best Hitter Ever as Feller Is Rated Above Johnson," *New York Times*, 10 July 1946, 26.

12. "Red Sox Take Pair as Williams Stars," *New York Times*, 15 July 1946, 17.

13. Bobby Doerr, Letter, 1999.

14. Ted Williams with John Underwood, *My Turn at Bat: The Story of My Life* (New York: Simon and Schuster, 1969), 126.

15. *Ibid.*

16. "What Williams Did," *Boston Evening Globe*, 7–16 October 1946.

17. Doerr, Letter, 1999.

18. Dave "Boo" Ferriss, Letter, 1999.

6. 1950
Philadelphia Phillies

From Whiz to Fizz and Back Again

Writing for the *New York Times* after the final game of the National League's 1950 regular season, Roscoe McGowen characterized the Philadelphia Phillies as "The Philadelphia Whiz Kids, who came so close to winning the ignominious title of the Fizz Kids."[1]

For the Phillies, the game played on Sunday, October 1, was an oasis within a desert of downfall and defeat. With it, the Phillies avoided a sudden-death playoff with the Brooklyn Dodgers for the National League pennant.

The Whiz Kids came to Ebbets Field for the final weekend of the campaign, holding a precarious two-game lead over their hosts. They lost the series opener on Saturday, and only a single, critical contest remained on the schedule. What had been a comfortable lead at the top of the National League a few weeks earlier was now within a loss of vanishing.

The 1950 Whiz Kids, sporting their new peppermint-stick uniforms, mixed the excitement and exuberance of youth with the steadiness of age and experience. They melded young, eager pitchers and hitters with seasoned and crafty veterans.

The Phillies averaged just under 26 years of age, and no team in the league fielded a more youthful lineup. Their five starting pitchers were younger still, averaging 23.8 years. On opening day, reliever Jim Konstanty and first baseman Eddie Waitkus were the only regulars over 30.

The infield featured Willie "Puddin' Head" Jones, who had been a rookie in 1949, at third base. Granny Hamner, in his third major league season, was solid at shortstop. Mike Goliat, who had come up from the minors in July 1949, was at second. He was learning a new position, having played third and first before arriving in Philadelphia. Waitkus, at first, was the veteran of the infield.

Richie Ashburn, in his sophomore season, patrolled center field, flanked by seasoned outfielders Dick Sisler and Del Ennis. Andy Seminick, another of the club's elder statesmen, was behind the plate. He had been with the club since 1943.

Right-hander Robin Roberts, who had made his major league debut on June 18, 1948, and had gone 15–15 in 1949, was projected to be the staff's leader. Some were expecting lefty Curt Simmons, who had struggled to a 4–10 mark the previous season, to become the number two man. Simmons, who had first appeared with the Phillies in late September 1947, had pitched mostly out of the bullpen in 1949 while the coaches tried to smooth out his herky-jerky, unorthodox motion. During the 1950 spring training, the Phillies' brass decided to let Simmons throw as he felt most comfortable, and the results were promising.

Other starters included veteran left-hander Ken Heintzelman, who posted a 17–10 record the previous season, Russ "The Mad Monk" Meyer who had come in a trade with the Chicago Cubs prior to the 1949 campaign, and a pair of rookies, Emory "Bubba" Church and Bob Miller. Konstanty, who had an undertaker as his personal pitching coach during the off-season, was the main man out of the bullpen.

Manager Eddie Sawyer, an erstwhile college professor, was in charge of blending youthful exuberance with veteran experience. Sawyer was in his third season with the Phils, who had given him his first major league managing opportunity when they promoted him from the Triple-A club in Toronto on July 26, 1948, to take over as the Phillies skipper.

The Phils had ended the 1949 season in third place, which was their highest finish since 1917 when they had placed second behind the New York Giants. Some thought the club could have climbed even higher. Coach Maje McDonnell was one of them:

> We came on strong in '49. If Waitkus hadn't been shot, we might have had a shot. We were coming, boy oh boy, we were coming. Good pitching, the kids were hitting and fielding. The attitude was terrific. We had such a good clubhouse. Good teams have good clubhouses. We had a lot of fun....
>
> That was the first time the Phillies had finished in the money in a lot of years. We all got our World Series share just before Christmas. It was about $800 a person and, boy, we were on cloud nine.[2]

McDonnell's reference to Waitkus was a reminder that the Philadelphia first baseman had been shot and seriously wounded on June 14 in a Chicago hotel room. The attacker, Ruth Ann Stenhagen, was a troubled 19 year old who had been infatuated with Waitkus while he was a member of the Cubs before his trade to the Phillies after the 1948 season.

After an extended period of recovery and an impressive spring training, Waitkus batted third for the Phils in the regular season opener against the Dodgers in Shibe Park. Before a record-setting, opening-day crowd of 29,074, Roberts beat Brooklyn's ace, Don Newcombe, 9–1. Goliat led the way for the home club, going 4-for-4. Waitkus, in his most important test since the shooting, went 3-for-5 and drove in a run.

The Phils won only six of the 12 games they played in April and were 2½ lengths behind the front-running Dodgers at the end of the first month of the race. Heintzleman and Meyer were struggling on the mound. On the final day of the month, a frustrated Meyer, known as the "Mad Monk," hit umpire Al Barlick with a ball and bumped him during a heated dispute about a close call. Meyer's actions brought him a seven-day suspension.

May was much better for the Whiz Kids. They went 16–9 and entered June in third place behind Brooklyn and the St. Louis Cardinals, a mere 1½ games behind the leader. And the Phils shaved a game off the lead in June with a 14–11 record. The Dodgers still sat at the top of the National League, but the Phils were only one rung below them.

Miller had been the surprise of the staff, winning his first eight decisions as a major leaguer. Church, another rookie, spent most of the first half of the campaign on the bench, but by mid–July he had joined the starting rotation.

On July 4, the Whiz Kids held a slim lead, and the Boston Braves had joined the Cards and the Dodgers in the closely bunched race. The Phils split a holiday doubleheader with the Boston Braves, and the Cardinals took over first place after taking two from the Cubs.

The Phillies opened a homestand on July 25 with a doubleheader against the Cubs. Church shutout the team from the Windy City, 7–0, on a three-hitter in the first contest, and Roberts posted a 1–0 victory in the nightcap. With the pair of wins the Phils regained first place.

From that point in the season, the Whiz Kids built toward the pennant—the pennant which would be the club's first since 1915 and the days of Grover Cleveland Alexander. During the homestand, the Phillies won 12 of the 16 games and expanded their lead.

By the middle of August, the Whiz Kids, showing no signs of weakening, were five ahead of the runner-up Dodgers. They posted a 20–8 record for the month and went into early September with a seven-game pad.

Simmons, a 17-game winner for the Phillies, pitched his final game of the season on September 6. A day earlier he had traded his Phils' red and white pinstripes for Uncle Sam's khakis, becoming the first major leaguer inducted into the Armed Forces during the Korean War. On August 1, he had received news of the impending activation of his National Guard unit, and he suspected that he would be unavailable to complete the campaign with the club.

Fellow pitcher Charlie Bicknell spoke about why he and Curt were in the National Guard:

> In '49 Bob Carpenter [the Phillies' owner] asked Curt Simmons and me to join the National Guard in Philadelphia, which was part of the 28th Infantry Division. The way he put it we had no choice. He was trying to protect his investment. So we both joined the National Guard and then the Korean War broke out. At that time there were two National Divisions that could be activated, go through basic training, and be ready for combat within a short period of time. They were the 28th and the division down in Oklahoma. So they activated our whole division. Of course, by that time the Phillies had sold me to the Braves [who sent him to the minors] on waivers.[3]

The schedule of activities for Simmons' National Guard unit made it possible for him to go to the mound on September 6 for one last time. Facing the Dodgers in Shibe Park, he took a 2–0 lead into the ninth inning, when things unraveled. Brooklyn rallied for three runs off Simmons and ace reliever Konstanty, and the Whiz Kids lost, 3–2, one of the three they dropped to the Dodgers in the series. The Phils' lead had been whittled to 4½ games. Following the game, Simmons left for basic training at Camp Atterbury in Indiana.

The Whiz Kids regrouped and charged back. By September 19, their sprint put them 7½ games ahead of the Braves. Brooklyn had fallen nine lengths off the pace.

At that point, the air once again started to seep—and then rush—out of the Phillies' high-flying balloon. Columnist Red Smith called it the "tallest, steepest, swiftest, dizziest, daredevil, death-defying dive ever undertaken by a baseball team."[4]

From September 19 until the final day of the season, the Phils won only three games and lost nine. The hard-charging Dodgers, on the other hand, were victorious 13 times, dropping only three contests during the span.

Questions abounded. Had Philadelphia's frightening fall been caused by a youthful response to pennant pressure? Had the Whiz Kids been playing over their heads during their second-half run for the National League pennant? How instrumental was the loss of Simmons' strong left arm down the stretch?

Two other young pitchers suffered debilitating injuries in the final weeks. In mid–September, Church's season ended after he was struck in the face by a line-drive off the bat of Cincinnati's Ted Kluszewski. The pitcher finished the year 8–4. Then, Miller came down with a "dead arm" and a bad back. Miller had first hurt his back on June 25 when he tripped up the stairs while carrying his luggage on the way to catch a train for Boston. Together, Church and Miller took 19 wins with them to the injury list. Whatever the reasons for their tumble, the Phils arrived at the final game of the National League campaign needing a victory.

The work horse of each staff went to the mound for the finale. Roberts, a 19-game winner, started for the Whiz Kids. He was making his sixth attempt to nail down the final victory in what he hoped might be his first 20-win season. But Roberts' luck appeared to have run out as the season closed: he was in the throes of a three-game losing streak.

On the Saturday before the last week of the season, Roberts pitched eight innings in a 3–2 losing effort against the Dodgers. In his next start on Wednesday, he lasted only four innings against the New York Giants, but did not pick up the loss in Philadelphia's 8–7 extra-inning defeat. The following day, the Whiz Kids' ace right-hander was back as the starter in the second half of a doubleheader against the Giants. He went nine innings, but again was on the losing end, 3–1. Three days later, he was going to the mound in the most important game of his young career.

Don Newcombe was given the ball by Brooklyn manager Burt Shotton. The Dodgers' ace was seeking his 20th win too, and sought to become the first African American to accomplish the feat. On the day Simmons had pitched his final game before heading off for military service, Newcombe had started both ends of the doubleheader against the Phillies. The iron-man feat was a symbol of his importance to the Dodgers. In the opener, he shutout the Whiz Kids, 2–0, giving up only three hits over nine innings. When the lineup card was posted for the second game, Newcombe's name was there again. He went seven innings and left for a pinch hitter with Brooklyn trailing, 2–0. The Dodgers' ninth-inning rally against Simmons and Konstanty produced his team's 3–2 victory.

The pair of final-game starters, who would face each other many times throughout their long and distinguished careers, hurled outstanding games. Newcombe surrendered the Phils' first run in the top of the sixth inning. Roberts gave up a run on a freakish homer by Pee Wee Reese in the bottom of the inning, tying the score, 1–1. Arthur Daley of the *New York Times* described Reese's short poke to right field:

> The ball climbed lazily into the air as Del Ennis back-tracked toward the fence. It looked for a moment as though he might catch it. Then it appeared as though it might carom back for a harmless single.
>
> Suddenly there was a gasp of utter disbelief from the multitude.... That silly, little white pellet moved gently over the upper edge of the fence, bounced indolently off the screen and screwily came to rest on the top edge of the wall.... It was a home run.[5]

By the bottom of the ninth inning, the warm sun had disappeared and Ebbets Field's lights were on. When Brooklyn came to bat, the score was still tied, 1–1. The Dodgers could have—and should have—won the game right there.

Cal Abrams led off and worked Roberts for a walk on a three-and-two pitch. Reese twice failed to bunt safely and then singled into left-center. Abrams was on second base, Reese was on first, and no one was out. Baseball strategy called for a sacrifice bunt, and the Phillies were expecting one. But Duke Snider lined Roberts' first pitch for a single to center. Ashburn charged the ball and fired a strike to Seminick at home plate to get Abrams, who was attempting to score the winning run. It was the play that saved the pennant for the Phils.

Ashburn had been anticipating a bunt and was in shallow center field. He said, "I wouldn't have been able to get Abrams if I were playing my normal position. At that, I was sort of surprised that Abrams didn't hold up at third."[6]

After the dust settled, Brooklyn had runners at second and third base with only one out. Jackie Robinson was intentionally walked to load the bases. The Dodgers were still one hit, one fly ball, one walk, one passed ball, one wild pitch, or one error away from a playoff for the championship of the National League.

With the pennant slipping from his grasp, Roberts got Carl Furillo on a pop out to first base on the first pitch. Ennis tracked down and caught Gil Hodges' long fly ball to the base of the scoreboard in right field to end the threat. The line score for Brooklyn's aborted ninth inning read: two walks, two hits, no runs, and three men left on base.

The Phils pitcher was the first batter scheduled up in the top of the 10th—and it was indeed Roberts, not a pinch hitter, who strode to the plate. He opened the inning with a single up the middle. No pinch-runner emerged from the dugout. If his turn at bat left any doubt, it was now clear that the game was Roberts' to win or lose.

Waitkus, after fouling off the first pitch in an attempt to lay down a sacrifice bunt, got the hit signal and promptly blooped a Texas Leaguer into short centerfield. With Whiz Kids on first and second base and no one out, visions of old heartbreaking scenes no doubt rose spectre-like before the season's largest gathering of Dodgers fans. There might have been the painful recall of Hugh Casey's pitch caroming off Mickey Owen's glove and rolling toward the Dodger dugout. Or, perhaps, some older folk may have remembered Bill Wambsganss spearing the line drive over second base to start the unassisted triple play which ended a Brooklyn rally in the fifth game of the 1920 World Series against the Cleveland Indians. That afternoon in 1950, the Flatbush faithful had already stuffed the memory of Abrams' costly out at home plate into their memory banks of frustrating finishes.

Ashburn attempted to move the runners along with a sacrifice bunt, but Roberts was forced out at third. The Dodgers and their faithful fans breathed a bit easier.

Left-handed hitting Sisler, who had pulled three singles to right field in the game, came to the plate with one away and two men on base. His father, George—a former major league great, a member of the Hall of Fame, and the head scout for the Brooklyn organization—sat in the stands. He was about to feel, as he put it, "awful and terrific at the same time."[7]

Sisler had almost not made it to his memorable moment. In the fourth inning he had reinjured his right wrist sliding into second base, an attempt at avoiding a force out on a ground ball by Ennis. The previous injury had sidelined him for two weeks in September, and he had only recently returned to the lineup. "For a few minutes I thought sure I would have to leave the game," he said later. "I landed on the wrist hard and a pain shot right up my arm. However it went away. What a lucky break for me. I didn't have to leave the game."[8]

It was a lucky break, too, for Philadelphia: Sisler's plate work proved fateful. In a letter nearly 50 years after the season, he recalled his decisive at-bat against Newcombe:

> We, the Whiz Kids from Philly, had men on first and second with one out. Newcombe had a count of one and two on me. I almost swung at a high away ball for ball one.
>   Then Newk got one a little closer but still high and away. I swung and it was a home run to straight left field [an opposite field home run]. What a thrill! The biggest of my career.[9]

Waitkus and Ashburn scored ahead of Sisler and the Whiz Kids led, 4–1.

Newcombe retired the next two Phillies, but the damage had been done. Roberts handled the Dodgers in order in the bottom of the 10th and left the mound a winner. He had started four games in a nine-day span, pitching 31 innings. The last 10 represented his finest effort. The Phils had captured their first pennant in 35 years.

Dick Sisler and the Whiz Kids celebrate the memorable home run (Corbis).

The regular season ended, as it had begun, with a Philadelphia victory over Brooklyn, with a Roberts win and a Newcombe loss. Roberts registered his 20th victory, and become the first Phillies pitcher to chalk up that many wins since Pete Alexander accomplished the feat in 1917. Newcombe would have to wait another year before reaching the revered milestone.

Brooklyn had another haunting memory to add to its storied history. Abrams summed it up succinctly, writing, "Dick Sisler's home run was a nightmare."[10]

Church, who was out for the season, remembered two events from the game that would stay with him for the rest of his life:

> One was in the top of the 10th when Sisler hit the home run off Newcombe. And the other was in the bottom of the 10th when Roberts got the last three outs. Those were the biggest thrills. There are a lot of people who play a lot of baseball and are never on a pennant winner.[11]

Al Cartwright, writing for the *Wilmington* (DE) *Evening Journal,* extolled the Whiz Kids' virtues:

> No team in any sport ever rode so high, or fell so hard, or came back the way the 1950 Phillies did, and when you add the way the club was born, how it was reared, the earthquakes it survived, then you've got a story that you'll never find in your neighborhood theatre.[12]

With Roberts [20–11] leading the way, the pennant-winning Phillies had a major-league leading 3.50 ERA. Konstanty set an all-time record with 74 appearances on his way to a 16–7 record.

Ennis was fourth in the National League's batting race with a .311 average and led the circuit with 126 RBIs. Ashburn was the next highest on the club with a .303 mark and a league-leading 14 triples. Seminick's .288 average was the best of his major league career.

A number of the Phils attributed their success to the leadership of their manager. Ennis praised him, saying, "Eddie Sawyer is the man chiefly responsible for our winning. He really knows how to get the best play from them. We all feel our best is hardly good enough."[13]

The City of Brotherly Love was ecstatic about its young band of National League champs. Their struggles during the latter half of September had been forgotten, and Sisler's blast on October 1 brought renewed optimism for the World Series. The Whiz Kids, who had come so close to not making it to the postseason, were poised to meet the American League champion New York Yankees. The future appeared bright for these young Davids as they prepared to slay October's Goliaths.

The upcoming Fall Classic was shaping up to be a matchup of intellectual types. Before his managerial career, Sawyer had been a college professor at his alma mater, Ithaca (N.Y.) College, where he had taught biology and coached football. His counterpart in the opposing dugout would be the "Ol' Professor," Casey Stengel, whose credentials were legendary.

Philadelphia mayor Bernard Samuel wanted the Series to be an experience available to everyone. Prior to its start, it was announced that

> Mayor Samuel has arranged ... for the installation of television sets in all parks, recreation centers and playgrounds. In the square surrounding City Hall it is proposed to install eight television sets with 21-inch screens.[14]

The World Series opened on October 4, in Shibe Park. The Yankees' pitching proved to be too much for the Phillies. Vic Raschi, Allie Reynolds, and Ed Lopat, a formidable veteran-threesome, and Whitey Ford, then a rookie phenom, silenced the Whiz Kids' bats in four straight games.

Konstanty, the season's top relief pitcher, was Sawyer's surprise starter in the opener. He pitched eight strong innings for the Phils but lost, 1–0. Roberts and Heintzelman pitched the next two games, which the Yankees also captured, 2–1 and 3–2.

The World Series ended in New York on October 7, when Ford became one of the youngest pitchers to win a Fall Classic game. The 5–2 victory was the first of his 10 career World Series wins.

The Whiz Kids' dream season was over. They had not played badly, but they had been swept in the World Series. Their final regular-season game with the Brooklyn Dodgers, in which was born the memory of Dick Sisler's game-winning, opposite-field home run, would have to be enough. And, 50 years later, it is.

Notes

1. Roscoe McGowen, "Phils Beat Dodgers for Flag; Win 4–1 on Homer in Tenth," *New York Times*, 2 Oct. 1950, 1.

2. Robin Roberts and C. Paul Rogers, III, *The Whiz Kids and the 1950 Pennant* (Philadelphia: Temple University Press, 1996), 194.

3. Roberts and Rogers, 243.

4. Red Smith, "1950: Philadelphia Phillies 4, Brooklyn Dodgers 1," in Charles Einstein, ed., *The Second Fireside Book of Baseball* (New York: Simon and Schuster, 1958), 343.

5. Arthur Daley, "The Flatbush Fantasy Ends," *New York Times*, 2 Oct. 1950, 28.

6. "Phillies Capture Pennant," *Wilmington (DE) Morning News*, 2 Oct. 1950, 20.

7. "Chip Off the Old Block," *New York Times*, 2 Oct. 1950, 27.

8. Joe Reichler, "Sisler Nearly Replaced Before Historic Homer," *Boston Evening Globe*, 2 Oct. 1950, 12.

9. Dick Sisler, Letter, 1988.

10. Cal Abrams, Letter, 1988.

11. Thomas Lavin, "Bubba Church: A Forgotten Member of '50 'Whiz Kids'," *Baseball Digest*, Oct. 1989, 69.

12. Al Cartwright, "A La Carte," *Wilmington (DE) Evening Journal*, 2 Oct. 1950, 28.

13. "Players Credit Sawyer for Pennant," *Boston Daily Globe*, 2 Oct. 1950, 12.

14. James P. Dawson, "Stampede for Tickets and Rooms as Series Fever Hits Quaker City," *New York Times*, 3 Oct. 1950, 36.

7. 1951 New York Giants

A Miraculous Recovery
and a Playoff Memory

The 1951 New York Giants completed spring training by following a circuitous route from the their Southern base in St. Petersburg, Florida, to the Polo Grounds. The Cleveland Indians made the junket with them, and the two clubs played an 11-game series along the way.

On Thursday, April 12, the Giants slammed the Indians, 13–6, in the eighth game of the set. A report by John Drebinger in the *New York Times* commented on the game and described manager Leo Durocher's hopes for the early part of the season:

> Cutting loose another devastating broadside, their fourth in the last five days, the Giants today flattened the Indians, 13–6. The victory gave Leo Durocher's band a lead of 5 to 3 in the series with Al Lopez' American Leaguers.
>
> A grand total of eighteen blows, including five home runs, two by Monte Irvin, one each for Bobby Thomson, Whitey Lockman and Clint Hartung, thrilled a crowd of 6182....
>
> One doesn't hear much these days of the Giants' young hurlers, George Bamberger, Norman Fox, Roger Bowman and George Spencer, which is a pity since all four were primed to make a strong showing this spring.
>
> However, so determined is Durocher to have his front line flingers ready for that hoped-for quick getaway that he simply hasn't been able to find the time to work the youngsters.[1]

New York captured the preseason series against Cleveland, winning seven games, losing three, and tying one. It was a strong finish to a successful spring training. The club's 19–12 record, in fact, was second best among the National League teams. Chicago, at 18–10, ended with a higher winning percentage.

There was growing optimism among Giants fans. In 1950, from mid–July on, New York had been the hottest team in the Senior Circuit. The Polo Grounders had finished in third place, five games behind the pennant-winning Philadelphia Phillies, who had defeated the Brooklyn Dodgers on the final day of the campaign to capture the flag. The Giants' spring training accomplishments had kept the excitement high as the new season approached.

One writer longed for an improbable déjà vu campaign:

> To expect major league baseball to come up with another pair of sizzling flag races ... seems a pretty large order.
>
> Yet, that is exactly what fans and experts are confidently looking forward to....
>
> Durocher ... has developed a hustling, fine-spirited group of players capable of doing any number of things exceptionally well. The mound staff, headed by Larry Jansen, Sal Maglie, Jim Hearn and Sheldon Jones, plus a rejuvenated Jack Kramer, an effective Dave Koslo and a fine crop of youngsters, is more than adequate.[2]

On April 17, the Giants were in Boston's Braves Field to open the National League's 75th season. Breaking a lengthy string of opening-day losses, the Giants handled both the Braves and their jinx, registering a 4–0 victory behind Larry Jansen's five-hitter.

The next day, Boston center fielder Sam Jethroe blasted a three-run homer off reliever Allen Gettel in the bottom of the ninth to bring the Braves an 8–5 win.

A Patriot Day doubleheader, an annual Beantown event, concluded the series. The Giants' Jim Hearn bested Warren Spahn, 4–2, in the opener. The second game went into extra innings, tied 12–12. In the bottom on the 10th, Boston's Earl Torgeson banged the ball off the center-field fence to score Buddy Kerr from third base with the winning run, ending the 13–12 slugfest which featured 12 extra-base hits.

With a 2–2 record, the Giants returned home to meet the Dodgers on April 20. The Polo Grounds, which had been the site of many fierce battles between the "Jints" and the "Bums," was not friendly to the home team. Dodger right-hander Don Newcombe went the distance in game one to lead Brooklyn to a 7–3 victory. They scored four runs in the fifth inning, three of them unearned. Brooklyn won by the same score the next day. Jackie Robinson had an outstanding day for the winners, belting a two-run homer, doubling home a third run, and scoring on an error after having stolen third base.

The third and final games of the set, each of which was played before more than 30,000 fans, also went to the boys from Ebbets Field. Carl Furillo's round-tripper off Sal Maglie in the 10th inning provided the Dodgers' margin of victory. Newcombe, who had come into the game in relief in the eighth, picked up his second win of the series.

Newcombe's appearance seemed to bear out an assessment of the Dodgers which had appeared in the *Times* before the season's opener. The article noted that though the vital offensive cogs represented by the likes of Robinson, Roy Campanella, Duke Snider, and Gil Hodges were still in place, the pitching might throw the proverbial wrench into the works:

> The pitching has bogged down and unless the imaginative and energetic [Chuck] Dressen can pull a few miracles he may run into serious difficulties. Don Newcombe and Preacher Roe are the top two but there is too much uncertainty behind the pair.[3]

The Dodgers had things working against the Giants, true; but the late-inning appearance of Brooklyn's ace—and so early in the season—seemed an indication that Chuck Dressen had indeed little faith in his second-tier moundsmen.

Following the three-game sweep by the Dodgers, the Giants had dropped four in a row, heading to Philadelphia where they were also blanked. The Giants wouldn't win again until April 30, in the final game of their second series with the Dodgers. Before the victory in Ebbets Field, they had dropped 11 straight games and their record was a dismal 3–12.

Arthur Daley, assessing the situation, wrote:

> The losing streak of the Polo Grounds tenants represents a far greater disaster than the faltering start a year ago. At that time the Silent Strategist [Durocher] was fumbling for the right combination in order to get his lineup set. He was still experimenting. But at this time the Taciturn Tactician knows that he has the best possible varsity on the field. And still he's deeply and incomprehensibly imbedded in last place.[4]

The Giants had not been in the postseason since the late 1930s; the Dodgers had been there a number of times. However, few teams had experienced as much postseason frustration as Brooklyn had in the previous five years. They had participated in the first-ever, best-of-three playoff in 1946, losing two straight games to the eventual World Champion St. Louis Cardinals. They made it to the Series the following year, but lost to the

New York Yankees, four games to three. In 1949 Brooklyn captured the National League flag on the final day of the season with a 10-inning victory over the Phillies, but lost the World Series to the Bronx Bombers in five games. In 1950, on the last day of the regular season, the Phils' Dick Sisler hit an extra-inning, game-winning home run to defeat the Dodgers and take the pennant. It was a heart-breaking defeat for the team from Flatbush, whose blistering charge to catch the front-running Whiz Kids fell short.

The Giants finished in third place in 1950 after two seasons of ending up in the fifth spot under Durocher's leadership. On July 18, 1948, Leo, then the Brooklyn manager, left the Dodgers and headed crosstown to the Giants, replacing Polo Ground legend Mel Ott. Right fielder Don Mueller remembered Durocher's approach:

> I know that when I joined the Giants in August 1948 Leo was the new mgr. and he cleaned house of the slow, long ball hitters. His plan was as always, singles, doubles, bunts, speed and defense ... but the rest fell in place.[5]

On May 15, the Dodgers were tied with the Braves for the top spot in the Senior Circuit, and the Giants were down in the standings with a 13–15 mark.

With the season in jeopardy, the Giants looked to their farm system for help, and they called up 20-year-old Willie Mays, who was hitting .477 for Minneapolis of the American Association. Outfielder Monte Irvin recalled the move:

> We were in 5th place in May of 1951. Willie Mays reported to us in Phila[delphia]. During the 3 game Series he got no hits but caught everything in the outfield, [and] threw out everybody that tried to score. After winning all three games we moved to the Polo Grounds that Friday nite and the first time up against Warren Spahn he hit a tremendous home run off the left-center field facade—he was on his way.[6]

By the end of the month, New York had climbed into fifth place, had evened their record at 21–21, and were only 4½ games behind the front-running Dodgers.

On June 3, after the Giants whipped the Pittsburgh Pirates, 14–3, Drebinger expressed some of the rediscovered enthusiasm for the club:

> The long-awaited big push of the Giants above the .500 mark may be regarded as definitely on its way. At least, it was moving at a dazzling pace at the Polo Grounds yesterday when Leo Durocher's minions belted Bill Meyer's bewildered Pirates to win, 14–3, behind Jim Hearn's six-hit hurling.

This notable achievement swept the two-game series for the Polo Grounders, moved them two lengths over .500 and into a virtual three-cornered tie [with the Chicago Cubs and the Braves] for third place.[7]

At that point in the campaign, Brooklyn's Robinson was leading the majors with a lofty .416 batting average. Four other Dodgers [Cal Abrams, Pee Wee Reese, Campanella, and Hodges] were hitting above. 300. Alvin Dark was the only Giants hitter that high, at .335. The pitching stats of the two clubs were a bit more even. Brooklyn's Preacher Roe led the circuit with a perfect 6–0 record, but New York's Maglie had posted an 8–2 start.

At the All-Star break, the Giants had climbed into second place. After reaching the .500 mark, they continued to play improved ball, going 22–15. The problem was that the Dodgers were even hotter, picking up 26 wins while losing 11 times. Although the Giants had moved up in the standings, they had fallen four lengths off the pace and were 8½ games behind the team from Flatbush.

From that point in the season until the second week of August, Brooklyn ran off a 10-game winning streak, and went 20–10 overall. The Giants struggled to a 16–15 record, sinking to 13 games behind the front-running Dodgers.

But on August 12, the Giants took a pair of games from the Phillies in the Polo Grounds. Maglie picked up his 16th win in the 3–2 opener, and Al Corwin pitched the Giants to a 2–1 victory in the nightcap. The day belonged to Irvin, who slammed a three-run homer off the screen in the upper stand in right field in the first game and then sprinted all the way from first base, on a rain-softened field, to score the winning run in game two on Bobby Thomson's double. The two victories would serve as the starting line for the Giants' amazing race to the pennant.

The next day, Whitey Lockman's three-run shot powered New York to a 5–2 win over Philadelphia.

The Dodgers had taken a three-game series from the Giants early in the season, and they had captured all three games played against New York over the July 4th holiday. When Brooklyn returned to the Polo Grounds on August 14 to open another series, the Dodgers ran into a red hot band of Giants.

In the opener, before 42,867 spectators, the home club picked up their fourth-straight win by the score of 4–2. An article in the *New York Times* indicated that, though the Polo Grounders' streak was not yet a serious threat to the Dodgers, "it was none the less sweet to Leo Durocher's charges, who had bowed six times in a row to their rivals from Flatbush."[8]

The trend continued through the series and beyond that. The New Yorkers beat the Dodgers in the final two games, and then went on to Philadelphia's Shibe Park where they took all three games. Following the final victory, a 5–4 come-from-behind win over the Phils, Louis Effrat writing in the *Times*, showed a glimmer of excitement about the Giants' fortunes. He explained that the victory, coupled with a Dodger loss, meant not only that "the Giants' longest winning streak [is] still alive—nine in a row—but the margin between first and second places has been cut to eight lengths. It's still a tremendous gap, but the New Yorkers certainly are lots healthier now than they were a month ago."[9]

The Polo Grounders continued their winning ways. On August 27, in the first game of a doubleheader against Chicago, the Giants picked up their 15th straight victory. After the Cubs took the lead 4–3 in the top of the 12th inning, the Giants roared back to score twice in their at-bat to claim the victory, 5–4, with Jansen going the distance. New York also took the nightcap, 6–3, for their second doubleheader sweep of the series.

The next day the Pirates halted the streak at 16 games, beating the Giants, 2–0. The Dodgers, whose record was 80–45, maintained a six-game lead over the rampaging Polo Grounders, who were 75–52. During New York's run, Mays provided both an offensive and defensive spark that had been missing earlier in the season.

Irvin mentioned another element playing a key part in the Giants' run—unity. "We became a family," he recalled. "If one player failed, the next player tried very hard to get the job done. That's why we beat the Dodgers."[10]

Thomson recently echoed the sentiment, saying, "We were a team of experienced competitors who knew how to play the game—fundamentally—we trusted each other and had confidence in each other."[11]

With a developing race in the National League, the pre-season dream of close pennant fights in both leagues was, for the first time, beginning to shape up. Three American League teams were in a dog fight for much of the campaign. On September 1, the Yanks held a one-game lead over the Indians, with the Boston Red Sox 4½ games back.

That day the Giants, with the help of a triple play, beat the Dodgers, 8–1. Mueller, not noted as a slugger, slammed three homers and drove in five runs to lead the way. The Dodgers' only tally came when Maglie, who picked up his 18th win, plunked Robinson with a pitch to force in a run.

Mueller's hot hitting continued the following game when he led the Giants to a 11–2 win over Brooklyn. He remembered the special moments:

[On] Sept. 1, in the Polo Grounds against the Dodgers I hit three home runs in a row. My wife was back at home in St. Louis getting ready to have our first son. [On] Sept. 2, I hit one home run and was at bat for the last time. [The count was] one ball and no strikes. Monte Irvin in the on deck circle called me back and said a telephone call said I had a son. I went back up and hit the next pitch for number 5 in two games.[12]

Brooklyn went home to Ebbets Field and rebounded, taking two from the Braves the next afternoon. The Giants split with the Phillies, giving a game back to Brooklyn.

Through the first three weeks of September, the Dodgers maintained a lead of three games or more. They split a series with the Giants, winning the opener, 9–0, with Maglie gaining his 20th victory. They dropped the second game, 2–1.

On September 21, Brooklyn ran into their 1950 nemeses, the Phillies, who topped the Dodgers, 9–6. Philadelphia took the second game of the series as well, by the score of 7–3, before dropping the finale, 6–2.

After the Giants beat the Braves the next afternoon, 4–3, on a ninth inning hit by Stanky, Brooklyn's lead was down to 2½ lengths.

Daley's article in the *Times* on September 25 seemed to concede the race to the Dodgers:

> Presumably the Dodgers and Yankees will meet in the world series next week but no guarantees can be made. Each hold a lead by moderately substantial margins for so late in the season....
>
> This is as good a time as any to pay tribute to the Giants for making so gallant a battle with the Dodgers. They whittled ten games off the Brooklyn lead since midsummer.[13]

According to Thomson, the Giants were enjoying themselves:

> It started slowly for us and [was] not fun because we weren't winning enough. The fun started naturally when we began to win and slowly creep up on the Dodgers. The real excitement was [the] last week of the season. Dodgers were in front, we couldn't afford to lose.[14]

The battle was not over, Daley's opinion notwithstanding, and it continued to heat up the rest of the way. In Boston the Braves slammed the Dodgers twice, 6–3 and 14–2, while the Giants were beating the Phils, 5–1. Then, both challengers for the pennant had high-scoring wins, with Brooklyn banging Boston, 15–5, and New York blasting Philadelphia, 10–1.

The next day, while the Giants were idle, Boston took the final game of their set from the Dodgers, 4–3. Roe was the losing pitcher, having gone into the game with a 22–2 record and riding a 10-game winning streak. A disputed play at home plate on which the winning run scored led to the ejection of Campanella and coach Cookie Lavagetto. In the eighth inning, with the score tied, 3–3, Bob Addis was on third base and Jethroe on first with no one out. The Dodgers brought their infield in, and Torgeson grounded to second baseman Robinson who threw home to Campanella in an attempt to get the sliding Addis. When Umpire Frank Dascoli sig-naled the runner safe, the Dodgers catcher and others gave him a piece of their minds, which led to the ejections. The Brooklyn lead was down to one-half game as they headed to dreaded Philadelphia.

On September 28, the Phillies topped the Dodgers, 4–3. The Giants did not play, and the two teams were deadlocked. The same day the Yan-kees clinched the American League pennant with 8–0 and 11–3 wins over the Red Sox. The opener was especially memorable as right-hander Allie Reynolds tossed his second no-hitter of the season.

On the next-to-last day of the Senior Circuit's pennant battle, pitch-ing took over when Brooklyn shutout Philadelphia, 5–0, with Don New-combe registering his 20th win. In Boston, New York beat the Braves, 3–0, behind Maglie's five-hitter and 23rd win.

From the start of the Giants' August streak, which had begun with the doubleheader sweep over Philadelphia, until the final game of the sea-son, the Polo Grounders compiled an amazing 36–7 record. The matchups with Brooklyn had been critical. New York catcher Wes Westrum remem-bered their head-to-head meetings, saying, "Of course [we] had to beat the Dodgers when we met them and did beat them six out of seven games in the drive to cut the lead.... Beat them when you meet them was our 'Bat-tle Cry.'"[15]

During that same span, Brooklyn played only three games over .500 at 25–22, leaving the Dodgers and the Giants deadlocked at 95–58 with one game to play.

On the regular season-ending Sunday afternoon, Durocher's Giants added to their amazing 50-day counterattack by winning, 3–2. In Philadel-phia the Dodgers fell behind the Phils early, 6–1. They had closed the gap to 8–5 when they received word the Giants had won in Boston. A Dodger loss would send another pennant flying out the window. Having led most of the campaign, it would have been a bitter pill for the players and the fans to swallow.

The Giants were celebrating on the train back to New York, aware that their adversaries from Ebbets Field were trailing the Phillies. Late in the trip the bad news reached the Giants: Brooklyn had scored three times in the top of the eighth inning to knot the contest, 8–8.

Dressen went to his bullpen and found Newcombe ready to come back, with less than 24 hours of rest, and try to shut down the Phils. Eddie

Sawyer summoned his ace Robin Roberts, who had pitched eight innings the previous day, and asked him to do the same to the Dodgers. During those years, it would not have seemed right had Newk and Robin not faced each other in both the season's opener and finale.

The game moved into the bottom of the 12th inning, and Robinson took control. He robbed Eddie Waitkus of a two-out, bases-loaded single, diving headlong and grabbing a whistling line-drive. In the top of the 14th, Robinson came to bat and hit a game-winning homer to assure Brooklyn of a tie for the crown. Newcombe yielded one hit in 5⅔ innings of relief. Roberts was the loser, pitching 6⅔ innings.

Daley wrote about the great Brooklyn comeback, lauding the team for their gutsy play: "Only a game fish swims upstream, and no set of superlatives could do justice to the magnificent courage of the Brooks for what they accomplished yesterday."[16]

For only the second time in the National League's long history, the season was extended beyond the normal 154-game schedule. A best-of-three series would determine which team would capture the flag and become the league's representative in the World Series. A flip of the coin awarded game one of the playoff on October 1 to Brooklyn and Ebbets Field.

It was a day when home runs were decisive—and a preview to a final and momentous baseball memory. Andy Pafko gave the Dodgers a lead in the second when he connected off Hearn. Thomson, the Glasgow-born Staten Islander, hit a two-run homer off Ralph Branca in the top of the fourth inning to put New York ahead to stay. Irvin's round-tripper off Branca in the eighth provided an insurance run in the 3–1 victory. Durocher's team took a 1–0 lead in the series, and many of the 30,070 fans—at least those from Flatbush—went home disappointed. The Giants had finished the regular season with seven straight wins, and now they had registered number eight.

Some years later, Jansen wrote about the manager's pitching strategy for the remainder of the playoff, saying:

> Leo [Durocher] called [Sal] Maglie and myself into his office before the second game and we talked about taking a chance with [Sheldon] Jones pitching and give Maglie the extra day of rest and relieve with me in the third game if Sal got in trouble. Sal and I had pitched a lot the last two weeks of the season and were tired.[17]

The manager's strategy did not work. Jones went to the mound in the Polo Grounds for game two. He would be the first of three New York hurlers to be battered by Brooklyn in their 10–0 barrage. Six weeks of the Dodgers' downhill struggles seemed to have turned around in that one-game onslaught, which featured home runs by Robinson, Hodges, Pafko, and Rube Walker, and 13 hits in all. On his 25th birthday, rookie right-hander Clem Labine, who took the hill for the most significant game of his young career with a 4–1 record, held the Polo Grounders to six hits in their own park.

An article in the October 3 edition of the *Times* drew from an earlier time to capture the significance of the current struggle:

> Those miracle-workers of the last war, the Seabees, had a motto to the effect that "We do the difficult immediately, the impossible takes a little longer." For more than six weeks the Giants have been operating on that principle and getting away with it astonishingly well. But in the second game of the play-off at the Polo Grounds yesterday the Dodgers stole their borrowed motto, their thunder and the ball game."[18]

The long National League campaign came down to a one-game playoff which took place on Wednesday, October 3, in the Polo Grounds before 34,320 spectators. The crowd was over 4,000 fewer than had been at the ballpark a day earlier to witness the Dodgers' romp over the local heroes. Perhaps many believed that the Giants' luck had run out.

Maglie, who had gone 5–1 against the Dodgers during the season, was the Giants' starting pitcher. He was in search of his 24th win in the most important game of the season. Newcombe, who had pitched 14⅔ innings against the Phillies the previous Saturday and Sunday, was on the hill for the Dodgers.

Brooklyn's Beautiful Bums continued their scoring ways of the previous day. In the top of the first inning they jumped out to a 1–0 lead, when Robinson singled to drive home Reese, who had walked. Newcombe protected the slim margin until the bottom of the seventh when Irvin tagged up and scored from third after Thomson flied out to center field.

The Dodgers quickly retaliated in the top of the eighth. Reese singled and went to third on a hit by Snider. Maglie's wild pitch allowed Reese to cross the plate with the go-ahead run, giving Brooklyn a 2–1 edge. Two more Dodgers scored before Maglie and the Giants got the third out.

The Giants went out in order in the bottom of the eighth. In the top of the ninth, Jansen replaced Maglie, and three Dodgers went down quietly.

With a three-run lead and three outs to go, Newcombe went to the mound to hoist another pennant flag for the Dodgers. The Brooklyn faithful began to smell victory. Giants fans were slowly losing hope of catching their archrivals and perennial adversaries. Durocher, who had tasted defeat as the manager of the Dodgers in the 1946 National League playoff, sensed that the same agony was about to grip him as skipper of the Polo Grounders.

Dark and Mueller led off the bottom half of the ninth with singles. Aroused Giants fans groaned when Irvin popped out. Two outs to go. It was then that those in the press box were given the following information: "Attention: Press World Series Credentials for Ebbets Field can be picked up at 6 o'clock tonight at the Biltmore Hotel."[19]

Lockman slammed a double to left, driving in Dark. The score was 4–2, and runners were at second and third base. Lockman described the situation, writing:

> Don Mueller had sprained his ankle on going into third base. During the time out, I recall that Freddie Fitzsimmons, our first base coach, walked down to second base and said two prayers, one for Mueller and the other for Bobby to get a hit.[20]

Dressen came to the mound. Newcombe had given him 8⅓ strong innings that Wednesday afternoon, after his pair of outings the previous Saturday and Sunday in Philadelphia. Brooklyn hurler Carl Erskine later recalled some of the details of the final inning, saying:

> Dressen, fearing that (Newcombe) might be tiring, got the bullpen going when the Giants got a man on. Branca and I were up throwing. When a second [sic] Giant reached base, Dressen called the bullpen and asked if we were ready. Clyde Sukeforth, the bullpen coach and catcher said, "They're both ready, but Erskine is bouncing his curve sometimes."
>
> "Let me have Branca," said Charlie.[21]

Erskine, recalling Dressen's choice of Branca, added, "I do think that the pitching change was influenced by the fact that Campy was hurt and not catching."[22]

Branca, who had been the losing pitcher in the opener, walked from the pen to the mound. If he could retire two Giants he would deliver the pennant to Ebbets Field. With first base open, Dressen decided against walking the next batter, Thomson, who represented the winning run.

Russ Hodges, the "Voice of the Giants," provided the audio of the next few, amazing moments of baseball history:

> So don't go away.... Light up that Chesterfield.... Stay right with us and we'll see how Ralph Branca will fare against Bobby Thomson.... Thomson against the Brooklyn club has hit a lot of long ones this year.... He has seven home runs.[23]

Branca's first pitch was a called strike. The second delivery, too, caught part of the plate. But this time, Thomson swung. Hodges had the call:

It's gonna be ... I believe ... the Giants win the pennant! The Giants win the pennant! The Giants win the pennant. The Giants win the pennant! Bobby Thomson hit it into the lower deck of the left-field stands! ... The Giants win the pennant and they're going crazy, they're going crazy! ... I don't believe it! I don't believe it! I will not believe it! The Giants—Horace Stoneham has got a winner! The Giants win it by a score of 5–4 and they're picking up Bobby Thomson and carrying him off the field![24]

Erskine, recalling the memorable at-bat, wrote:

The pitch Thomson hit was up and in—just where the pitch should have been. The pitch he took for a strike was a low fastball—right in his power. All of this [is] to say that destiny was siding with the Giants.[25]

The three-run homer gave the Giants a 5–4 victory and catapulted them to the top of the National League standing—blasting the Brooklyn Dodgers out of the World Series. "Delirium broke loose below Coogan's Bluff," wrote the *Boston Globe*'s Hy Hurwitz. "Men wept with joy. Women wept too."[26] The resurrected Giants had come back from the dead again. That had been the story of the regular season, and it had just become the story of the playoff as well.

Shortly after the game, Thomson described the rush of feelings that were pounding within him:

I didn't run around the bases—I rode around 'em on a cloud.
It felt as if I was actually living one of those middle-of-the-night dreams....
I heard yells...I saw paper flying...I noticed people jumping in the air but through it all I just kept riding high on that cloud.[27]

Years later, he reflected again on the miraculous moment:

It boils down to a great rivalry between the Giants and the Dodgers—and rivalries are what create interest and excitement among the players and fans and media. The Dodgers were razzing us from the dugout. It looked hopeless and I felt dejected. A few hits and suddenly the stage is set. I stayed loose, but determined, and got lucky and hit one.[28]

It was a home run that came with such impact that the memory of it was burned deeply into the minds of fans throughout the baseball world. Lawrence Ritter and Donald Honig, in *The Image of Their Greatness*, proclaim, "It was at that moment, ... that the name of Bobby Thomson would be etched and associated forever with a swing of the bat so stunning and incredible as to make believers of dreamers everywhere."[29]

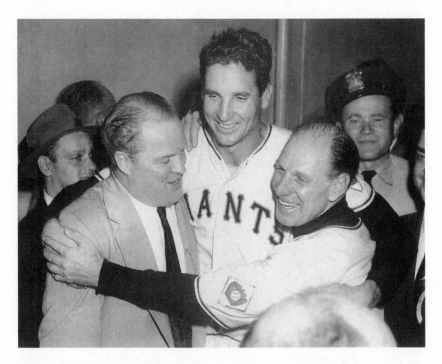

Manager Leo Durocher hugs Bobby Thomson and club owner Horace Stoneham after the "Shot Heard Round the World" (*The Sporting News*).

Branca's fateful pitch brought him notoriety that would dog him for the rest of his life. Following the loss, his pain was evident:

> Amid a scene of silent despair brief moments after the game, Branca sat on a staircase in the center of the Dodger dressing room, still in uniform, with his dark curly-haired head sunk between his knees. He was not crying, for he was beyond tears.[30]

Years later he mused on the eternal nature of one pitch, saying, "A guy commits murder and he gets pardoned after 20 years. I didn't get pardoned.... It's just like an alcoholic. You're going to have to live with this until they put you in the ground."[31]

A few of the Giants brought notable regular season statistics into the World Series. Dark's 41 doubles led the majors, and Irvin's total of 121 RBIs was best in the league. The Cardinals' Stan Musial topped the Senior Circuit with a .355 batting average, and Irvin was fifth at .312. Maglie [23–6] and Jansen [23–11] led the majors in wins, and Sal was second-best in the Senior Circuit with a 2.93 ERA.

The World Series began in Yankee Stadium on October 4, one day after the final game of the playoff. It was an overcast afternoon, and the lights would have to be turned on. Manager Casey Stengel was hoping to nail down his club's third consecutive championship. The Bronx Bombers sent Allie Reynolds [17–8], their double no-hit pitcher, out to mute the Giants' bats. Veteran left-hander Dave Koslo with a 10–9 record carried the hopes of the Polo Grounders.

Reynolds' troubles began in the top of the first inning when the Giants scored twice, capped by an Irvin steal of home. The New York outfielder had a 4-for-5 day as he led the visitors to a 5–1 win before a crowd of 65,673 in the Bronx. Reynolds lasted six innings, surrendering eight hits, all five runs, and seven walks.

Irvin continued his hitting spree the following day, going 3-for-4. But his heroics were not enough to defeat the Yankees and lefty Eddie Lopat, who had gone 21–9 during the regular season.

A drive by Yankees' first baseman Joe Collins, the Yanks' eighth hitter in the lineup, just reached the right-field stands in the second inning for a homer to lead the Bronx Bombers to a 3–1 win over the Giants and Jansen.

The Polo Grounds welcomed the World Series for the third game. A record crowd of 52,035 was there to root for their Jints. A five-run fifth inning, highlighted by Lockman's three-run homer, propelled the Giants to a 6–2 victory and a 2–1 lead in the Series. The Yankees' major accomplishment that afternoon was to hold Irvin hitless, lowering his Fall Classic average to .583.

After a day of rain, the Yankees tied the Series with a 6–2 victory in the Polo Grounds. Reynolds returned to form, allowing eight hits again but going the distance for the 6–2 win. Joe DiMaggio's home run and single in victory overshadowed Dark's three doubles in defeat.

The Bronx Bombers, behind Lopat, routed the Giants, 13–1, in the final game played in the Polo Grounds. A five-run third inning put the Yanks out of reach of the Giants, and they continued to roll up the score.

The Polo Grounders had rebounded from their 10–0 embarrassment at the hands of the Dodgers in the National League playoff; they did not do it against the Yankees in the World Series. Back in the Bronx, the home club won, 4–3, wrapping up the Fall Classic and bringing an end to the Giants' wonderful campaign.

The season was over for Durocher's club. It could have ended one week earlier had it not been for Thomson's historic last. In *The October Heroes*, Irvin recalled the waning moments of the Giants' final game against the Yankees. The Polo Grounders had scored twice in the top of the ninth, cutting the Yankee margin to one run. With a man on third and two out, Durocher called on Sal Yvars to pinch-hit for Henry Thompson. Irvin confessed,

> We were sitting on the bench wondering if we had any more miracles left in our bag. And for a second we thought we did. Sal really ripped one. He sent a screaming line drive out to right field. Hank Bauer went rushing for it and as he did he lost his footing. He slipped and fell, but some how he caught the ball and held on to it. It was a hell of a catch.[32]

That was the last out. The Yankees had captured the 1951 World Series.

But the Giants, said Irvin, despite their disappointment were not wholly unsatisfied with themselves:

> I'll tell you the truth, as much as we wanted to win the Series, we didn't feel that badly let down. We were still thinking about the play-off against the Dodgers. That was our year, right there, when Bobby hit that ball.[33]

Notes

1. John Drebinger, "Giants Crush Indians with 5 Homers in 18-Hit Assault; Dodgers Defeated," *New York Times*, 13 Apr. 1951, 29.

2. John Drebinger, "Tight Races Loom in Major Leagues," *New York Times*, 15 Apr. 1951, sec. 5, 2.

3. *Ibid.*

4. Arthur Daley, "Touching All Bases," *New York Times*, 1 May 1951, 37.

5. Don Mueller, Letter, 1999.

6. Monte Irvin, Letter, 1989.

7. John Drebinger, "Hearn Turns Back Pirates at the Polo Grounds, 14–3," *New York Times*, 3 June 1951, sec. 5, 1.

8. Joseph M. Sheehan, "Giants Topple Dodgers with 3-Run First; Yankees Defeat Senators," *New York Times*, 15 Aug. 1951, 30.

9. Louis Effrat, "Giants Down Phillies for Ninth Straight as Dodgers Are Routed by Braves," *New York Times*, 20 Aug. 1951, 29.

10. Monte Irvin, Letter, 1999.

11. Bobby Thomson, Letter, 1999.

12. Mueller, Letter.

13. Arthur Daley, "What's the Score?" *New York Times*, 25 Sept. 1951, 36.

14. Thomson, Letter, 1999.

15. Wes Westrum, Letter, 1989.

16. Arthur Daley, "Achieving the Impossible," *New York Times*, 1 Oct. 1951, 28.

17. Larry Jansen, Letter, 1989.

18. Arthur Daley, "Still a Dead Heat," *New York Times*, 3 Oct. 1951, 44.

19. "Wishful Thinking," *Boston Daily Globe*, 4 Oct. 1951, 16.

20. Whitey Lockman, Letter, 1989.

21. Carl Erskine, Letter, 1989.

22. Carl Erskine, Letter, 1996.

23. Russ Hodges and Al Hirshberg, *My Giants* (Garden City, New York: Doubleday, 1963), 113.

24. Hodges and Hirshberg, 113, 114.

25. Erskine, Letter, 1996.

26. Hy Hurwitz, "Thomson's Homer Climaxes Giants' Saga," *Boston Daily Globe*, 4 Oct. 1951, 1.

27. Bobby Thomson as told to the United Press, "Rode 'on a Cloud' on Tour of Bases," *New York Times*, 4 Oct. 1951, 42.

28. Bobby Thomson, Letter, 1988.

29. Lawrence Ritter and Donald Honig, *The Image of Their Greatness* (New York: Crown Publishers, 1979), 248.

30. John Griffin, "Like World's End for Branca," *Boston Daily Globe*, 4 Oct. 1951: 18.

31. Donald Honig, *The October Heroes* (New York: Simon and Schuster, 1979), 69.

32. Honig, 80, 81.

33. *Ibid.*, 81.

8. 1964
Philadelphia Phillies
The Missed Opportunity

The 1964 Philadelphia Phillies were rolling along on the way to the franchise's third appearance in the World Series, hoping that they would also pick up their first-ever World Championship. They had made it to the Fall Classic in 1915, during the days of Hall of Famers Grover Cleveland Alexander, Dave Bancroft, and Eppa Rixey, but had lost to the Boston Red Sox, 4–1. They also got there in 1950, but Eddie Sawyer's Whiz Kids dropped all four games to the New York Yankees in a well-played and hard-fought series.

In 1964 the Phillies were well on their way to the postseason until their September struggles swept them out of the lead and cleared the way for two teams to pass them down the stretch. The St. Louis Cardinals finally captured the National League flag on the final day of the campaign.

The Phils opened the season with a two-game series against the New York Mets in Connie Mack Stadium, Philadelphia. On April 14, they defeated the Mets, 5–3, and they went on to pick up their second win the following day with a 4–1 victory. Leaving for Chicago, the Phils were 2–0 and had spent the first two of the 134 days they would reside in first place that season.

Philadelphia beat the Chicago Cubs in the season's first game in Wrigley Field before losing to them the next day. They won 10 of their first 12 games, with rookie third baseman Richie Allen from Wampum, Pennsylvania, delivering six home runs. Allen was playing a new position, but it did not appear to affect his hitting.

The Phillies, under the guidance of manager Gene Mauch, acknowledged as one of the most knowledgeable skippers ever, sat at the top of the 10-team National League until May 3, when the San Francisco Giants took the lead for 12 days. The two teams alternated, moving in and out of first place during the next several weeks.

On the final day of the month, the Giants and the Mets staged a monumental doubleheader in Shea Stadium. San Francisco picked up two victories, 5–3 and 8–6, after 32 innings of baseball spread out over 10 hours and 23 minutes before 57,037 fans. The second game was not decided until the 23rd inning and after seven hours and 23 minutes of play. In terms of time played, it was the longest game in major league history. Though the contests ate up the hours, few fans found reason to wander from their seats:

> They saw baseball rarities like a two-man triple play, ... they saw 12 pitchers share in two strike-out records—36 in one game and 47 in one day, ... [and] finally, they saw ... Gaylord Perry of the Giants and Galen Cisco of the Mets. They pitched an entire game in relief—10 innings for Perry and nine for Cisco—in a duplicate of the 15-inning struggle in San Francisco two weeks ago.[1]

On June 1, Philadelphia was 21–15 and held a half game lead over San Francisco. Three days later, they were victims of left-hander Sandy Koufax's third career no-hitter, as the Los Angeles Dodgers dropped the Phils, 3–0. San Francisco continued Philadelphia's woes by sweeping the home team in a three-game set, 5–3 in 11 innings, 4–2, and 4–3 in 10 innings. However, after the Giants returned to Candlestick Park, they fell on their own hard times, and on June 11, the Phillies climbed back into the lead for 17 days.

At the time, the league-leaders were without a .300 hitter. Allen led the club with a .294 average, and Johnny Callison was next at .289. The Philadelphia pitchers were faring much better. Jim Bunning was leading the league with a 1.09 ERA and lefty Chris Short was in the third spot with a 1.99 mark.

A momentous event took center stage on June 21, when Bunning pitched his second career no-hitter, this one a perfect game. The 32-year-old, college-educated stockbroker, who also happened to be an outstanding, 6'3" right-handed pitcher, stymied the Mets, 6–0. Bunning had come to the Phillies during the off-season in a trade with the Detroit Tigers. His approach during the "perfecto" was contrary to the usual baseball protocol, which forbids pitchers from talking about the feat while it's underway:

Jim Bunning firing for the Phillies (NBL).

He chatted happily about it since the fourth inning ... with even better results than the first one in 1985 [a no-hitter against the Red Sox], when he turned to his teammates and yelled:

"Protect that no-hitter, boys, start diving for everything."[2]

On May 18, Bunning had hurled a one-hitter against the Houston Colt .45s. Eleven days later, he had a perfect game against the same club for 6⅔ innings. When left-fielder Wes Covington did not get a good jump on a soft liner in his direction, the ball dropped in for the Colt .45s' first hit. Houston went on to score five times in the next inning. The Phils manager made a move in the Mets game to try to prevent the same thing from happening again. In an effort to strengthen the defense, he moved Cookie Rojas to left, taking Wes Covington out of the game, and plugged in Bobby Wine at short.[3]

Everything fell in line on Father's Day, 1964, and Bunning had his perfect game. He had given a special present to his seven children.

After the Giants ran off a string of 12 wins in 14 games to climb back to the top, the Phillies flew to the "Stick" for a three-game series. On July 3, 22-year-old right-hander Ray Culp stopped San Francisco, 5–1. On Independence Day, Bunning raised his record to 9–2 and continued his holiday form, going 11 innings and nailing down a 5–2 victory. Allen tripled home the go-ahead run and Covington followed with a homer to provide the margin of victory. Left-hander Dennis Bennett completed the sweep, with a masterful 2–1 win over Giants ace Juan Marichal.

Philadelphia's league-leading record was 47–28 and the Giants, as a result of their three losses to the Phils, had dropped to second with a 47–31 mark. Cookie Rojas, who was proving to be a valuable utility man, led the Phils with a .326 average. Allen had crept over the .300 mark, hitting .303. Short was 7–4 and had taken over the Senior Circuit's ERA lead with a 1.58 mark.

That completed the first half of the campaign, and the clubs took their annual break for the All-Star Game. Callison turned into the game's hero by hitting a ninth-inning, three-run homer to bring a 7–4 victory to the National Leaguers.

The break was not good for the Philadelphians, and they proceeded to lose six of the eight games after the resumption of play. San Francisco nudged ahead again, but for only four days.

The Phillies, behind Art Mahaffey, beat the Pittsburgh Pirates, 7–5, on July 16. They took over the top spot again, and this time they would stay there until September 27.

On July 11, 50 years to the day that the 1914 Miracle Braves started their march from the basement to the pennant, St. Louis was in fifth place with a 40–41 record and were 10 games out of the lead. The Cardinals announced a shake-up on July 17: President August A. Busch, Jr., had fired general manager Bing Devine and business manager Art Routzong. Although Devine was gone, a trade he had made on June 15, when the Cards were 28–30 and tied for seventh spot, proved to be critical in the Cardinals' drive to the pennant. The general manager had engineered a deal with the Cubs which brought 24-year-old outfielder Lou Brock to

St. Louis in exchange for pitcher Ernie Broglio, a 28-year-old veteran right-hander. When the speedy Brock, who was in his third full season at the major league level, left Chicago he was batting .251. With the Cards he went on to hit .348, played outstanding defense in the outfield, and proved to be a vital member of his new club.

Six days after Devine's firing, and after having dropped three straight at home to the Pirates, the Red Birds had a 47–48 record, and were 10 games out of first place. Their climb to the top was about to begin as they would go 46–21 the rest of the way.

The Phillies played steady baseball through the second half of July and August. On the final day of August they were 78–51 and held a 5½ game lead over Cincinnati.

Philadelphia added right-handed power to its lineup, acquiring Frank Thomas from the Mets on August 7. He put together a .302 average, hit seven homers, and knocked in 28 runs while playing 32 games with his new club. On September 8, he suffered a broken right thumb diving back into second base, and he made only one more appearance [on September 25] with the Phils that season. General manager John Quinn purchased Vic Power from the California Angels in an attempt to fill the void created by the loss of Thomas.

The Reds were fighting more than their closest competitors that season: Their manager Fred Hutchinson was battling terminal cancer, which had been discovered the previous winter. Beloved by the team, it was a difficult time for many of the players. He entered the hospital for treatment on July 27 and handed over the club to Dick Sisler, who had been Philadelphia's hero in 1950 when he hit a dramatic homer to clinch the pennant on the final day of the season. Hutchinson rejoined the team on August 4, but was re-admitted to the hospital nine days later. Although he was back with the Reds near the end of the month, Sisler ran the club the rest of the way. Hutchinson, who was affectionately called the "Bear," died during the offseason.

On September 16, Houston beat the Phils, 6–5. Bunning, who had defeated the Colt .45s four times during the season, started the game with only two days rest. He had beaten the Giants in San Francisco on September 13.

The Phils were 90–60 and 6½ games in front of the Cards and the Reds, with 14 days remaining in the season and 12 games left to play. Their magic number was seven.

Mauch has pleasant memories about the season to that point, writing, "For the first 150 games nobody or no team ever enjoyed what they were doing and each other more. They knew how to play."[4] He also valued the players' intelligence and maturity: "If we were playing the Cubs, they would practice bunting down the first base line to make Ernie Banks field the ball, not Ron Santo at third. They did what they had to do to win."[5]

The Phillies came home after a four-game split on the West Coast against the Dodgers. Bunning, with his usual three days of rest, won the series finale. He went the distance in the 3–2 victory and raised his season's record to 18–5. Short was 17–7, but had dropped to second place in the ERA race behind Koufax, who at 1.74 bettered slightly Short's minuscule 1.92.

Although some would say it began with Bunning's appearance against the Colt .45s, it's more likely that Philadelphia's fatal decline started on September 21.[6]

Mahaffey went to the mound that day against Cincinnati to open the Phils' final homestand. He suffered a tough loss, 1–0, and the club lost a bit of their grip on first place, when Chico Ruiz stole home, with Mahaffey throwing the ball away, in the top of the sixth for the only run of the game. John Tsitouris pitched the gem for Cincinnati. The next day, the Reds blasted Short for six runs in 4⅓ innings, on their way to a 9–2 win. It was his roughest outing of the year to date. As reported in the *New York Times*, "The Cincinnati Reds raised eyebrows all over the National League tonight by knocking off the Philadelphia Phillies for the second straight time. They now trail Philadelphia by 4½ games."[7]

Bennett took a 6–4 loss in game three, with Vada Pinson powering two homers which were good for four runs.

Things didn't improve for the Phillies when the Milwaukee Braves came to town. Milwaukee captured game one, 5–3, with Bunning dropping his second straight decision. Prior to that, he had won 10 of 11 games and was 6–0 at home. The next day, September 25, Short went 7⅓ innings, surrendering three runs, only one of which was earned. The Braves and the Phillies went to the 12th inning before Milwaukee took a 7–5 victory. It was a heartbreaking loss that saw the Phillies lead through seven before the clubs traded runs, knotting the score until an error gave the contest to the Braves.

The game marked a continuation of Mauch's new approach to using his pitching staff. The Phils manager, who was unable to speak because of a strained voice which had resulted from a shouting match with an umpire in the third game of the Dodgers series, still had his mental wheels going at full speed. He had decided to go with a three-man rotation to use Short and Bunning on two days' rest. The experiment had begun with Bunning in Houston, and now Short was taking part. Chris pitched well in his first try at a quick comeback, but the result was the same as Philadelphia suffered its fifth straight defeat.

On September 26, the Phillies were ahead, 4–3, going into the top of the ninth against the Braves, but Rico Carty's three-run triple led to Milwaukee's 6–4 win. The Phils' lead over the Reds had evaporated to one-half game. Cincinnati, who had won seven in a row, was in hot pursuit, and the Cardinals were only one game behind.

Bunning was back on two days' rest. Philadelphia took an early 3–2 lead, but Jim could not stop either Milwaukee or the stunning slide. The Braves pummeled him and four other Philadelphia pitchers for 22 hits in the final game of their series sweep, 14–8. Callison had a three-homer day for the losers, who saw Cincinnati take over the top spot. The stunned Phillies, who had seen their dream of the postseason become a nightmare, had gone 0–7 during the homestand and had fallen to second.

Philadelphia went to St. Louis to face the Cardinals, who sat one spot below them in third place. At least they were getting away from the City of Brotherly Love's growing flock of boo-birds, who were aiming their disappointment at most of the team. They were the same ones who, for most of the season, had been unmerciful toward the young Allen, who was having defensive troubles at third base.

Mauch's pitching strategy had not kept the Phillies at the top of the league. Neither Bunning nor Short had won a game while pitching with two days' rest, and the Phils had lost their lead. Some believed that Mauch had panicked and had gone to his strategy because he was afraid to use any but his top two pitchers. Danny Cater, a rookie outfielder at the time, was one of them, saying, "I liked Gene Mauch, but I think he tried to clinch the pennant too fast by changing the pitching rotation. The last 12 games Bunning and Short were pitched every other day."[8]

During the final one and a half months of the season, critics would later point out, Cardinals manager Johnny Keane had only three pitchers he felt he could rely on—Bob Gibson, Ray Sadecki, and Curt Simmons—yet he did not go to an altered rotation. (The Cards' fourth starter was veteran Roger Craig, who had come from the Mets in 1964. He had registered a forgettable 10–24 mark with New York in 1962, the club's first year.)

Short went to the hill with two days rest to open the three-game set, and he was bested, 5–1, by Gibson, the Cardinals ace. It was St. Louis' sixth straight win and Philadelphia's eighth consecutive loss. With the victory, the Cards dropped the plummeting Phils into third place.

The next day, September 29, the Cardinals topped the Phillies again, 4–2, and the Reds lost to the Pirates. The Philadelphia pitching staff was in shambles. Cincinnati and St. Louis were both 91–67 and shared the National League's top rung.

In the final game of the series, Simmons, who had been the Cardinals' steadiest pitcher down the stretch and had won his last five decisions, administered his former club an 8–5 defeat, going 6⅔ innings before surrendering his first hit. Bunning, back after only two day's rest, was the losing pitcher as the Phils were dealt their 10th defeat in a row. The Phillies did not help their own cause, committing four errors and tossing a wild pitch.

Since Simmons' arrival in St. Louis during the 1960 season, the 35-year-old lefty had gone 16–2 against Philadelphia. When he topped the Phils, 8–5, in the final game of the series, it resurrected powerful memories of an earlier potential disaster for many long-time Philadelphia fans. The veteran left-hander had been in a pennant fight with the 1950 Whiz Kids, and although the club made it to the World Series with a dramatic victory over the Brooklyn Dodgers on the final day of the regular season, he wasn't with them. Simmons, a 17-game winner that season, was gone by September 6, the first major leaguer inducted in the military for the Korean War.

In 1964 things were getting so tight at the top of the National League that president Warren Giles made plans for possible two-team, three-team, and four-team playoffs.

Although the Phillies were looking up from third place, they still had a shot at the title. They broke their 10-game losing streak on October 2, beating the Reds, 4–3. Short, working with three days rest, went 6⅓ frames, giving up three runs—only one of them earned—but he did not pick up the victory. The Mets took two from the Cards, walloping them, 15–5, in the second game.

Entering the final day of the season, St. Louis and Cincinnati had identical 92–69 records. Philadelphia was one game behind at 91–70. The following analysis of the variety of possibilities appeared in the *New York Times*:

> If St. Louis defeats New York and Philadelphia defeats Cincinnati, St. Louis will be league champion. If New York defeats St. Louis and Cincinnati defeats Philadelphia, Cincinnati will win the pennant. If Cincinnati and St. Louis both win, they will tie for the pennant and engage in a three-game play-off. If they both lose [and Philadelphia wins], a three-way tie will result, necessitating a round-robin play-off.[9]

New York held a 3–2 lead over St. Louis in the top of the fifth, but then the Cards took over, romping over the Mets, 11–5. Ironically, it was Philadelphia who ended all the speculation, dashing Cincinnati's hopes of maintaining the tie by thumping the Reds, 10–0, behind Bunning, who was going on three days' rest.

St. Louis was in the World Series for the first time since 1946, when they had defeated the Red Sox in seven games. In 1964 they would capture a second Fall Classic crown with a 4–3 margin over the Yankees.

Philadelphia went home. Allen took a .318 average with 29 home runs and 91 RBIs with him. He also carried away both the Baseball Writers' Association and *The Sporting News* Rookie of the Year Awards. Rojas finished at .290, Covington at .280, Tony Gonzalez at .278, and Callison at .274 with 31 homers and a team-leading 104 RBIs. Short finished with a 17–9 record and a 2.20 ERA, the fourth best in the league. Bunning narrowly missed the 20-win mark, closing the campaign at 19–8, with 219 strikeouts and a low 2.63 ERA.

Members of the 1964 club still have strong feelings about the season and their part in it. Culp, who was removed from the rotation down the stretch (either because of an injured back or because he had been given an extended stay in Mauch's doghouse), was asked how he felt about how the season had gone. He wrote simply, "It was a very disgusting year for me. It was very long."[10]

Bennett, who hurt his arm and missed a number of starts, had good memories about the season and Mauch:

> Nobody expected us to be a contender, so we took a lot of teams by surprise. We were a young team and just went out and played the game. It was a season of highs and lows. Everybody on the team contributed.... It was the most exciting season of my career.
>
> The big thing about the team was everybody pulled for each other. There was no animosity on the team. I think Gene did a great job of managing. I know in the 3 years I played for Gene was when I learned the game.[11]

First baseman John Herrnstein recalled the squad's slow recognition of what was happening to them:

> Of the 10 losses in a row when we dropped from first place—we had chances to win 7 of them, but just didn't get the job done. I never sensed panic among the players, just disbelief at what was happening. I don't think any one of us felt we were capable of ever losing 10 in a row. We had been too good all year for that to happen.[12]

Commenting years later about the collapse, Bunning, who had become a congressman from Kentucky, put it bluntly:

> We blew it. It was a total team effort in '64 and we blew it together; that includes manager, coaches, trainers, and all personnel on the ballclub....
>
> We had not had a slump in the whole season [until the one in September]. There are a lot of reasons for it. You can go back and find out that we

hadn't had a day off in 40-games and the Phillies rescheduled some games when we were playing pretty well for later in the season when we could draw more people, [not] realizing an off day might have saved our lives during that stretch of losing.[13]

It would be another 12 years before the Phillies found their way to the postseason, and another 16 before they sat atop all of baseball.

Notes

1. Joseph Durso, "New York Drops 5–3, 8–6 Contests," *New York Times*, 1 June 1964, 35.
2. "Perfect-Game Pitcher," *New York Times*, 22 June 1964, 31.
3. "Mauch Acts to Aid Bunning by Closing Old Disaster Area," *New York Times*, 22 June 1964, 31.
4. Gene Mauch, Letter, 1999.
5. Steve Wulf, "The Year of the Blue Snow," *Sports Illustrated*, 25 September 1989, 80.
6. Wulf, 79.
7. Joseph Durso, "Reds, with O'Toole, Subdue Phils, 9–2, Trail by 4½ Games," *New York Times*, 23 September 1964, 59.
8. Danny Cater, Letter, 1999.
9. "Dept. of Utter Confusion," *New York Times*, 4 October 1964, sec. 5, 1.
10. Ray Culp, Letter, 1999.
11. Dennis Bennett, Letter, 1999.
12. John Herrnstein, Letter, 1999.
13. Brent Kelley, "An Interview with Congressman Jim Bunning," *Sports Collectors Digest*, 2 March 1990, 160.

9. 1969 New York Mets and Chicago Cubs

A Miracle Comeback and a Painful Comedown

Baseball avoided a strike in 1969. During the off season, the Players Association had rejected an offer from management, saying that the players wanted an additional increase in health care, life insurance, and pension benefits. Short of that, they would drop their contracts unsigned and take up placards, instead. Bowie Kuhn, the new commissioner, was able to secure new pension concessions from the owners, however, and with the players satisfied by their gain, the season began on time.

Besides Kuhn, there was a lot new in the game. There was a new club in another country, Canada, as the Montreal Expos joined the National League. The Senior Circuit also welcomed the San Diego Padres as part of the two-team expansion in each league. The American League added the Kansas City Royals and the Seattle Pilots.

The additional teams necessitated that the 12 clubs in each loop be divided into two divisions. Both leagues were divided into East and West, with the winner of each division to play in the October League Championship Series, which would decide the circuit's pennant winner. Those two teams would go on to meet in the World Series. The regular season had been expanded to 162 games for each team.

There were eight new major league managers, one of whom received much of the attention: Ted Williams. He had put his bat down and was prepared to lead the Washington Senators throughout the campaign.

Richard M. Nixon was the country's new president, and he had the honor of throwing out the first pitch on April 7 at the Senators opener against the New York Yankees. Thing were a bit difficult for him at the start. He arrived at his box and discovered that the seal of his office read, "Presidnt of the United States." Then he dropped the ball when it was given to him for the ceremonial first pitch, and he had to retrieve it as it rolled at his feet. He had made out better during his appearance in 1959, when he had performed the honors as the vice president, standing in for President Dwight Eisenhower.

Major league pitchers found something new and different, too. The height of the mound had been lowered from 15 inches to 10 inches in an attempt to aid the hitters, who hit a dismal .230 in the AL and .243 in the NL during the '68 campaign. Also, umpires had been instructed to create a smaller strike zone. A strike would be a pitch that crossed the plate on a plane no higher than the batter's arm pits, no lower than the tops of his knees. In an effort to speed up the games, pitchers would have to deliver the pitch in under 20 seconds when the bases were unoccupied. Failure to do so would result in the umpire calling a ball.

Kuhn had replaced William "Spike" Eckert, who had served only three years before being forced out of office by dissatisfied owners. Kuhn was at opening day in Robert F. Kennedy [R.F.K.] Stadium in Washington, the new name of D.C. Stadium. Following the opener, he had plans to travel the country and appear at the home openers of many of the major league clubs.

He wasn't at Chicago's Wrigley Field on April 8, but a record-setting opening day crowd of 40,796 was. One of them was comedian Jimmy Durante, who was in attendance as a guest celebrity. Chicago's captain, Ron Santo, introduced Durante and draped him in a Cubs' jacket.

The Cubs won the opener in the 11th inning when Willie Smith, a 30-year-old veteran pinch hitter, entered the game and slammed a two-run homer. His shot gave Chicago, who was trailing 6–5 at the time, a 7–6 victory over the Philadelphia Phillies. Phil Regan picked up the win in relief, and 38-year-old first baseman Ernie Banks hit two homers to drive in the Cubs' first five runs.

With the swing of Smith's bat:

> Up in the WGN Radio booth, exuberant, excitable Vince Lloyd sprang to his feet, nearly knocking over his play-by-play partner Lou Boudreau, and began bellowing, "Willie hits one! High! Deep rightfield! This could be! This is a home run! A home run for Willie Smith and the Cubs win! Holy Mackerel!"
>
> Right next door, in the WGN-TV booth, Jack Brickhouse was torturing his tonsils too—shouting his famous jubilant "Hey! Hey!" as he does every time the Cubs hit a homer.[1]

Chicago went on to sweep the three-game series against Philadelphia with 11–3 and 6–2 wins. Billy Williams' four doubles, which tied a major league record, were the key blows in the Cubs' 11–3 victory, as Bill Hands registered his first win of the season.

Chicago's pitching excelled in the opener of the three-game set with the Expos, as the Cubs won, 1–0, in 11 innings. Joe Niekro pitched the first nine and gave up six hits. Ted Abernathy followed him to the mound and threw three hitless frames to pick up the win. Williams singled home Don Kessinger with the winning run in the bottom of the 12th. Chicago dropped the next game to Montreal, 7–3, with Ferguson Jenkins absorbing the club's first loss of the season. However, the Cubs rebounded and won the rubber game, 7–6, and Regan picked up his second victory in relief. Chicago ended its first homestand with two wins over Pittsburgh, and they left for St. Louis with a 7–1 mark.

On April 20, they extended their record to 11–1, before suffering their second loss in the second half of a doubleheader with the Expos in Montreal.

Manager Leo Durocher's Cubs were off to an eye-catching start in the new National League East, and they were eagerly hoping for a return to the postseason. Chicago had not been there since 1945, during the war years, when they lost the World Series to the Detroit Tigers in seven games. One had to go all the way back to 1908 to find a Cub team which had won the Fall Classic.

The New York Mets opened their season in Shea Stadium, losing to the expansion Expos, 11–10. They picked up wins the next two days with 9–5 and 4–2 victories over the league's new entry from Canada. After a 6–5 loss to the St. Louis Cardinals, however, the Mets' bats went silent, and they dropped two more to St. Louis, 1–0 and 3–1, with ace right-hander Bob Gibson administering the loss in the final game of the series.

New York split two games in Philadelphia and dropped two in Pittsburgh. They bounced back and picked up a pair of victories in St. Louis and, on April 17, they stood 5–7.

At least the Mets knew one thing for certain. For the first time in their history they wouldn't finish lower than sixth place. With the new divisional setup, that was as low as they could sink. From 1962 through 1965, the Mets knew only the National League's basement. They rose to ninth in 1966, but were back in the cellar in 1967. Their fellow expansion team, the Houston Colt .45s [they became the Astros in 1965], finished higher than New York each year until 1968, when the Mets climbed out of the cellar and claimed ninth place, with Houston taking over the basement.

For the first 155 days of the campaign, the Cubs flag atop Wrigley

Field's center-field scoreboard fluttered in the wind above those representing the other five teams in the National League's Eastern Division.

On May 1, Chicago was 16–7, and one month later they were 32–16 and held a 7½ game lead over the runner-up Pittsburgh Pirates. Randy Hundley and Kessinger were hitting .306, and Williams was at .302. Banks was leading the league with 41 RBIs.

The Cubs strung together a trio of shutouts on May 11, 12, and 13: left-hander Ken Holtzman blanked the San Francisco Giants, 8–0; Jenkins followed with a 2–0 win over San Diego; and Dick Selma, a hard-throwing right-hander the Cubs had acquired in an early season deal with the San Diego Padres, whitewashed his former club, 19–0, to complete the string. Selma had spent 1965–68 with the Mets before going to San Diego, where he appeared in only four games.

Chicago had picked up a number of late-game wins as evidenced by the fact that their two top relievers, Abernathy and Regan, were 4–0 and 5–2 respectively. The club's top starter was Holtzman, who had a stretch of 33 scoreless innings during the month and was 8–1.

On June 1, the Mets sat in third place with a 21–23 mark and trailed Chicago by nine games. Cleon Jones was leading the league in batting with a .369 average, but Bud Harrelson's .286 was the next Met in line. Tom Seaver had posted a 7–3 record, but the club's best ERA, 2.50, belonged to left-hander Jerry Koosman, who had won only one game in four decisions.

The Mets' position above the middle of the pack surely seemed a dizzying height for the ball club. It had been a long climb to contention.

The Mets entered the 1969 season as a 100–1 shot to win the National League pennant. Gil Hodges, who had suffered a heart attack the previous September 24, had recovered and was back managing the team, but only time would tell how much stress and strain he could take from his club.

The 1969 Mets players were nameless to most fans, and only a few were coveted by other clubs. There was interest in two of their young pitchers, Koosman and Seaver, and in Jones, one of their outfielders.

As Nolan Ryan said, "Our Opening Day lineup didn't figure to scare anyone: Tommy Agee in center field, Rod Gaspar in right field, Ken Boswell at second base, Cleon Jones in left field, Ed Charles at third base, Ed Kranepool at first. Jerry Grote was the catcher, Bud Harrelson played shortstop, and Tom Seaver pitched."[2]

Over in the Windy City, Chicago's theme song, "Hey, Hey! Holy Mackerel," had become a rallying cry. Early in the season, Santo's heel-clicking was added to the Cubs' repertoire. Following an important victory over the expansion Expos, Santo expressed his excitement in a novel manner:

For some reason, and to this day I don't know what was going through my mind at the time, I ran down the left field line, listening to the cheers from the fans, and for no particular reason, I jumped into the air—and clicked my heels. It was reaction. It was out of jubilation. One click of the heels from an emotional Italian. I never had done that before—ever. Little did I realize it would be associated with me for the rest of my life.[3]

Santo's heel-clicking became the rage. Soon he was doing double and triple clicks after victories, and some spectators were trying to imitate him. It excited the fans; soon, it enraged opponents. The Cubs captain begun to see an increasing number of brush-back pitches as pitchers sent him a message about what they thought of his victory celebrations.

Chicago's 1969 season had started in a manner which raised Banks' hopes. He was the perennial optimist, who always seemed to see a pennant on the horizon during an extended winning streak.

Williams, the sweet-swinging left-hander, had also been waiting years for the Cubs to field a winner. He was in his ninth full season in Chicago and, on June 29, he was honored on Billy Williams Day in Wrigley Field. In the first game of a double header with the Cardinals, Williams tied Stan Musial's consecutive-games-played streak of 895; in the second game, Billy broke the mark. On his special day, Williams hit two triples, two doubles, and a single to lead the Cubs to a sweep of the Cards. And the fans, including the 41,060 who had come to the ballpark to honor Williams that day, were also getting excited, hoping that this would be the magical year for the club.

The Cubs and the Mets faced each other in a pair of three-game series in July. The two clubs had met eight times earlier in the season, and Chicago led the year, 5–3.

There was growing antagonism between the Cubs and the Mets; the two clubs didn't like each other. In May, they had engaged in a beanball battle in one of their games, and the bad feelings carried over.

George Vecsey of the *New York Times*, catching the importance of the upcoming series, wrote:

It has taken them 7½ years, 439 victories and 771 defeats, but today the Mets finally begin an important series.

At 2:05 P.M. at Shea Stadium, they start a three-game series with the Chicago Cubs, the only team ahead of them in the National League's Eastern Division.[4]

On July 8, the Mets, behind Koosman and in front of 55,096 fans, won one of the biggest games in their history, scoring three runs in the ninth inning to shock the Cubs, 4–3. Until the fatal ninth, Jenkins, who had been a 20-game winner the previous two seasons, had held New York to one hit, Kranepool's home run in the fifth. In the Mets' final at bat, the Cubs' 6'5", 205-pound right-hander gave up three doubles before Kranepool singled to score the winning run. The Mets had cut the Cubs' lead to four games.

The following day, things got even better for the Mets. The mushrooming excitement about their unbelievable challenge for the division's top spot drew the largest crowd in Shea Stadium history. Seaver provided a masterpiece for the 59,080 fans in the Mets' Flushing home. He went 8⅓ innings before the Cubs managed a baserunner. Rookie outfielder Jim Qualls drilled a solid single to left-center field between Jones and Agee. Seaver retired the next two batters, and the New Yorkers had a 4–0 victory. Tom had not gotten his no-hitter, but he had his 14th victory against only three losses. It was the Mets seventh straight win and the Cubs fifth loss in a row. Chicago's lead was three games, and New York was only one behind in the all-important loss column.

Prior to the series finale, Banks emerged from the dugout, greeting the new day with his eternal optimism:

Tom Seaver on the hill for the Mets (NBL).

"Happy Thursday," he chirped in greeting.... "What about those Mets? ... Wasn't that a magnificent game that Tom Seaver pitched? And he's such a nice young man as well as being a great pitcher. He has the same assurance that Robin Roberts had and is as smooth and as compact a pitcher."[5]

The Cubs took a bit of the glow off the Mets' big series with a 6–2 win in game three. Durocher's charges came from a 2–1 deficit by scoring five runs in the fifth inning. Qualls started the rally with a double and, before the inning was over, the Cubs had four more hits, including a two-run homer by Santo. The Mets also committed two damaging errors in the uprising. Hands picked up the victory to go 10–7 for the season.

Following the series, the Cubs returned to Wrigley to take on the Phillies. Chicago won three of the four games. The Mets headed to Montreal and took the final two games there after dropping the opener.

On July 14, the top two teams hooked up again, but this time it was in the Windy City. In game one, the Cubs won a measure of revenge, beating Seaver, 1–0, before 40,252 fans. It was Seaver's first loss since May 25, after winning eight straight. Hands, with ninth-inning relief from Regan, took the win. Chicago's lone run came as the result of Kessinger's one-out bunt single, a hit-and-run ground out, and Williams' single. The victory stretched the Cubs' lead to 5½ games.

The final two games in 54-year-old Wrigley Field on Chicago's North Side went to the team from Flushing. Met shortstop Al Weis' three-run homer, his first of the year and only his fifth in eight seasons, sparked the New Yorkers to a 4–3 win. The Mets beat Jenkins again the next afternoon. They jumped all over him, scoring six times in the first inning to set the wheels in motion for the 9–5 victory. Weis' homer in the fifth gave the hot-hitting shortstop his second in two days and his sixth in eight seasons. The Mets, led by Weis, had captured their second two-out-of-three series in nine days from the division leaders.

On July 20, as the Cubs were looking down from the top of the National League East, the rest of the world was looking up at the moon. That night, Eagle, the Apollo 11 lunar module, touched down on the moon, and Neil Armstrong and Edward "Buzz" Aldrin took their famous steps on the previously uncharted surface.

The second game of the doubleheader in Philadelphia between the Cubs and the Phils was stopped for five minutes in the third inning to celebrate the space accomplishment. Chicago had taken the opener, 1–0, behind Jenkins, who raised his record to 13–7. They went on to also capture the nightcap by the score of 6–1. Selma went the distance for his 10th win against four defeats.

Chicago held a 4½ game lead and Selma said, "With those guys on the moon tonight and me pitching, no way we can lose."[6]

The Cubs had something of an ally in the president of the Phillies, Bob Carpenter. At President Nixon's White House reception before the July 23 All-Star Game in Washington, D.C., Carpenter confessed:

> If the Phillies can't win... I'm pulling for the Cubs because of just one man— Phil Wrigley. He's one pioneer who puts baseball ahead of everything—his team, his hopes. If something isn't good for the complete game, you'll never sell it to him. A man with such ideals deserves nothing but the best, and in Phil's case that would be a pennant.[7]

The Cubs got hot during the first three weeks of August, going 12–4. They extended their lead to 8½ games over the Cards, who had taken over second place and were 9½ in front of the Mets.

Durocher installed Jim Hickman as Chicago's regular right-fielder on August 3. Hickman, who was the second oldest player on the team after Banks, had been platooning in right. His bat came alive and he powered the Cubs during the final two months of the campaign, hitting 14 of his 21 home runs.

On August 19, Holtzman pitched a no-hit, no-run game against the Atlanta Braves, and Santo's three-run homer off knuckle-baller Phil Niekro in the first inning produced all of the day's scoring. The blast also extended Santo's league-leading RBI total to 97. Holtzman was aided by the wind blowing in from left field, especially on a towering drive by Hank Aaron in his second at-bat. The wind kept the ball from ending up in the bleachers, guiding it instead into Williams' waiting glove. There were also outstanding fielding plays by second baseman Glenn Beckert and shortstop Kessinger which kept the no-hitter intact.

During warmup, Holtzman had realized that his curveball and change-up weren't

Ferguson Jenkins, the Cubs mainstay (NBL).

working and all that he had was his fastball. His 90-plus heater and the defense behind him took him a long way.

Now a 23 year old with the 14–7 record, Holtzman spoke about his memorable day on which he had thrown 112 pitches: "About the sixth inning I thought I was running out of gas and when I got to the dugout I asked coach Pete Reiser to watch me out there—to check my speed to see if I was losing any ... I never heard anything from Reiser, so I just kept throwing fast balls."[8]

Everything seemed to be going Chicago's way. Beckert was swept up in the excitement and optimism, saying, "It was just great. The entire city of Chicago was aware of the Cubs. Every place you would go it was 'Cubs.' It was just great being able to be there at that time. Something I will never forget."[9]

While Chicago was rolling, New York was struggling. From July 30 through August 12, the Mets won only seven of the 17 games they played. Rookie Gary Gentry, who was seeking his 10th win, Koosman, and Seaver each suffered two losses and picked up only two wins among them. Seaver had developed a stiffness in the front of his right shoulder, and it was affecting his throwing.

On July 30, their home doubleheader against Houston, the Western Division's fifth-place team, greased the slippery slope for the Mets. The Astros thumped them, 16–3, in the opener, scoring 11 runs in the ninth inning. Even with the Mets' undistinguished past, it was the highest scoring output against them in one inning in the franchise's history. In the disastrous final frame, Denis Menke and Jim Wynn hit grand slams—that, too, set a record. It was the first time it had happened in the National League's 94 years of operation. About an hour later, Houston put 10 runs on the scoreboard in the third inning of the second game on their way to an 11–5 romp.

During the Astros' 10-run splurge, a frustrated Hodges burst from the dugout on his way not to the mound, but to left field to talk with Jones, who had not hustled to get a ball hit into the left-field corner. When Hodges headed back to the dugout, Jones followed a few steps behind him, with his head bowed. Art Shamsky hustled out to left to take his place.

Perhaps the Mets had viewed the day as the occasion to remember times past when Stengel was at the helm. Casey, who early in the club's history had asked, "Can't anybody here play this game?" was celebrating his 79th birthday.[10]

Chicago's success, which had taken them through mid–August, continued to raise the hopes and expectations of the Cubs and their faithful fans. They had beaten back the Mets' charge and had regained a comfortable lead in the NL East. New York had given it a good shot but, coming off their play early in August, their vision of beating the odds and capturing the pennant was dimming.

However, following Holtzman's gem, Chicago's hopes began to take a turn toward the ultimate disaster. On August 27, after Chicago had dropped five of seven games, their fragile lead was two games, the smallest it had been since May 9. They made one final dash, a five-game winning streak. When they moved 5½ lengths in front of the Mets on September 2, it appeared to some that all was well in Wrigley Field. In the clubhouse, the Cubs' song, "Hey, Hey! Holy Mackerel!" was blaring again.

Chicago took off on an eight-game losing streak and finished the campaign going a dismal 8–18. They lost a three-game set at home to Pittsburgh early in the streak. The Pirates' Steve Blass bested Holtzman, 9–2, in the opener. The next afternoon, Pittsburgh blasted Chicago, 13–4. The most painful defeat was the series finale in which the Cubs held a 5–4 lead with two outs in the ninth. The Pirates' Willie Stargell homered off Regan, and the Bucs went on to pick up a 7–5 win in 11 innings.

Durocher assessed the Cubs' slide, saying, "We went into a complete slump.... It wasn't just one or two guys. It was everybody and every department. Hitting, pitching and fielding all went bad."[11]

The Mets slowly but surely regained their winning ways. Starting in the middle of August, the Mets reeled off 18 wins with only six defeats. Beginning on August 9, Seaver won 10 games in a row as the soreness in his right shoulder went away as mysteriously as it had come.

The red-hot New Yorkers and the ice-cold Cubs hooked up for two games in Shea on September 8 and 9. Seaver had picked up his 20th win a couple of days earlier, becoming the first Met ever to reach the lofty goal. Chicago had not yet fallen from first place, but their lead had shrunk to 2½ games.

Before the start of the first game with the Cubs, Arthur Daley wrote in the *New York Times*:

> When Ol' Case originally characterized the Mets as "amazin," he was using the word in a pejorative sense. But they have truly become amazing. They leaped all the way from bad to good, bypassing mediocrity and thereby tilting the baseball world on its axis....
> Amazin'? You said it, Casey.[12]

Koosman beat the Cubs and Hands, 3–2, fanning 13 in the series opener, which was played before a crowd of 43,274 on a dreary and rainy night. Nate Oliver, who had joined the Cubs in May after five seasons with the Los Angeles Dodgers, a year with the Giants, and a brief stay with the Yankees, remembered the game:

> They were passing out white handkerchiefs to fans as they entered Shea. During the seventh-inning stretch, all the lights except the emergency lights were turned off and the crowd stood, waved their handkerchiefs and sang "Bye, Bye, Leo" [to the tune of "Goodbye, Ladies"]. That was a very sad night for me.
>
> During most of the season, we believed in ourselves. But at the end we began to doubt our abilities and believed all the bad things the Chicago press was writing about us. We were unable to turn it around.
>
> The way things turned out, to this day I believe we were Chicago's biggest disappointment. A sign of how strong we were was that we had six starters in the All-Star Game that summer.[13]

And it was that night, when the Cubs were starting to believe in their vulnerability, that at least two of the North Siders came face to face with what they believed an omen of their darkening fate:

> That night, I [Santo] was in the on-deck circle waiting to face Koosman. I was studying Billy Williams at the plate when all of a sudden, a black cat jumped out of the third base stands! He ran in front of me, stopped to stare and headed toward our dugout, where he glared at Leo, who was stooped on the front step of the dugout. Then he headed back into the stands.
>
> I don't like to walk under ladders; I throw salt over my shoulder and don't light three cigarettes on one match. I especially don't like black cats in my path.[14]

Seaver followed the next night, before 58,436 screaming fans, with a 7–1 win, slicing Chicago's lead to one-half game. Jenkins, who was the loser, had come back with two days' rest as Durocher shuffled his rotation to allow Holtzman to observe the upcoming Jewish holiday of Rosh Hashanah.

The next day the Mets won a doubleheader over the Expos. Those victories, coupled with a Chicago loss to Philadelphia, vaulted New York into a one-game lead. At 10:13 P.M. on September 10, the Mets reached the high-water mark in their eighth year of existence. In Wrigley Field, the Cubs' favorite flag was lowered one notch and it would not be hoisted above New York's blue and orange banner the rest of the way.

Ryan remembered the thrill of the second game:

> On September 10 I was given one of my rare starts. I went the distance, striking out 11 and giving up just three hits as we beat Montreal, 7–1. That was

a satisfying moment for me because it gave us a one-game lead over the Cubs, and the applications for tickets to the World Series started coming in.[15]

Leonard Koppett, writing in the *New York Times* expressed the area's excitement:

> The ultimate height has been scaled after seven humiliating years only partially soothed by laughter, and never again can it be said that the Mets have never been on top. "We're No. 1, we're No. 1" chanted the 32,512 in Shea Stadium last night, and that moment can never be taken away from them or from Met supporters everywhere.[16]

Things only got better for the Mets—if better was at all possible. At times during the summer of '69, the Mets had been much closer to the pack than many thought they had any right to be. At other points along the way, they could be found as many as 9½ games behind the front-running Cubs. Now, in an amazing fashion, they had reached the top. From that point forward, they went 16–5, including an eight-game winning streak. They clinched the division's title on September 24, before 54,928 Mets lovers.

At the conclusion of the game, a wild celebration erupted in Shea Stadium as fans charged onto the field, removing the bases, home plate, and pulling up chunks of sod to serve as mementos of the unbelievable.

On October 2, which was the final game of the regular season, they met the Cubs again. The previous afternoon they had beaten Chicago, 6–5 in 12 innings, raising their record to 100–61. Their lead had ballooned to nine games over the club that had led the division most of the way.

The Cubs held a whopping 46–26 margin over the Western Division rivals. A loss to the Mets on the final day would leave Chicago with a 45–45 mark against the clubs in their own division.

For what it was worth, the Cubs beat the Mets in the regular season's finale, 5–3, and they finished 46–44 against the Eastern clubs.

For the Chicago players, whose dreams of going to the postseason had not come to reality, there were some impressive personal statistics to carry away from 1969. Two pitchers had 20-win seasons, with Jenkins going 21–15 and Hands finishing with a 20–14 record. Jenkins was Durocher's workhorse, starting 42 games, completing 23, and relieving in another. It was the first time that two Cubs pitchers had won at least 20 games since 1935, when Bill Lee went 20–6 and Lon Warneke was 20–13. Holtzman finished 17–13.

Santo produced 123 RBIs, and Banks drove in 106. Williams extended his National League consecutive-games-played streak to 982 games. With the club struggling down the stretch, Williams hit .304 in September, but the remainder of the team batted a dismal .219.

Kessinger had some thoughts about the way the season went and offered a possible explanation for the slump:

> The best of times and the worst of times.... We had a lot of talent and experience. Perhaps, the best talent in baseball! ... It was a wonderful year. I have never experienced a relationship between the players and the fans or between the players themselves that existed that year. I feel terrible for the wonderful fans that we came up short.... We were tired from all the day games, and slumped at the wrong time.[17]

Pitcher Rich Nye commented on his experiences in 1969, echoing Kessinger's thoughts on team fatigue:

> The season was a high point in my career. First place for 5½ months. Chicago was truly buzzing.
>
> We were getting career years from Kessinger, Hundley, Hickman, Beckert; we were strong up the middle with excellent defense; the pitching of Dick Selma added to Hands, Holtzman and Jenkins was very strong.
>
> [But] we played tired. Leo [Durocher] had played his starters with little rest. The reserves were not being kept fine-tuned. For myself I might pitch 4 or 5 days in a row in relief, then sit for 2–3 weeks. It was poor management of the personnel.[18]

Rookie catcher Ken Rudolph was yet another who leveled the finger of blame at Durocher:

> Most players had outstanding years until they all tired out from not getting enough rest. You have 25 players, use 25 players not 15 or 17. I enjoyed the season overall because it was my first year. However, it was very difficult to sit and watch those last few games.[19]

The Mets were going to the National League Championship Series and, they hoped, on to the Fall Classic. The 1914 Miracle Braves had come from the basement in July to capture the National League's flag. In 1951 the New York Giants had come from 13½ games behind in August to capture the pennant. In 1969 the Amazing Mets had come from nowhere.

New York's top two pitchers, Koosman [17–9] and Seaver [25–7], a lefty and a righty, were being cast in the mold of Spahn and Sain and of Koufax and Drysdale. The moundsmen and Mets magic had been the basic ingredients in the miracle.

The club brought an anemic .242 team batting average into the National League Championship Series to face the Braves, who despite geography, had won the West. Once again the Mets were the underdogs.

The miracle continued during the Mets' march to the pennant. When the pitching faltered, New York's bats came alive just in time to rescue the club. They captured the National League Championship Series, beating the Braves in three straight games by the scores of 9–5, 11–6, and 7–4.

The American League champion Baltimore Orioles were waiting to take on the Mets. They had decimated the American League East, winning 109 games and romping to a 19-length win over the field. They followed their regular season's success by handling the Minnesota Twins in three games. The Orioles needed 12 innings to win the first, 4–3, and 11 innings to capture the second, 1–0. The final game was more in Baltimore's style. They pounded Minnesota, 11–2.

Daley, writing in the *New York Times*, presented a widely held belief: "It's somewhat obvious that Baltimore is the best team in baseball. It has the same beautiful balance of the old-time Yankees of the Ruthian era— explosive hitting, slick defense and overpowering pitching."[20]

Baltimore was one of the most talented teams of the modern era. No one was quite sure what to make of New York. Many were not even convinced that the Mets were the best team in the National League in 1969. But no one could deny that they were there to play in the World Series.

The opener was played on October 11th in Memorial Stadium, and a pair of 20-game winners, Seaver and Mike Cuellar, faced each other in Memorial Stadium. Don Buford led off the bottom of the first inning with a home run, giving the Orioles a quick 1–0 advantage. He also contributed a run-scoring double in the fourth to support Cuellar in the 4–1 victory.

The Mets' stellar pitching had lost some of its luster in the National League Championship Series. And now against the O's, Seaver tired in the early innings, continuing the pattern that had appeared unexpectedly against the Braves. Baltimore's victory delivered "reality" to New York's doorstep: "The Mets' propensity for amazing everyone with their endless supply of miracles was halted with disconcerting abruptness."[21]

Koosman went to the mound the next day and attempted to regain momentum for the Mets. He held Baltimore hitless through six innings. In the next 2⅔ frames he surrendered two hits and a run before being relieved by Ron Taylor. Koosman left the game with a 2–1 lead, and Taylor retired Brooks Robinson on a roller, leaving the Series even at one game apiece.

The Mets returned home to friendly Shea Stadium, to "Magic Land," in Flushing for game three on October 14. From the middle of August through the National League Championship Series, they had won 23 of the 28 games played there. On an overcast afternoon, Gentry, with relief-help from Ryan, shut out the Orioles on four hits, 5–0. The renewed vigor of New York's pitching was a major factor in the victory.

The rest of the third game was owned by Agee. As Buford had done in Baltimore in game one, Agee led off the bottom of the first inning with a home run over the fence in left-center field. But Agee's offense was only part of the story. It was on defense that the game belonged to the 27-year-old center fielder.

In the fourth inning, after Gentry had fanned Paul Blair, Frank Robinson lined a shot to left field, and Jones made a diving trap of the ball. It was ruled a single. Boog Powell singled to right, moving Robinson to third. Brooks Robinson was Gentry's second strikeout victim in the inning. Then Elrod Hendricks tagged an opposite-field liner to left-center. Agee sprinted across the grass and, with his glove stretched across his body, made an outstanding grab for the final out.

The catch would stir memories of some of the other great grabs from the past—Mays of the Giants, Gionfriddo and Amoros of the Dodgers. Agee of the Mets was added to that group, and he was not finished yet. In the opinion of many, the best was still to come.

Hendricks opened the seventh with a long fly to Agee. Davey Johnson, the Oriole infielder who would become the manager of the Mets in 1984, also flied out to center. With two away, Gentry walked three straight Orioles: Mark Belanger, Dave May, and Buford. Hodges brought in Ryan to replace Gentry. Blair was the first hitter he faced. Ryan recalled the at-bat:

> Blair was digging in, and I guess I should have brushed him back or wasted a pitch, but I was anxious to get out of the inning. I wound and threw a fastball up and over the plate. Blair made contact. The instant the ball left his bat I knew it was trouble. I turned, and the ball was headed to the warning track in right center—extra bases, I thought. Tommie Agee, who had made a tremendous catch earlier in the game, kept running to his left and toward the fence. I guessed he had no chance to catch the ball even if he reached it. He reached the ball just as it was about to hit the edge of the dirt on the warning track. Diving, skidding on one knee, Agee gloved the ball just inches off the ground. Three outs! Blair was at second base when Agee caught the ball, and might have had a shot at an inside-the-park home run.[22]

The pair of amazing catches were instrumental in the Mets' 5–0 win. Weaver, the Orioles manager, credited Agee with the victory, stating, "He batted in one run for them, and took five away from us."[23]

Buoyed by Agee's heroics, the Mets took a 2–1 lead into the fourth game. It was a lead they wouldn't relinquish in their rush to their first championship.

On October 15, game four went 10 innings before Seaver picked up the 2–1 victory. Ron Swoboda provided the special memory in that contest. The Mets went into the top of the ninth holding a 1–0 lead. With one away, Frank Robinson singled to left for the Orioles. Powell followed with a single to right field, with Robinson sliding into third base. That set the stage for Swoboda's heroics. Seaver remembered:

> On my first pitch to Brooks [Robinson], I got the fastball up, but it wasn't tight enough. It was over the plate where he could get his bat on it. He ripped a line drive to the opposite field, fairly shallow in right-center.
>
> The instant Brooks hit the ball. I knew that, even if it were caught, the tying run was going to score from third. And I started worrying, immediately, about the tie-breaking run....
>
> I watched, fascinated by the race between Ron [Swoboda] and the ball. I should have been moving somewhere, backing up third or backing up home, but my fielding instincts, everything Rod Dedeaux [Seaver's college coach at the University of Southern California] had drummed into me, weren't working. Besides, I wasn't certain whether the ball was going to go through or be caught or be trapped, and I didn't know for sure where I should be moving.
>
> The ball started to sink toward the ground, and Ron left his feet and dove and jabbed out his glove backhanded. The ball hit the glove. It stuck.
>
> And then, even more remarkable than the catch, which was pretty remarkable, Ron rolled over, displayed the ball to the umpire and came up throwing. He didn't have a chance to catch Frank Robinson, but he was trying, not conceding a thing, exactly the way we'd been playing all year.[24]

The Mets got out of the inning with the score tied, 1–1. They Mets broke the deadlock in the bottom of the 10th and picked up a 2–1 victory.

After the game, Swoboda commented on the ninth-inning dilemma he faced in deciding whether to charge Brooks Robinson's quick-falling fly, which might easily have gotten by him, or play it on the bounce, conceding Frank Robinson's run: "You just have to take the chance you can reach the ball.... So I just go as far as I can and pray. If there's even one chance in a thousand to catch it, I'm going to try."[25]

Some 20 years later, Swoboda answered a question about the catch and remarked philosophically, "Just imagine a game you played as a child becoming the vehicle to your wildest adult dreams!"[26]

In game five, Baltimore broke on top, 3–0. Swoboda's sliding save had been instrumental in delivering defeat to the Orioles the previous day. Shoe polish and a home run by a player who had hit only three others in the two previous seasons brought doom to Baltimore in the final game of the World Series.

In the bottom of the sixth, Jones argued that he had been hit by a pitch from Dave McNally. At the batter's request, the umpire examined the baseball and found shoe polish on it. Compelled by the evidence, the arbiter awarded first base to Jones. Donn Clendenon immediately followed with his third round-tripper of the Series, closing the gap to 3–2. Later, Weis hit a dramatic two-run homer to break a 3–3 tie, only his seventh round-tripper over an eight-year span.

The impossible dream came true at 3:17 p.m. on a sunny and cool fall afternoon when Jones caught a fly ball off the bat of Johnson. The final score of the Series-clinching fifth game was 5–3.

The celebration began, and Mets fans, as William Legget wrote, were beside themselves with hope and joy:

> When the Mets finally clinched the championship, a blizzard of ticker tape settled over Manhattan; and at Shea Stadium fans pulled up chunks of turf, festooning themselves with the magic sod as if its new-established healing qualities could cure all their fears and ills as merely walking upon it had cured those of their heroes.[27]

Mets pitcher Don Cardwell, who went 8–10 during the season, gave his thoughts about the club's success:

> Every day we had a new hero. Someone always came through to make a brilliant play or to get the clutch hit. The pitching staff worked very effectively too. We decided we could win it all, and we did. ... We played without multi-year contracts and mega-buck salaries. We played for the sheer joy of playing the game.[28]

Taylor lauded Hodges, crediting the manager with making sure "every player knew his job and what was expected of him. The team began the year as competitive, became a contender and a champion in one year."[29]

The Mets had been *Amazin* since their inaugural season. The term was used to described the way they butchered and betrayed the great American pastime. But sometime during the 1969 season, when many were looking the other way, a magic transformation had taken place. The team came to believe, the fans came to believe and, then in October, the baseball world believed. And *Amazin* came to mean "miraculous," "unbeatable," "unbelievable," and "world champion."

Notes

1. Billy Williams with Irv Haag, *Billy the Classic Hitter* (Chicago: Rand McNally, 1974), 117.

2. Nolan Ryan and Harvey Frommer, *Throwing Heat* (New York: Doubleday, 1988), 55.

3. Ron Santo with Randy Minkoff, *Ron Santo: For Love of Ivy* (Chicago: Bonus Books, 1994), 77.

4. George Vecsey, "Mets and Koosman Face First-Place Cubs as 3-Game Series Opens Today," *New York Times*, 8 July 1969, 47.

5. Arthur Daley, "Descent from Cloud Nine," *New York Times*, 11 July 1969, 24.

6. Rick Talley, *The Cubs of '69* (Chicago: Contemporary Books, 1989), 77.

7. Ernie Banks and Jim Enright, *Mr. Cub* (Chicago: Follett, 1971), 165.

8. "Cubs Win on Holtzman's No-Hitter; Mets 1–0 Victors on Agee's Homer in 14th," *New York Times*, 20 Aug. 1969, 53.

9. Glenn Beckert, Letter, 1999.

10. Arthur Daley, "Bypassing Mediocrity," *New York Times*, 7 Sept. 1969, sec. 5, 2.

11. Edgar Munzel, *Official Baseball Guide for 1970* (St. Louis, MO: The Sporting News, 1970), 127.

12. Daley, "Bypassing Mediocrity," sec. 5, 2.

13. Nate Oliver, Telephone Conversation, February 2000.

14. Santo with Minkoff, 83.

15. Ryan and Frommer, 57.

16. Leonard Koppett, "Mets Are First! They Top Expos, 3–2, in 12 Innings and 7–1, as Cubs Bow, 6–2," *New York Times* 11 Sept. 1969, 56.

17. Don Kessinger, Letter, 1999.

18. Rich Nye, Letter, 1999.

19. Ken Rudolph, Letter, 1999.

20. Arthur Daley, "Bypassing Mediocrity," *New York Times*, 7 Sept. 1969, sec. 5, 2.

21. Arthur Daley, "The Bubble Bursts," *New York Times*, 12 Oct. 1969, sec. 5, 2.

22. Ryan and Frommer, 62, 63.

23. Harold Kaese, "Agee's Two Circus Catches Spark Mets, 5–0," *Boston Globe*, 15 Oct. 1969, 1.

24. Tom Seaver with Dick Schaap, *The Perfect Game* (New York: E.P. Dutton, 1970), 146, 147.

25. Joseph Durso, "Mets Triumph, 2–1, on Error in 10th; Lead Series by 3–1," *New York Times*, 16 Oct. 1969, 58.

26. Ron Swoboda, Letter, 1989.

27. William Leggett, "Never Pumpkins Again," *Sports Illustrated*, 27 Oct. 1969, 14, 15.

28. Don Cardwell, Letter, 1999.

29. Ron Taylor, Letter, 1999.

10. 1978 Boston Red Sox

A Comedown and
the Bambino's Curse

Every time the Boston Red Sox put themselves in position to contend for the postseason, devoted Bosox fans, who have suffered through their team's past failures, hold their collective breath and cling to hope one more time. Down through the years, these loyal Bostonians and other dedicated souls have read stories, heard tales, or had the opportunity to be there themselves to see it happen. The stories were about the many disappointing times when things just didn't work out the way they thought they would—the way they were supposed to, Sox fans secretly believed.

In 1918 the Red Sox defeated the Chicago Cubs, four games to two, to win the World Series. Between then and 1978, Boston won the American League pennant in 1946, 1967, and 1975, only to lose the Fall Classic each time in seven games. Only the Cubs, who had not caught baseball's brass ring since 1908, could claim a more frustrating legacy.

Some blame the "Curse of the Bambino" whenever the Red Sox break the hearts of their faithful followers. Financially strapped Boston owner Harry Frazee sold Babe Ruth to the New York Yankees after the 1919 season for $100,000 and a $300,000 mortgage on Fenway Park. He shipped the Red Sox's former 20-game winning pitcher-turned-outfielder, who had stunned the baseball world in 1919 by slamming 29 home runs, to the team that generations would know as Boston's fiercest rival. The Yankees, with Ruth's magic leading them, won their first-ever world championship two years later and were on their way to a lengthy period of dominance. Perhaps the Red Sox would never be forgiven for such a dastardly act.

In 1975 the most recent memory of a lost opportunity was etched in the psyche of Red Sox fans. They had been brought to the heights of hope only to be dropped into the valley of despair one more time.

In the sixth game of the World Series, Carlton Fisk hit a majestic 12th-inning home run high into the night sky and over Fenway Park's Green Monster to bring Boston a 7–6 victory, tying the Series with the Cincinnati Reds.

After Fisk's memorable rescue, there was hope, excitement, and anticipation in Fenway as the two clubs prepared for the deciding seventh game. Many in the crowd, no doubt, had a clear vision of the Bosox short-circuiting the Big Red Machine and riding Fisk's clutch homer to the championship. The Red Sox broke on top, 3–0, helped by four walks by Cincinnati left-hander Don Gullett. Those would be Boston's final runs of the season. With the score tied, 3–3, and two outs in the top of the ninth, lefty Jim Burton threw a pitch low and away to Joe Morgan. The Reds' second baseman reached with one hand and hit a chip shot off the end of the bat, lobbing it over the infield. It dropped in front of center fielder Fred Lynn, and Ken Griffey, Sr., who was on third base, scored the go-ahead run.

There was no more Boston magic. They went quietly in their final at-bat. It was one more near miss for the Bosox. It was another World Series championship that might have been.

The 1978 season, the 78th for the American League, was kicked off on April 5. The opener was played indoors at night in Seattle's Kingdome. The two-year-old Mariners bested the Minnesota Twins, 3–2. The Cincinnati Reds, who had traditionally opened the major league season, had to wait a day to play their first game.

The Red Sox, who had finished the 1977 campaign tied with the Baltimore Orioles for second place and 2½ games behind the Yankees in the American League East, didn't get a fast start from the gate in 1978. They were 1–3 after each of their four starting pitchers threw his first game.

The Chicago White Sox scored a pair of runs in the bottom of the ninth inning off reliever Dick Drago to pick up a 6–5 win over the Red Sox in their curtain-raiser. Mike Torrez, who had left the Yankees as a free-agent after the 1977 season and had signed a $2.5 million contract to pitch for Boston, went the first six innings, giving up four runs and 10 hits.

Dennis Eckersley, who had come from Cleveland in a March 30 trade, was on the mound for the Bosox in their second game in Comiskey Park. Eckersley was holding a 5–2 lead when he left after seven innings. Chicago scored four times in the bottom of the eighth off Bill Campbell to take another 6–5 win from the Bosox.

Dick Drago, Manager Don Zimmer, and Carlton Fisk confer at the mound (Boston Red Sox).

The third game was put in the hands of lefty Bill Lee, and he shutout the Pale Hose, 5–0. In Boston's first victory, the "Spaceman" allowed seven hits while going the distance. Jim Rice had three hits, including his first career homer in Comiskey, to lead the Red Sox.

The Olde Town Team moved on to Cleveland for its next game, and manager Don Zimmer gave rookie right-hander Allan Ripley the starting nod. When Ripley was relieved after eighth innings, the teams were dead-locked, 4–4. Reggie Cleveland surrendered the Indians' final run in their last at-bat to bring the 5–4 victory. Boston stood 1–3 for the campaign.

Torrez picked up his first win in his second start, beating the Indians, 6–3. Home runs by Lynn and Rice and Jerry Remy's two-run single sparked the Sox.

On April 14, Boston played its home opener, and the Sox tripped the Texas Rangers, 5–4 in 10 innings. Eckersley threw 9⅔ effective innings and left the game with the score tied, 4–4, in the top of the 10th. Drago, who would make 36 appearances out of the bullpen in 1978, finished the Rangers' at-bat by retiring the one batter he faced and picked up the decision when the Red Sox scored in the bottom of the inning. Butch Hobson's homer in the eighth had helped Boston come from behind to tie the game. In the 10th, Rice's wind-blown 395-foot single to the base of Fenway Park's right-field wall scored Hobson from third base with the deciding run.

The defending world champion Yankees played their home opener on April 13, carrying a 1–4 record from their first road trip. It was a great day of celebration in the "House That Ruth Built. Two retired Yankees—Mickey Mantle and Roger Maris—took part in the pre-game festivities. Maris had not been at the stadium in the 12 years since his trade to the St. Louis Cardinals after the 1966 season.

The present-day Yanks picked up their second victory of the season, beating the White Sox, 4–2. Reggie Jackson's three-run homer in the first inning got New York off to an exciting start. The last time he played in the Bronx he had hit three home runs on three pitches off a trio of Los Angeles pitchers in game six of the World Series to help the Yanks finish off the Dodgers.

Reggie Bars, the new candy in town, were given to the fans as part of the opening day festivities. Hundreds of them were hurled from the stands as Reggie made his trot around the bases after his homer against the White Sox.

During 1977, turmoil had engulfed the team. Owner George Steinbrenner, manager Billy Martin, and Jackson had been the stars on the "off-Broadway" stage, delivering their lines of direct challenge, insinuation and innuendo. On the day before the start of the new season, Martin appeared to be at ease: "Martin is autographing baseballs from a carton on his desk, serenely putting his signature alongside those of Reggie Jackson, Thurman Munson and other high-salaried players whose real or imagined feuds helped keep the team in turmoil last year."[1]

On May 1, Boston was in second place with an 11–9 record. They were three lengths behind the division-leading Detroit Tigers. New York was one-half game behind the Bosox in third place. The Red Sox went on an 11–2 run, and, by the middle of the month, they had passed Detroit and sat at the top of the American League East with a 22–11 mark. Lee was 5–0 and Torrez was 5–1. Rice was pounding the ball at a .364 clip with 11 homers, and Lynn was hitting .324.

Boston and New York did not meet for the first time until June 19, over two months into the season. The Red Sox were in first place with a 45–20 record, and Baltimore sat in second. New York, with a 37–26 mark, was third, seven games behind the front-runners.

The Bosox took the first game of the series in Boston, 10–4, Left-hander Tom Burgmeier pitched 5⅓ innings of strong relief after taking over for Luis Tiant who gave up all four Yankees runs in the fourth inning. The Red Sox scored six times in the eighth to break a 4–4 tie.

The Yankees rebounded the following day and picked up a 10–4 victory against Torrez, who went to the mound with a 10–2 record. Before the series opener, Torrez had commented about the Bosox's promising season:

> We've had guys getting hot at different times this year.... Hobson carried us early, then Rice carried us, then [Dwight] Evans got hot. We haven't had everyone contributing all at the same time. But I see signs of everyone starting to get hot together. If this whole club gets hot in the next two or three weeks, really you can forget about it.[2]

The second game was pay-back time for the Bronx Bombers, who clobbered the Boston starter by scoring seven runs in the fourth. Torrez had won two World Series games for the Yankees the previous season before defecting, via free agency, to Beantown.

Game three went into Boston's win column, 9–2. Eckersley, a 23-year-old right-hander, picked up his first win in four seasons against the Yankees while Jim Beattie, Dick Tidrow, and Catfish Hunter were bombarded by Boston's bats. Rumors abounded of Steinbrenner's dissatisfaction with the team and, especially, with Billy Martin.[3]

The two clubs met five days later in New York for a two-game set. Before the first matchup, Steinbrenner gave a vote of confidence to his manager. Following a meeting between George, Billy, and Yankees president Al Rosen, Steinbrenner reported,

> This should end the speculation that has been developing of late concerning Billy's job. It was a solid, air-clearing session. Everything was discussed in considerable detail. I think that Al and Billy got a lot of things ironed out. In fairness to Billy, I think this commitment to him is warranted in view of his cooperative attitude at the meeting.[4]

Boston went out and defeated New York, 4–1, extending their lead over the Yanks, who had climbed into second place, to 9½ games.

The following day, the Bronx Bombers gained a split of the series, defeating the Bosox, 6–4, in 14 innings. Graig Nettles' two-run blast off Drago, who had pitched 4⅓ scoreless innings for the Red Sox, sealed the victory. Left-hander Ron Guidry, who led the majors with a gaudy 12–0 record didn't pick up the win, going six innings and surrendering four runs. Sparky Lyle, with three innings of shutout relief, registered his sixth victory against a single loss.

On July 2, Rice was trailing only the Twins' Rod Carew in the American League batting race with a .325 average. The Boston outfielder's 23 home runs were tops in the loop. Lynn trailed Rice by a single point at .324. Torrez's 11–3 mark represented the club's top winner, and Tiant [7–1] and Lee [8–3] had the team's lowest ERAs at 2.83 and 2.91 respectively.

New York traveled to Boston for games on July 3 and 4. Eckersley beat the Yanks for the third time in 13 days in the opener, 9–5, as Carl Yastrzemski and Fisk drove in three runs apiece.

The Fourth of July game was rained out, and New York left Beantown in third place, nine games behind the Red Sox.

Although New York had hoped to put the turmoil of the previous season behind them, they did not succeed. It continued and played itself out in the front office, in the clubhouse, and on the field. Through midseason, the Bronx Bombers did not mount a serious challenge to the Red Sox. Only Guidry's outstanding 13–1 record had kept the Yankees' faint hopes alive.

The pivotal point in the season for the Bronx Bombers was the latter part of July. Jackson had been seething since June 26 when he was demoted from full-time right fielder to part-time designated hitter. On July 17, he was promoted from the sixth position in the batting order to his preferred clean-up spot. Martin's decision to move Jackson up in the order on that particular day was interesting if not strange. The Yankees were scheduled to face Kansas City lefty Paul Splittorff, who had spurred the manager's decision to bench the left-handed hitting Reggie in the fifth game of the American League Championship Series the preceding October.

Martin justified his July 17 decision, saying:

> He's starting to swing the bat decently lately…. And the way we're going now, maybe hitting fourth will make him happier. And if it helps him and makes him happy, maybe he'll hit better and we'll win some games and make me happy."[5]

In the bottom of the 10th inning, Jackson came to bat with the score tied, 5–5. No one was out and Munson was on first base. Martin flashed Reggie the bunt sign. Kansas City pitcher Al Hrabosky's fastball sailed by the batter's head. With the infield drawn in, the manager wiped off the bunt signal and told Jackson to hit away. On the second pitch, Reggie attempted to sacrifice. Dick Howser, the third-base coach, ran toward home plate to confer with the batter about the missed sign. Jackson informed Howser that he was going to bunt anyway. Ignoring the manager's signal, he attempted to lay the ball down two more times. His second try produced a foul pop to the catcher, Darrell Porter, for the first out of the inning.

After the game, Martin, still livid at his indignant player, flung a clock radio and a beer bottle against the clubhouse wall. Reggie expressed his anger about being the designated hitter, charging, "How can they say I'm a threat to swing the bat? I'm not an everyday player. I'm a part-time player."[6]

The incident earned Jackson a hefty five-day suspension and a $9000 fine. New York won four games during his absence and the fifth upon his return, when Martin refused to put him in the lineup.

On July 23, Martin was still at odds with Jackson. He had also heard that, earlier in the season, Steinbrenner had considered trading managers— Martin for the White Sox's Bob Lemon. While waiting at Chicago's O'Hare Airport for a flight to Kansas City, Billy lashed out at his two adversaries, Jackson and Steinbrenner, telling reporters, "The two deserve each other.... One's a born liar, the other's convicted."[7]

The next day in Kansas City, the Yankees' embattled skipper resigned before Steinbrenner could fire him. Lemon, who earlier in the campaign had been dismissed by Chicago, was hired by the Yankees owner to lead the struggling Bronx Bombers. The aftershock was felt on July 29 at the Old Timers' Game in Yankee Stadium, when Steinbrenner announced that he had rehired Martin to manage his club in 1980!

But at least for the remainder of the 1978 season, Lemon would be at the Yankees' helm. He brought calm to a hostile battlefield. As Nettles, New York third baseman, said:

> It wasn't Billy's fault, but as long as he was there, the turmoil would have kept going.... Lem was the perfect guy for that team at that time. He just kept things loose and easy, no commotion, and let us play. That's all we needed."[8]

On July 19, the Bronx Bombers were in fourth place, 14 games behind Boston. Whether or not it was the Bambino's Curse, something bought a number of the Yankees a measure of improved health and dealt the Red Sox players the reverse during the latter part of the campaign. The Yanks had begun the season with "too much" pitching, and the injury jinx had hit and decimated the staff. A struggling and sore-armed Hunter mended, posting a 6–0 record for the Yanks in August with a 1.64 ERA. The Red Sox's Rick Burleson, Fisk, Lynn, Hobson, and George Scott came up with nagging problems.

When Boston went to New York for a pair of games on August 2 and 3, they were in the midst of their worst slump of the season, having gone 3–11. Over the same two-week period, the Yankees had won 12 of 16 and had sliced 7½ games from the Bosox's 14-game lead.

Murray Chass, writing in the *New York Times*, sensed a change in Boston's demeanor, noting "the incredible, invincible, insurmountable Boston Red Sox returned to Yankee Stadium last night and there was something conspicuously missing—their incredible, invincible, insurmountable look."[9]

The first game of the series, which was interrupted by rain twice, was suspended after 14 innings because of the American League's 1:00 A.M.curfew. The Red Sox had battled back from a 5–0 deficit and had tied the game, 5–5, in the eighth inning on a sacrifice fly to deep center field by Yastrzemski, which enabled Rice to score. The two clubs were back at it the following night, and Boston won the suspended game in the 17th inning on run-scoring singles by Burleson and Rice.

The Bosox captured the nightcap, 8–1, in a rain-shortened game. Torrez picked up his 13th win and Rice drove in three runs with a single and a home run. Symptomatic of the Sox's slump was the fact that Rice's homer was only his second in 34 games. Lynn helped in Boston's win, slamming a three-run shot.

The Bronx Bombers' bats were silenced by Bosox pitching. The home club had scored five times in the first three innings of game one, and then managed only one unearned run over the next 20 frames.

Boston's sweep of the Yanks in two straight dropped New York into fourth place, 8½ games off the pace. The Red Sox had not faced Guidry, who was beaten the next night by Baltimore for only his second loss of the season. The major leagues' leading pitcher, looking back on the Boston series, said the Yankees knew they had allowed what might have been their best opportunity to strike at the knees of the Sox, and that the balance of their season would be defined by focused, aggressive play: "We were the defending champs, and the general feeling was, if we were going to lose, let's lose with dignity, let's make it close."[10]

Over the remainder of the season, the Yankees never lost more than two in a row, going 41–14 the rest of the way.

Boston's darkest hours came during the period between August 30 and September 16, their second lengthy slump, when they won only three games and had lost 14.

On September 7, the Bronx Bombers came to Fenway to open a four-game series. The matchup turned into "the [Second] Boston Massacre." The Yankees torched the Sox in a four-game annihilation which left the Beantowners dead-tied for first place and Fenway fans in mourning. What had been a comfortable Boston lead in the American League East had disappeared. What had been a time for optimism in and around Boston was devolving into despair over another missed opportunity. Perhaps the Curse was working its black magic again.

It wasn't just the losses that were so difficult for Boston to swallow; it was the way New York had done it, by the scores of 15–3, 13–2, 7–0, and 7–4. The Yankees rattled 67 hits around "friendly Fenway," while the hometown Sox managed only 21.

A week later Boston visited New York. On September 16, a 3–2 defeat was the Sox's sixth straight loss to New York and left them 3½ games behind the front-running Bronx Bombers.

The next day, Eckersley, with bullpen help from Bob Stanley, stopped the Yankees and the streak by the count of 7–3. While the New Yorkers were rushing to a pennant on the wings of their amazing and historic comeback, the Red Sox had just begun to mount a phenomenal recovery of their own. They went to Detroit and Toronto during the next-to-last week of the campaign and gained ground on the league-leading Yankees.

On Sunday, September 24, one week before the end of the regular season, New York held a one-game lead over Boston with seven remaining to be played. Following their Sunday encounter in Toronto, the Red Sox would close with the Tigers and the Blue Jays in Fenway Park. After a final game in Cleveland, the Yankees were scheduled to finish at home against Toronto and Cleveland, the division's two weakest teams.

Neither team could afford to lose and neither team did—until the last afternoon of the regular season. Zimmer's rejuvenated Red Sox won all seven games, knowing that to lose even one would probably seal their doom. They closed the season picking up victories in 12 of their final 14 games, and they were still one monumental game behind, and one length from a chance to retrieve all that had been lost during their disappointing slide from the American League East's lead.

After Tiant shut out Toronto, 5–0, in the Bosox's 162nd game, there was nothing to do but hope that Cleveland would close their season with a win over New York. Hunter did not have his "August sharpness," giving up five runs in 1⅔ innings. Rick Waits pitched the Indians to a 9–2 victory, becoming something of a celebrity in Boston. The Red Sox had gained a tie for the Eastern Division flag.

The American League East would require a one-game playoff in Boston to crown its champion. *Sports Illustrated* billed the showdown as baseball's recasting of the *Iliad*, with the Yankees the invading, mighty Danaäns, and Fenway the great walled city of Troy. And no one, least of all the players, failed to appreciate all that was at stake. "This probably is the only way it should be settled," Carl Yastrzemski said. "But I feel sorry that either team must lose. The two best teams in baseball, the greatest rivalry in sports. There should be no loser."[11]

For the Red Sox, 1978 brought back memories of 1948. Cleveland had lost and Boston had won on the final day of the regular season, 30 years earlier. That had created a tie for the American League pennant between those two teams and brought about the first-ever Junior Circuit playoff. Cleveland won that game.

October 2 was a glorious early autumn day in New England. Each starting pitcher had a special goal for the game beyond winning the flag. Guidry, entering the game with a 24–3 record, wanted to guarantee a happy conclusion to his incredible American League season. Boston's Torrez, who had struggled through a 40-day drought down the stretch without a win, welcomed the opportunity to try to pitch his new team into the postseason. Perhaps he alone might suppress the Curse; after all, the only three pitchers to have beaten Guidry that season were also named Mike—Caldwell, Flanagan, and Willis.

Yastrzemski homered in the second inning, putting the Red Sox on the hand-operated Fenway Park scoreboard. Rice produced a run-scoring hit to add to the lead in the sixth.

Rice had put together a wonderful season. The Boston slugger led the league in hits (213), triples (15), home runs (46), total bases (406), RBIs (139), and slugging percentage (.600). By finishing third in the American League's batting race with a .315 average, he narrowly missed out on the Triple Crown, but did capture the league's coveted Most Valuable Player Award.

Going into the top of the seventh, Torrez was protecting a 2–0 advantage, having surrendered only two hits. Chris Chambliss and Roy White singled to start things off for the Bronx Bombers. They watched as Torrez got the next two Yankees out. Bucky Dent, the ninth hitter in the New York line-up, came to bat, bringing a .243 average and four home runs to the plate with him.

Dent took the first pitch for a ball. He fouled Torrez's second delivery off his ankle. While Bucky was hobbling around the batting area on his throbbing ankle, Mickey Rivers grabbed Dent's bat. He had the bat boy replace it with a new Roy White model. It was later learned that Rivers had been trying to convince Dent to make the switch, but to no avail. With Bucky in agony, Mickey had the chance he needed.

Bucky swung at Torrez's next pitch, and the Red Sox announcer gave the fatal account: "Deep to left, Yastrzemski will not get it. ... It's a home run!"[12] Dent had lifted a three-run fly ball into the netting just over the top of the Green Monster. As reported in the *Boston Evening Globe*, Dent's *blast* was "a 306' home run over a fence 305' away."[13]

The Yankees took the lead, 3–2. Yastrzemski later recalled the tragic moment and lamented:

When he first hit the ball I thought it was an out. I just kept going back— and then when it slid over the wall it just almost nicked the back part of the wall. I couldn't believe it. ... It's probably the one time I hated Fenway Park, on the Bucky Dent home run.[14]

Dent's home run landed a bit to the right of where Fisk's dramatic homer had struck the foul pole in game six of the 1975 World Series. Fisk's shot had brought ecstasy to Fenway; Dent's was a blast of doom.

Stanley replaced Torrez. Before he could get the third out, Rivers walked and Munson doubled-in the fourth run. An inning later, Jackson homered for what would become the decisive run, putting the Yankees ahead by the margin of 5–2.

Fenway spirits received a brief boost in the bottom of the eighth, when the Red Sox scored twice off Goose Gossage on RBI singles by Yastrzemski and Lynn.

With Boston trailing, 5–4, they came to bat in the last of the ninth, hoping for one more comeback. With one out, Burleson walked, and Remy followed with a shot to right field. As Yankee outfielder Lou Piniella moved toward the ball, it suddenly disappeared in the bright sunlight, and he extended his arms in panic, but the ball bounced in front of him. He was able to field it on the first bounce and made a throw back to the infield. Burleson, who was rounding second base, decided not to chance going to third and headed back to the bag. That proved to be a critical break for the Yankees. Rice followed with a long fly to Piniella, which was deep enough to advance Burleson to third. Certainly, had Burleson already been on third when Rice hit the ball, he would have scored the tying run.

One out remained. Yastrzemski, probably the most poignant symbol of the struggles of the Red Sox through the years, came to bat. He took a hefty cut at a Gossage pitch, and made contact.

> The ball had floated into the air, the laziest sort of a pop up and a certain out, whether the third baseman was Graig Nettles or the kid next door.
> And as Nettles grabbed the ball, amid the stunned silence of Fenway Park, you thought, This isn't the way it should end. Not like this. Not with Yaz making the final out.[15]

The game was over. Yaz wept in the training room. He had driven in two runs with a single and a homer, but he had ended the season with a futile pop fly to third base. Perhaps, Nettles' glove had gobbled up the 39 year old's final chance to play for a world champion.

A headline in the *Boston Globe* put the painful loss in perspective, at least from the point of view of Beantown's battle with futility. It read: "Destiny 5, Red Sox 4."[16]

Notes

1. "Martin: No Discord on Yankees Expected," *New York Times*, 7 April 1978, 19.
2. "A Big Change in Year for Red Sox," *New York Times*, 20 June 1978, sec. 2, 15.
3. Murray Chass, "Red Sox Rout Yankees, 9–2, Under Steinbrenner Scrutiny," *New York Times*, 20 June 1978, sec. 2, 7.
4. "Red Sox Defeat Yankees, 4–1; Martin Gets Some Job Security," *New York Times*, 27 June 1978, sec. 3, 11.
5. Murray Chass, "Hunter Knocked Out; Yanks Lose 5–1 Lead," *New York Times*, 18 July 1978, sec. 2, 13.
6. Bert Randolph Sugar, *Baseball's 50 Greatest Games* (New York: Exeter Books, 1986), 109.
7. Murray Chass, "Martin Raps Steinbrenner, Jackson and Jeopardizes Job," *New York Times*, 24 July 1978, sec. 3, 1.
8. Moss Klein, "Miracle Finish in '78 Still Vivid for Yankee Fans," *Baseball Digest*, August 1988, 79.
9. Murray Chass, "Yanks, Red Sox Tied at 5–5 as Curfew Suspends Play," *New York Times*, 3 August 1978, sec. 2, 5.
10. "Klein, Miracle Finish...," 80.
11. Peter Gammons, "There's Life After Death," *Sports Illustrated*, 9 October 1978, 35.
12. *Heroes and Heartaches* [Videotape], Phoenix Communications Group, 1987.
13. Leigh Montville, "So What? We're Used to Waiting," *Boston Evening Globe*, 3 October 1978, 29.
14. *Heroes and Heartaches*.
15. Ray Fitzgerald, "A Run for the Money," *Boston Globe*, 3 October 1978, 1.
16. Ernie Roberts, "Destiny 5, Red Sox 4," *Boston Evening Globe*, 3 October 1978, 32.

11. 1987 Toronto Blue Jays

An Ignoble Seven-Day Collapse

In 1987 the Toronto Blue Jays began their second decade of play and were picked by some to win their second American League East championship. During the season, Toronto was in and out of first place. In late September they climbed back to the top of the Eastern Division and built what appeared to be a comfortable lead with only seven games to play. But it proved not to be enough.

Toronto was awarded a place in the American League on March 25, 1976, when the Junior Circuit expanded to 14 teams. For a while it appeared as if the San Francisco Giants would be moving to the Canadian city and join Montreal in the National League. That plan was short-circuited when the Giants were sold and the new owners kept the club in the Bay Area.

It was a long building process for the expansion Blue Jays. From 1977, when they began play, through the 1981 campaign, Toronto finished all alone in the basement of the seven-team Eastern division. In 1977 the Jays lost 107 games and finished 45½ games behind the division-winning New York Yankees. In 1982 the Cleveland Indians joined them in the cellar.

Toronto's breakout year was 1983 when they posted the franchise's first winning season with an 89–73 record. They finished in fourth place and were within nine games of the front-running Baltimore Orioles.

The following year, Toronto had the same record and climbed to the runner-up spot behind the division-winning Detroit Tigers.

The Blue Jays reached the pinnacle of the AL East in 1985 with a 99–62 record. They nipped the Yankees by two games and were sparked by right-handers Doyle Alexander, who was 17–10, and Dave Stieb, who went 14–13 with a league-leading 2.48 ERA. Lefty Jimmy Key had a 14–6 mark, and Dennis Lamp, who started only once in his 53 appearances, put together a phenomenal 11–0 record out of the bullpen. Outfielders George Bell and Jesse Barfield led the offensive production with 95 and 84 RBIs. Tony Fernandez, playing in his third major league season, provided sensational defense at shortstop and hit .289.

Toronto got off to a fast start in their first postseason appearance, winning three of the first four games against Kansas City, who had captured the American League West by a game over the California Angels. The Royals battled back and took the next three games to capture the 1985 American League Championship Series and then went on to defeat the St. Louis Cardinals and become World Champions.

That was a memorable season for the Toronto franchise; the following campaign left something to be desired:

> The Blue Jays story is like a movie playing in our heads. "The Drive of '85" was a box-office smash, with all the ingredients for a hit. It won rave reviews for its outstanding cast of great heroes, swashbuckling action, likable characters, and above all, a great story with a happy ending. And can't you see that memorable finale in fine detail? You know the one: when the Oscar-winning leading man George Bell falls to his knees after catching the last out of the [regular] season as co-star Tony Fernandez leaps on him in joy and the Blue Jays win their first division title....
>
> The heroes of '85 finished fourth last year. That's not bad by previous standards, back in the days when our Jays were an expansion club just hoping to be noticed in the cattle call of also-rans.[1]

In 1986 the Blue Jays were under the leadership of rookie manager Jimy Williams, who had been a Toronto coach for six seasons and then replaced Bobby Cox after he left to become the Atlanta Braves' general manager. The Jays had a disappointing year and fell to fourth place with an 86–76 record, even though a number of the players had improved offensive statistics during the disappointing season. Barfield led the majors with 40 home runs, Fernandez was third in the league with 213 hits, the most ever by a shortstop. Bell had his highest average at .309 and drove in 108 runs.

The pitchers did not have the same success. In 1985 Alexander, Key, Lamp, and Stieb had accounted for 56 wins; in 1986, they won just half than number. Alexander was gone to Atlanta before the season was over. Relievers Mark Eichhorn and Tom Henke were the only bright spots on the pitching staff. Eichhorn burst on the scene with 69 relief appearances, a 14–6 record, 10 saves, and a 1.72 ERA. Henke had his best season, putting together a 9–5 record with 27 saves to play a key role in 36 of the team's 86 victories.

Murray Chass, in the *New York Times*, previewed the 1987 season, and predicted that a Dave Stieb–led Toronto would finish first in an American League East otherwise so weak in pitching that "to find a solid starting-pitching rotation, one might have to select pitchers from at least three different teams."[2]

Stieb had been a staff leader since going 17–14 in 1982, three seasons after joining the club. He followed with 17, 16, and 14-win seasons before falling to 7–12 in 1986. The club's success in 1987, as Chass suggested, depended in large measure on Stieb being able to regain his winning ways.

Manager Jimy Williams (Toronto Blue Jays).

Chass went on to mention some of the changes that had occurred on the Jays' roster. Damaso Garcia, Cliff Johnson, and Buck Martinez had departed, and their places had been taken by younger players such as rookies Greg Myers, Fred McGriff, Mike Sharperson, and Matt Stark. As the campaign progressed, only McGriff would play a major part in the club's success.

For the first time in major league history, the season's first pitch was thrown outside the United States. On April 6, in Exhibition Stadium, Toronto supplanted Cincinnati, the traditional site of the opener. The Reds kicked off their season later in the day.

The Blue Jays beat Cleveland, 7–3. Lloyd Moseby and Willie Upshaw, two of Toronto's elder statesman, homered for the winners. Fernandez hit a run-scoring triple, and Barfield and Sharperson added run-scoring doubles. Key went six innings, followed to the mound by Eichhorn and Henke. Henke had been working out of the Jays' bullpen since 1982. With the aid of his 98-mph fastball, he had become the club's late-inning ace.

The Blue Jays, behind Jim Clancy, beat the Indians the following day, 5–1. Upshaw homered again for the winners, and Barfield also smacked a four-bagger. Clancy, who was the second player chosen in the 1976 expansion draft and had been pitching for Toronto since his major league debut in July 1977, had gone 14–14 with a 3.94 ERA in 1986.

In the series finale, Cleveland blasted Joe Johnson as the Indians beat the Jays, 14–2. The 25-year-old righty, who had come from the Braves the previous season and had gone 7–2 with his new club, gave up seven runs in four innings. When the Indians' 42-year-old Steve Carlton relieved 48-year-old Phil Niekro in the sixth inning, it was the first time that two 300-game winners pitched for the same team in the same game.

Toronto went 12–8 during the opening month of the campaign and were in third place on May 1, 5½ games out of the lead. The fast-starting Milwaukee Brewers [18–3] sat at the top of the division, and the Yankees were four games behind them with a 14–7 record.

A month later, New York and Toronto had both passed the Brewers. The Yankees, who were 31–19, were two lengths in front of the Jays, who stood at 28–20.

After dropping a 2–0 decision to the Seattle Mariners on June 1, Toronto took off on a club-record 11-game winning streak. Bell's home run ignited a four-run second inning which led the Jays to a 4–3 win over the Mariners.

Toronto took the series finale, 7–2, behind Stieb. The veteran right-hander, who had started the season by going 0–2, won his fourth in five games to raise his record to 4–3. Cecil Fielder homered and had three RBIs for the winners. Fielder, who had come up from the Jays' Double-A club in Knoxville of the Southern League in mid–July of 1985, had hit .311 with 4 homers and 16 RBIs during the stretch run. The following season, the 6'3", 230-pounder spent most of the campaign with Triple-A Syracuse of the International League.

On June 5, the Orioles came to Toronto to open a three-game set. The Blue Jays swept the O's, with the middle game, which took over four hours to complete, being the most exciting. Barfield ended it with a 3-run homer in the bottom of the 11th to bring the Jays an 8–5 win.

The red-hot Blue Jays went to Yankee Stadium, trailing the Bronx Bombers by one-half game. After they smacked the Yanks, 11–0, they were all alone in first place. Stieb and Eichhorn combined for the shutout in the rout of the Bronx Bombers, with Stieb's win his third in a row, a feat he hadn't accomplished since June 1984. A big fifth inning in which Toronto, who led, 1–0, scored seven times cemented the victory. McGriff, a former Yankee farmhand, and Bell, who had two homers in the game, reached the seats in the inning. Bell's pair of four-baggers raised his season's total to 20.

Toronto took the next game, 7–2, behind John Cerutti. The Blue Jays' left-hander fulfilled a teenager's dream when he faced and beat Ron Guidry, who had been the Yankees ace when John was pitching in high school at

Christian Brothers Academy in Albany, New York. Cerutti went on to pitch for Amherst College and, after his graduation, he was the Jays' first round pick in the 1981 draft. He arrived in the majors near the end of the 1985 season, then spent time in Syracuse the following season before returning to Toronto in mid–May. He pitched himself to a 9–4 record with a 4.15 ERA after being called up from Syracuse.

Following the Jays' win, a positive Upshaw remembered the disappointment of 1985:

> We were pretty embarrassed about that... We want to win again. We're very capable, and if we win the division, we think we can go further.
>
> We've thought about it quite a bit, but we know there's still a long way to go.[3]

Williams also commented about the past and the present, echoing Upshaw's cautious optimism:

> I think we're a better club than '85... We have a deeper bullpen. But that still doesn't mean we're going to win it. We have guys who should be better players [since 1985]—Bell, Barfield, Fernandez—but you still have to go out and execute.[4]

Key pitched Toronto to a 4–1 win in the third game, and the Blue Jays left New York with a 2½ game lead.

Toronto's bullpen had been a major strength to that point in the season. The Jays starters had completed only eight games, and the club had not lost a game when they led going into the eighth inning.

On June 11, the Blue Jays took their eight-game winning streak to Baltimore, where they added three more wins before dropping the series finale to the O's, 8–5.

Eight was the winning number during the series. In the opener, Bell banged a pair of home runs for the sixth time in the season to lead the Jays to an 8–6 win. Johnson, who had struggled early in the campaign, raised his record to 3–5.

Bell, the 27-year-old Dominican native who first appeared in the majors with Toronto in 1981 and became the Jays' regular left fielder in 1984, was in the midst of a hot streak. In the three games in New York and the opener in Baltimore he had collected 10 hits in 18 at-bats, blasted five homers, and driven in 14 runs.

In a league dominated by sluggers, Bell was making a name for himself:

Scouts and pitching coaches talk about Bell's bat speed, that element of a batter's swing that produces power. "His bat goes through the strike zone as fast as anyone," [California pitching coach Marcel] Lachemann noted. Tom House, the Texas Rangers' pitching coach, said that Bell is "as good a low-ball hitter as I've ever seen in the league."[5]

Toronto took game two, 8–5, and followed the next day with an 8–2 victory. Cerutti, who raised his record to 4–2, started the third game in place of Stieb, who experienced tightness in his shoulder while warming up in the bullpen. Fernandez went 4-for-5, hit a homer, and scored three runs.

Following the loss to Baltimore, who won for the first time in 11 tries, Toronto held a three-game lead over New York.

The Blue Jays lost their edge during the remainder of June. They also lost the division lead while going 6–9. The Yankees put on a spurt with an 11–4 mark to take over the top spot.

On June 28, New York paid a visit to Exhibition Stadium, hoping for pay-back. Toronto held a narrow three-percentage-point lead before the series began. Six left-handed starters were scheduled to go to the hill for the teams during the three-game set. Dennis Rasmussen, Guidry, and Tommy John were on tap for the Yanks while Cerutti, David Wells, and Key were Williams' choices for the Jays.

Neither starter lasted long in the opener, which was a strange and unpredictable game. Cerutti, who had beaten the Yanks earlier in the month, was blasted from the mound after pitching 1⅓ innings and being tagged for eight runs. Rasmussen lasted longer, but he watched an 11–4 Yankee lead disappear in the seventh as the Jays jumped in front, 14–11. Dave Winfield's grand slam in the top of the eighth provided the Yanks their final 15–14 margin of victory.

The following day, Guidry, the 37-year-old left-hander who was trying to regain his mound prowess, bested Wells and led the New Yorkers to a 4–0 victory.

The finale brought back the weirdness of the opener. Key and John both had good outings, with the Jays' lefty going into the eighth and the Yanks' southpaw pitching seven innings and leaving with a 1–0 lead. New York tied it, 1–1, in the eighth and neither team scored again until the top of the 12th, when the Jays' normally steady bullpen fell apart and the Yankees scored five times for a 6–1 victory.

New York accomplished what it came to town to do, and they left Canada with a three-game lead and renewed optimism for the season, as expressed by Yanks first baseman Don Mattingly:

George Bell powers the Blue Jays (Toronto Blue Jays).

It's nice to get them back.... "Revenge" is a word you could use to describe it. They took it to us in New York pretty good, but we came here and won three straight. It's like Winnie [teammate Dave Winfield] said: We've got the whole family back now.[6]

At the All-Star break, the Yankees were 55–34 and had maintained their three-length lead over the Blue Jays, who were 51–36.

Three Jays were chosen to participate in the All-Star Game in Oakland on July 14. Bell, who was hitting .293 with 29 home runs and 76 RBIs, was chosen by the fans. Boston Red Sox manager John McNamara added Fernandez [.310] and Henke [0–4, 17 saves, and a 2.81 ERA] to the squad.

All three saw action in the Mid-Summer Classic, which went longer than any previous matchup before a run was scored. In the top of the 13th inning, Montreal's Tim Raines, who was already 2-for-2, tripled in two runs to bring the National League a 2–0 victory. In the marathon, Bell went 0-for-3, Fernandez was 0-for-2, and Henke worked 2⅔ scoreless innings.

During July, while New York was going 15–11 and Toronto was putting together a 15–12 mark, Detroit was surging, winning 17 and losing 9. The Tigers had closed the gap and were in third place. They were only three games out of the lead and one-half game behind the Blue Jays.

After Toronto dropped a 3–0 decision to Cleveland on August 1, they won five of their next six games, including a three-game sweep in Chicago.

Third baseman Kelly Gruber led Toronto to a 14–3 win in the opener of the White Sox series. After hitting a home run in the fourth inning, he doubled and singled two innings later as the Blue Jays sent 10 men across the plate.

On August 7, after trampling the Indians, 15–1, Toronto took over first place when the Tigers shutout the Yankees, 8–0. In the Jays' victory, Stieb picked up his fifth win in a row, and Bell and McGriff banged home runs to spark the offense.

Toronto's stay at the top was short-lived as they lost the next day to Cleveland, and New York beat Detroit. But in the see-saw American League East division, the Blue Jays were back in first after their next game. Toronto's Cerutti won his seventh straight in a 5–1 win over the Indians, and the Tigers thumped the Yanks, 15–4.

The Jays stayed in the lead until August 19 when Detroit took over. By that time Stieb had pitched his seventh straight win, and Bell had knocked in his 100th run. Phil Niekro had been acquired from the Indians on August 9 to bolster the pitching staff, and had lost his first start in a 10–3 defeat at the hands of the White Sox.

From August 19 until the end of the month, Detroit either sat in first place or was tied with Toronto for the division lead. Two series between the Jays and the Oakland A's, who were waging a fierce battle with the Minnesota Twins for first place in the Western Division, highlighted that stretch of time. Toronto and Oakland each took three games in their head-to-head meetings. Cerutti and Stieb saw their streaks come to an end, and Niekro dropped his second decision with his new club.

The Blue Jays entered September one game behind the Tigers. Both clubs had won 77 games, but Toronto's 54 losses were two more than Detroit had suffered.

Toronto started September with a five-game winning streak in Exhibition Stadium and then added another victory in Milwaukee before dropping their first game of the month.

Exciting, extra-inning victories were the order as the Jays' ran toward the pennant. On September 1, they topped the Angels, 4–3, in 10 innings. Barfield's double to right field scored Toronto-born rookie Rob Ducey with one out in the 10th. An inning earlier, the miraculous Fernandez had made a game-saving play at shortstop.

Stieb was hit hard and lasted only three innings in the second game against the Angels, but Toronto rallied from behind to tie the matchup, 5–5. Bell's opposite field home run with a runner on base in the eighth put the Blue Jays ahead to stay.

After a day off, the Mariners came to Toronto for three games. In the opener, Fielder's pinch-hit home run in the bottom of the 10th provided the winning margin in the Jays' 6–5 victory.

On September 5, Mike Flanagan made his first start for Toronto. The veteran left-hander had been acquired from Baltimore on August 31 and was pitching for only his second team in his lengthy major league career. He had been 3–6 with the Orioles in 1987 before changing uniforms. After the Blue Jays signed Flanagan, they released Niekro, who had made three appearances for Toronto and had an 0–2 record.

A number of clubs, including the Yankees, had shown interest in Flanagan before he signed with Toronto. But in the end it was the persistence of Blue Jays GM Pat Gillick, who had spent the better part of three weeks talking with the Orioles' front office, that landed the pitcher North of the Border.[7]

Flanagan's first start for his new club was impressive. He scattered four hits over 7⅔ innings to lead Toronto to a 3–0 win. He retired 14 consecutive Mariners during one stretch of the game.

The final game of the series went into extra innings before the home club notched a 3–2 victory for their fifth straight win. Upshaw's bases-loaded single off the left-field fence with two out in the bottom of the 11th scored the winning run. Toronto's victory, coupled with Detroit's 9–3 loss to the Texas Rangers, gave the Jays a half-game lead in the East.

The winning streak continued in the opener in Milwaukee's County Stadium. The Jays' three-run rally in the eighth helped deliver the 5–3 victory. Fernandez, who was leading Toronto in batting average, singled to drive in the first run, and then Brewers' left-hander Dan Plesac threw a pair of wild pitches to allow the final two tallies of the inning. Reliever

Duane Ward, who had been 0–2 with the Braves and Blue Jays in 1986, pitched one inning and picked up his first major league victory. With the win, Toronto sat at the top of the league with an 82–54 record. Detroit was right behind at 83–55.

Milwaukee captured the final two games of the series, both by the score of 6–4. In the second matchup, Clancy held a 4–2 lead going into the seventh. He gave up an inning-opening single to Paul Molitor, the Brewers' top hitter, who had a 39-game hitting streak stopped on August 28. Molitor's hit off Clancy broke his 0-for-19 slump. Williams summoned Ward from the bullpen. Ward could not hold the lead, and Wells and Henke were also called to try to put out the fire, which wasn't snuffed until Milwaukee put the winning run on the board.

Prior to the September 11 start of a three-game series in Toronto between the Jays and the Yanks, Chass, in the *New York Times*, wrote about how the two clubs had been affected differently by injuries:

> Counting this year and the previous two, the five-man nucleus of the Blue Jays' everyday lineup has played 96 percent of the team's games, missing an average of six games per player per season, or a total of 91 games.
>
> The Yankees, by contrast, have seen their five-man nucleus miss 139 games this season alone, an average of 28 per player.[8]

It was an important set for the Yankees, who had spent 65 days in first place, more than any other American League East club. Recently, they had begun to fade in the race for the division title.

In the opener, the Yanks got men on base but could not score enough of them, leaving 13 runners stranded. Fernandez had a three-hit day for Toronto, but the key blow was delivered by Ernie Whitt in the bottom of the 10th inning. The Jays catcher drove a 2-and-2 pitch from Dave Righetti into right field to score the winning run in the Blue Jays' 6–5 victory. Flanagan gave up two earned runs in 5⅓ innings in his second outing with Toronto, and Wells picked up the win with 1⅔ innings of relief.

There was no suspense the next day as the Blue Jays bombed the Bronx Bombers, 13–1. Whitt blasted two home runs and had a career-high six RBIs. Key went eight strong innings and raised his record to 16–6.

New York won the finale, 8–4, but they had lost more ground as the Jays took two of the three games played in Exhibition Stadium.

On September 14, Toronto had their hitting shoes on in the opener with Baltimore, blasting the Birds, 18–3. In the process of winning the game, they set a major league record by slugging 10 home runs. The hot-hitting Whitt blasted three and Bell and Rance Mulliniks each added two round-trippers. Cal Ripken, Jr., was replaced defensively in the eighth inning when the O's manager—his father Cal, Sr.—sent in a substitute. The switch snapped Cal's 8,243 consecutive-innings streak. He had played every inning of 908 consecutive games.

The Blue Jays captured the second game, 6–2. The hot-hitting Whitt homered again, which meant that each of his last six hits was a home run. His streak ended when he doubled later in the game. Moseby, who had one of the round-trippers the previous day, homered again and added a triple to his day's totals. Flanagan delivered another strong outing, going eight innings without surrendering a run.

Toronto finished the sweep of the Orioles with a 7–0 win behind Key, who worked seven innings. It was Baltimore's ninth consecutive loss.

The Jays were tied for the lead when they opened a four-game series against the Yanks in New York on September 17.

Cerutti started for the Blue Jays in the first game, but he did not retire a Bronx Bomber while giving up three earned runs. Toronto came back and tied the contest but eventually lost, 6–5, and fell out of the division lead. Six Toronto pitchers paraded to the mound, and Henke took the loss, dropping his record to 0–6.

The Blue Jays captured game two, 6–3. A football game a few days earlier between Grambling and Central State of Ohio for the benefit the Urban League had chewed up the turf, and a day of rain before the start of the second game of the series turned the Stadium's playing surface into a quagmire, making every play a challenge. Williams, Toronto's manager, filed a protest before the start of the game, but, after the Jays won, he withdrew it.

When conditions had not improved for the next game, Williams filed another protest. This angered Yankees owner George Steinbrenner, who shot back, saying, "I apologize to him for the field...but I think his actions stink."[9]

Toronto lost to the Yanks' Bill Gullickson, 4–2. That, coupled with Detroit's 5–2 win over Milwaukee, dropped the Jays 1½ lengths off the pace. Alexander had pitched the Tigers to the victory. Doyle, the 37-year-old hired gun Detroit had picked up from Atlanta on August 13, raised his record to 7–0. The right-hander had pitched for Toronto from mid–1983 through the middle of 1986 when he was sent to the Braves. Besides his 17 wins in 1985, he had gone 17–6 the previous season and had led the league with a .739 winning percentage. Before leaving Atlanta for Detroit in August, Alexander had a 5–10 record.

Detroit lost the next day and Toronto topped New York, 6–2, reducing the Tigers' lead to one-half game. Bell's two-run homer in the fourth, which was his 46th and raised his RBI total to 128, put Toronto ahead. In the seventh, Charlie Moore, who was in his first season with the Jays after 14 campaigns with Milwaukee, hit a run-scoring, bloop single and rookie Nelson Liriano banged a two-run shot to break a 2–2 tie and give the Jays a 5–2 lead.

Toronto went to Baltimore, where they swept the Orioles again in a three-game set. It was Bell's series. In the opener, he singled home the winning run in the top of the ninth to provide the margin of victory in the 2–1 Blue Jays win. The following day, he again drove in what proved to be the deciding run when he singled in the eighth to ignite a 5-run rally which led Toronto to a 8–4 decision. In the finale, Bell homered as the Jays beat the O's, 6–1, for their fourth straight victory.

The Blue Jays returned home to welcome the Tigers for an all-important matchup. Toronto's winning streak had hoisted them back to the top with a one-half game advantage.

The opening game on September 24 brought the Jays very mixed results. While winning, 4–3, behind Flanagan and in front of 42,436 excited fans, they lost Fernandez for the rest of the season. The injury bug had struck.

In the third inning, Tony suffered a fractured right elbow when Bill Madlock slid hard into second base. The injury required surgeons to wire the elbow together.

Rookie Manny Lee, who had seen only limited major league action, took over for Fernandez, the club's top hitter and its outstanding and exciting defensive shortstop. Williams, when he was asked about Lee before the start of the next game, said "Manny is a good shortstop, a good major league shortstop... And to me, he's a better-looking hitter than I have ever seen him."[10]

Williams' words were prophetic. Going into the bottom of the ninth, the Blue Jays had been shutout, 2–0, by Detroit starter Frank Tanana, who had not won a game in over a month. With one out, Barfield singled off Tiger reliever Dickie Noles. Rick Leach followed with a pinch-hit double off Willie Hernandez to put runners at second and third. It was time for Lee to make like Fernandez. The rookie lined the first pitch down the right-field line for a triple, which scored both runners to tie the game. Detroit manager Sparky Anderson ordered a pair of intentional walks to load the bases and set up a force play at home. Moseby hit a ground ball to Tiger second baseman Lou Whitaker, who fired it past catcher Mike Heath in an attempt to nail Lee at the plate. On the wild throw, Manny scored the winning run in the 3–2 victory. Toronto's lead was 2½ games. It was the first time since July 16 that the two clubs had been separated by more than a game and a half.

The next night, with the second-largest home crowd in Toronto history cheering, the Jays picked up their third consecutive one-run, come-from-behind decision over Detroit. Trailing 9–7 in the ninth, they scored three times in their last at-bat to pull off a 10–9 win. With no one out, Barfield started it again with a bloop double. Upshaw followed with a single, and reliever Mike Henneman hit Leach to load the bases. Juan Beniquez, who had come from the Royals in July and had been a designated hitter, slammed a double to left-centerfield on a 3–2 pitch to clear the bases and provide the comeback victory.

Toronto was in the driver's seat. Their lead now at 3½ games, they had won seven in a row, and only seven games remained to be played.

Barfield was feeling good about the prospects for the rest of the campaign:

> I have felt since spring training that this team was somehow going to do it....
> Everyone is coming up with the big hits... I came in the dugout after they scored three runs in the first and somebody, I forgot who it was, told me we'd be in double figures. A little late but we got there.[11]

On September 27, Detroit took the first of those seven games in the series finale at Exhibition Stadium. It was another one-run thriller, but this one went into the Tigers' column, 3–2, in 13 innings. Alexander, who was 8–0 with a 1.40 ERA, worked 10⅔ innings while giving up two runs, only one of which was earned. The Jays had been three outs away from sweeping the series when Kirk Gibson homered in the ninth to tie the game, 1–1. Both teams scored a single run in the 11th, and Gibson's bloop single in the 13th drove in the game-winner. At the time, it was only one loss in a long season. In retrospect, it was the beginning of the end for the Blue Jays.

Milwaukee came to Toronto, and they were not good guests, taking three from the Jays by the scores of 6–4, 5–3, and 5–2. Toronto had lost four in a row, and their lead was down to a single game when the Brewers left town.

During the series, the injury bug struck again. On September 29, in the middle game of the set, Whitt was injured in the sixth inning while breaking up a double play at second base. In the collision with Molitor, the Jays catcher cracked two ribs on his left side, knocking him out of action for the rest of the campaign.

Toronto entered the final series of the season against the Tigers in Detroit with a one-game lead and a patched-up lineup. Three youngsters were being called on to help keep the Jays at the top of the division. Along with Lee, Myers was in the lineup, behind the plate, and Liriano, who had taken over for Garth Iorg, was at second. As late as August 24, the three-some had made up the middle-defense for sixth-place Syracuse of the Triple-A International League.

Along with the injuries, Bell, the Jays' leading power-hitter with 47 home runs and 134 RBIs, was mired in a hitting slump. He had managed only one single during the Blue Jays' four-game losing streak.

A cool drizzle fell during the first game in Detroit on the Friday night of the final weekend of the regular season. Bell went 0-for-4 and was unable to move along any of the five runners on base during his at-bats. Lee put the Blue Jays ahead, 3–0, in the top of the second with a three-run homer, but that was all the scoring punch the visitors could muster off Alexander, who was helped by four double plays and extended his record to 9–0. Scott Lusader's two-run homer in the bottom of the second brought Detroit to within a run, 3–2. In their next at-bat, the Tigers' Alan Trammell hit a solo shot to tie the game, and then a run scored on a double play to give Detroit the lead. In the eighth, Toronto had runners on first and second with no one out against Henneman, who had relieved Alexander, but Bell hit into a forceout and Beniquez grounded into the Tigers' fifth double play of the day. Detroit took the opener, 4–3. The two teams were tied with identical 96–64 records.

Snow showers were predicted for the Saturday afternoon matchup in venerable Tigers Stadium. It took 12 innings before Detroit picked up a 3–2 victory before a sellout crowd and won the sixth straight one-run game between the two clubs. Against a drawn-in infield in the final frame, Trammell, who had been mentioned as co-favorite with Bell for the league's MVP Award, slashed a screaming single between Lee's legs to score Jim Walewander with the deciding run. Third baseman Mulliniks did not fault Lee, saying, "He didn't have any time to react.... He did everything he could. The ball just skidded."[12]

Detroit sat at the top of the heap again, and one game remained. The Blue Jays prayed for a playoff; the Tigers wanted a flag. Toronto's pitching coach, Al Widmar, who had held a similar position with the Philadelphia Phillies in 1964, was hoping not to repeat the outcome of that earlier season.

The Tigers pitchers had nearly silenced the Blue Jays' bats during the last three games between the two clubs. In 34 innings, Toronto had been limited to six earned runs. On the final day of the campaign they didn't score any.

Larry Herndon's second-inning home run over the left-field fence off Key was the only run Tanana needed as he pitched the Tigers to the American League East championship, 1–0. A huge mistake in the fourth inning hurt Toronto's chances and was an example of the club's recent frustration. Williams, trying to get some offense going, called for a hit-and-run with Fielder, who was quite slow of foot, on first base. Lee missed the sign, and Fielder, who had taken off for second, was an easy out.

With two outs in the ninth, Iorg hit a weak grounder back to Tanana, and he made an underhand toss to Darrell Evans at first for the final out of the game. It was a climactic end to an exciting game and an equally exciting season.

Bell wasn't the only Blue Jay who had struggled down the stretch. Barfield finished with only three hits in his final 24 at-bats, and Beniquez didn't manage to get a hit in his last 15 plate appearances.

The Tigers, who had lost 19 of their first 30 games and were as many as 11 games out of first place, were the comeback champions. The Blue Jays had only the memory of a painful comedown to take with them into the winter.

"The contest was the conclusion of an ignoble collapse," wrote the *New York Times'* Roy Johnson. "The troubled Blue Jays owned a three-and-a-half game lead over the second-place Tigers just one week ago, but endured one of their worst slumps of the year, suffering from injuries and an absence of timely hitting. They lost their final seven games of the season, including the final three here, where they stranded a total of 25 baserunners."[13]

Peter Gammons, in *Sports Illustrated*, also noted the historic nature of Toronto and Detroit's battle for the flag, a battle he proclaimed comparable to those in 1951, 1964, and 1967:

> In a pulsating 11-day drama that began with the Toronto Blue Jays leading the Detroit Tigers in the American League east by a half game, baseball's two winningest teams met seven times. For them, there was no wild-card escape hatch or any other postseason route except first-class transportation home in time for Columbus Day. Every game was decided by one run, four in the winner's final at-bat.[14]

The Blue Jays' season was over, but a number of players had continued their trend of offensive improvement from the previous year. Bell who hit .308, powered 47 home runs, and had a league-leading 134 RBIs, was named the American League's Most Valuable Player. Fernandez finished with 186 hits for a .322 average. Barfield contributed 28 homers and drove in 84 runs. Key led the staff with a 17–8 record and tied Houston's Nolan Ryan for a major league-best 2.76 ERA. Stieb recovered from a slow start and arm woes to put together a 13–9 mark, and Cerutti finished 11–4. Eichhorn had a major league–high 89 appearances out of the bullpen, a 10–6 record, and a 3.17 ERA. Henke allowed 2.49 earned runs per game and led the league with 34 saves, despite a deceptive 0–6 record. The statistic that mattered most, however, was the club's disappointing second-place finish after almost having the division crown for themselves.

Notes

1. "Looking Forward, Looking Back," *Blue Jays Special Edition Yearbook, 1987*, 6.

2. Murray Chass, "Mediocrity of the West Has Enveloped the East," *New York Times*, 5 April 1987, Sec. 5, 8.

3. Michael Martinez, "Blue Jays Singing Different Tune This Year," *New York Times*, 10 June 1987, Sec. 4, 29, 30.

4. Martinez, "Blue Jays Singing...," Sec. 4, 30.

5. Murray Chass, "It's the Season of the Heavy Hitters," *New York Times*, 13 July 1987, Sec. 3, 4.

6. Michael Martinez, "Yanks Polish Off Jays in 12th, 6–1," *New York Times*, 2 July 1987, Sec. 2, 5.

7. Murray Chass, "Baseball S O S: Stretch Pitching," *New York Times*, 6 September 1987, Sec. 6, 2.

8. Murray Chass, "Jays Good at Avoiding Injuries," *New York Times*, 10 September 1987, Sec. 2, 14.

9. Murray Chass, "Gullickson Forces Blue Jays 1½ Back," *New York Times*, 20 September 1987, Sec. 5, 3.

10. Joe Sexton, "Jays Stun Tigers in Ninth, 3–2," *New York Times*, 26 September 1987, 51.

11. Joe Sexton, "Blue Jay Rally in 9th Shocks Tigers, 10–9," *New York Times*, 27 September 1987, Sec. 5, 1.

12. Roy S. Johnson, "Big Loss Puts Jays in a Hole," *New York Times*, 4 October 1987, Sec. 5, 4.

13. Roy S. Johnson, "Miracle Finish? Incredible Flop? Tigers Win It," *New York Times*, 5 October 1987, Sec. 3, 1.

14. Peter Gammons, "Out!" *Sports Illustrated*, 12 October 1987, 22.

12. 1989
Baltimore Orioles

An Exciting Comeback
Falls a Bit Short

The 1989 baseball season piqued the emotions, prodding its faithful to extreme, wavering responses—from amazement to disbelief, from boundless optimism to despair.

On April 7, 21-year-old left-hander Jim Abbott, born without a right hand, made his major league debut with the California Angels, becoming only the 10th player since 1965 to play his first professional game at the major league level. Abbott, who had jumped straight from the campus of the University of Michigan to the big leagues, went on to post a 12–12 season's record, start 29 games, and finish with a 3.92 ERA.

Baseball fans cheered in amazement as Abbott competed with the best in the game; they also watched with disbelief and disappointment as Pete Rose, the all-time hit leader, fell from his lofty pedestal to banishment from the game. On August 24, Major League Baseball released an agreement signed by Commissioner A. Bartlett Giamatti and Rose which said, in part:

> Peter Edward Rose acknowledges that the Commissioner has a factual basis to impose the penalty ... accepts the penalty imposed on him by the Commissioner and agrees not to challenge that penalty in court or otherwise.
>
> The banishment for life of Pete Rose from baseball is the sad end of a sorry episode. One of the game's greatest players has engaged in a variety of acts which have stained the game, and he must now live with the consequences of those acts. By choosing not to come to a hearing before me, and

171

by choosing not to proffer any testimony or evidence contrary to the evidence and information contained in the report of the Special Counsel to the Commissioner, Mr. Rose has accepted baseball's ultimate sanction, lifetime ineligibility.[1]

On August 10, Dave Dravecky returned to the mound for the San Francisco Giants. After undergoing surgery the previous October to remove a cancerous desmoid tumor from a muscle near his left shoulder, Dravecky had courageously battled back from the disease. He had rebuilt his body, strengthened his spirit, and returned to the mound for the Giants. In his first major league appearance since the surgery, the left-hander pitched a dramatic 4–3 victory over the Cincinnati Reds. Five days after baseball fans had joyously witnessed his personal triumph, they watched in horror as he writhed in agony after breaking the humerus bone in his left arm while delivering a pitch against the Montreal Expos. Later, Dravecky fractured the same bone in another spot in a freak on-the-field accident during the Giants' celebration after winning the National League pennant. What had been cause for optimism had become bleak once again.

Baseball witnessed Dravecky's courage in August. A month earlier, the game had been stunned by a story of despair. In July former Angels pitcher Donnie Moore shot and wounded his wife. He then turned the gun on himself and took his own life. Three years earlier, in 1986, with the Angels one out away from winning the American League pennant, he had served up the memorable home run to Boston Red Sox outfielder Dave Henderson. The round-tripper kept the Bosox's hopes alive, and they went on to capture the flag. Moore never recovered from that historic defeat.

Baseball welcomed Giamatti as its new commissioner on April 1. Prior to becoming the game's top administrator, he had served as the National League president for two years. The scholar and former president of Yale University was a life-long lover of the great American pastime. Before taking over as the commissioner, he spoke about what his approach would be:

> I don't think of myself coming in and suddenly issuing a stern order for everybody to grow up and behave. I don't think it would materially change anybody's life.
>
> People respond to example and deeds more than they do to preachments. I think you have to put yourself on record and you have to express your goals and ideals, but the mere act of saying it is not to have done it all.[2]

One of Giamatti's hopes was that he would become the "fans' commissioner." His love of baseball had made him an interpreter and an ambassador of its greatness to others. When he wrote about it, he helped many understand how this kid's game served as a symbol of life itself.

But then, on September 1, a brief, televised special report announced that Giamatti, 51, had died. Life had been taken from him, and he had been taken from the game.

The Oakland Athletics and the San Francisco Giants won their League Championship Series and faced each other in the Fall Classic, which was dedicated to the memory of Bart Giamatti. Ironically, the two cities were linked by the Bay Area Rapid Transit system, or BART.

The first two games of the Series were played in the Oakland Alameda County Coliseum with the A's winning by the scores of 5–0 and 5–1.

The third game was scheduled to begin in Candlestick Park in the late afternoon of Tuesday, October 17. The October day brought Indian-summer weather to a ballpark often ridiculed for its chill factor even in summer. Many of the 62,000 fans in the sold-out "Stick" were moving to their seats, and a huge television audience had just joined the festivities. ABC-TV sportscasters Al Michaels, Jim Palmer, and Tim McCarver were in the booth on the stadium's second level, and fellow-announcer Joe Morgan was down on the field preparing to interview Willie Mays, who would be throwing out the ceremonial first pitch. The A's and the Giants were gathering in the dugouts, awaiting the introduction of the players. And at 5:04 P.M., PDT, a massive earthquake rolled up and down the San Andreas Fault from its epicenter near Santa Cruz. San Francisco was in its path, 75 miles to the north. The park shook, the center section of the Bay Bridge collapsed, I-880 in Oakland fell in upon itself, and fires broke out all over the Bay Area.

The breadth of the disaster caused by the earthquake, which registered 7.1 on the Richter scale, was revealed slowly to those in Candlestick. Transistor radios and a few miniature TVs brought the grim news to fans in the park. Because of power outages, the vast majority of people in the immediate vicinity of the quake did not hear reports or see pictures of the death and devastation which had happened all around them.

By the next morning it was clear that it would be some time before the series could be resumed. Interim baseball commissioner Francis "Fay" Vincent, Jr., stood behind a podium in the St. Francis Hotel and announced the postponement of Wednesday night's game. Putting the World Series in its proper perspective, he said, "Obviously there's been a substantial tragedy in this community.... Baseball is not the highest priority to be dealt with. We want to be very sensitive, as you would expect us to be, to the state of life in this community. The great tragedy coincides with our modest little sports event."[3]

During the regular season, as baseball fans were experiencing the highs and the lows, and the pleasure and the pain of the game, fans witnessed an unexpected comeback in the American League East. The surprising Baltimore Orioles led the field most of the way, only to meet the disappointment of being knocked from first place near the end of the campaign.

Murray Chass, writing in the *New York Times* about the upcoming 1989 season, described the Toronto Blue Jays as the American League East's most talented team and tapped them to finish at the top of the division. He unceremoniously relegated Baltimore to the cellar.[4]

The Orioles had been the basement's regular tenants the previous two seasons. In 1987 they had finished with a 61–101 record, and a year later, after starting 0–21, they went 54–107 and once again served as the division's doormats.

Frank Robinson replaced Cal Ripken, Sr., as the O's manager early in the 1988 season. Under his guidance, the club finished 34½ games

behind the first place Red Sox, and Baltimore's .238 team batting average was the major leagues' worst. Their pitchers hadn't fared any better, producing a 4.54 ERA, which was the highest in the majors. Nothing pointed to a resurgence by the club whose 15 years of glory had ended at the conclusion of the 1983 season. It had been downhill since then.

On opening day, April 3, President George Bush, who was accompanied to the game by President Hosni Mubarak of Egypt, threw out the first pitch to get Baltimore's new season underway.

Manager Frank Robinson (Baltimore Orioles).

The Orioles picked up their first win, beating the Red Sox, 5–4. Cal Ripken, Jr.'s three-run homer in the sixth inning put the O's on top, 4–3. Boston tied it in the seventh, and the game went into extra innings. Rookie Craig Worthington's single in the bottom of the 11th inning scored Mickey Tettleton with the deciding run. Tettleton, who had become a free agent after being released by Oakland following the 1987 season, then picked up by Baltimore and signed to a Triple-A contract, went on to have an outstanding season. Another acquisition, Brian Holton, who had been acquired in the trade which sent Eddie Murray to the Los Angeles Dodgers, pitched 4⅓ innings to register the victory.

Roland Hemond, Baltimore's vice president of baseball operations and general manager at the time, recalled the club's exciting start:

> Opening day set the tempo for things to come. Dan Shaughnessy, in the *Boston Globe*, said—in a tongue-in-cheek fashion—that [Roger] Clemens would pitch a no-hitter against the Orioles in the opener.
>
> Rookie Steve Finley was hurt when he crashed into the wall making a catch on a drive by Nick Esasky. He had to leave the game after the third inning. He was taken to the hospital and his arm was put in a sling. At the end of the game, after Worthington hit the game-winning homer, Finley was on the field celebrating, leading the cheers and still in his uniform. That was the kind of spirit we generated that year.[5]

The Orioles were not scheduled to play the following day, and they were rained out in Baltimore the next night. They closed out the Boston series on April 6 with their second win, a 6–4 decision over the Bosox. Outfielder Phil Bradley, who had come from the Philadelphia Phillies and was expected to be a major addition to the club, drove in the tie-breaking run with a single. The Orioles sat alone at the top of the AL East with a 2–0 record.

They traveled to Minnesota where they lost their first two games to the Twins, dropping the O's out of their briefly held division lead. They picked up an 8–1 victory in the series finale with Jeff Ballard pitching seven impressive innings. First baseman Randy Milligan's three-run homer and Ripken's two-run shot were the key blows off Minnesota left-hander Frank Viola, who had won the 1988 American League's Cy Young Award.

Baltimore lost three of its next four games, but made a recovery near the end of the month, and, on May 1, they were back on top of the AL East. However, they were not there alone, as the New York Yankees and the O's had identical 12–12 records. The other five teams in the division were below the .500 mark.

Toronto struggled early in the campaign, and manager Jimy Williams was fired on May 15 in an effort to change the club's direction. The firing came on the heels of a three-game sweep of the Blue Jays by the Twins, who had lost 13 of their previous 17 games prior to the weekend series. Minnesota crushed Toronto, 13–1, in the final game, dropping them to 12–24 as they remained in a tie for the basement with the Detroit Tigers.

The Jays' executive vice president and general manager Pat Gillick convinced a reluctant Cito Gaston, the club's hitting coach, to take over as the interim skipper. Toronto's plan was to lure ex–Yankees manager Lou Piniella to take over for Gaston. Piniella was still under contract to New York, and George Steinbrenner wanted significant reimbursement in terms of top Blue Jays prospects for releasing his former manager. For a period of time, negotiations continued between the two clubs.

On May 26, after Baltimore beat the Cleveland Indians, 5–2, and the Angels dropped the Red Sox, 5–0, the Orioles, with a 22–21 mark, climbed back into the top spot with a half-game lead over the Beantowners. In Baltimore's win, Ballard notched his eighth victory to go 8–1, which matched his 1988 rookie season's win total. Larry Sheets drove in a pair of runs with a homer and a single to power the O's to their fourth consecutive win.

The Junior Circuit's Eastern Division teams would be tightly bunched most of the season. After May 26, the Blue Jays, Red Sox, Yankees, Indians, and Milwaukee Brewers would take turns moving in and out of second place. However, during the next three months, none of them would unseat the Birds of Baltimore, who had claimed the catbird seat at the top of the division.

Toronto was unable to wrest Piniella from Steinbrenner and the Yanks, and, on the final day of May, Gaston was named the club's manager for the rest of the campaign.

Because the Orioles had the worst record in the majors in 1988, they received the first pick in the 1989 amateur draft. So it was that on June 5, they did something no team had done before: they made the first draft pick while sitting in first place at the time. The O's chose Ben McDonald, a 6'7", fireballing right-hander who was a product of Louisiana State University. McDonald was expected to make it to the majors quickly.

On draft day, the Blue Jays sat in sixth place with a 23–31 record and were only one game ahead of the cellar-dwelling Tigers. They were celebrating their exciting comeback against the Red Sox in Fenway Park the previous afternoon. Down 10–0 to the Bosox, they had battled back to pick up a 13–12 decision on Junior Felix's two-run homer in the top of the twelfth inning.

Back home, the Blue Jays experienced the excitement of playing their first game in Toronto's spectacular SkyDome. After having played in Exhibition Stadium since the franchise's first season in 1977, the new stadium, with a retractable roof, the world's largest scoreboard, a Hard Rock Café, a 348-room hotel, and seats for 53,000 spectators, could not turn the Blue Jays' fortunes around. They lost to Milwaukee, 5–3.

While the Jays were falling to the Brewers, the O's were thumping the Yankees, 16–3, in the House That Ruth Built, in the Bronx. It was Baltimore's eighth straight victory and their 13th in their last 14 games. Their only loss had been a 1–0 defeat at the hands of the Indians in Cleveland. The Orioles, with a 31–22 record, had stretched their lead over the Indians to five games.

Peter Gammons, writing in *Sports Illustrated*, attributed Baltimore's turnaround to their improved defense, citing their aggressive play and noting that the club, with nearly a third fewer errors than the league's next-best defense, was on course to finish as the AL's most surehanded club ever.[6]

Baltimore pitcher Mark Thurmond gave a similar assessment:

> We added four defensive outfielders (Steve Finley, Phil Bradley, Brady Anderson and Mike Devereaux), along with two heady catchers (Tettleton and [Jamie] Quirk), which enabled us to be one of the best defensive teams in 1989. We were close to the bottom in defense in 1988.... It was an unbelievable turnaround.[7]

And as the Oriole defense sparkled, their fans started to believe. Hemond recalls, "As the momentum got going, it became the 'Why-not?' year. T-shirts appeared with that slogan."[8]

The Orioles' five-game lead was the biggest of any of the majors other three division leaders. However, the lead had to be viewed in the proper perspective, which Chass did in a *New York Times* article:

> Long the dominant division, the East has plummeted severely into a state of mediocrity, or worse. When the Orioles reached a 26–22 record on the last day of May, the 59th day of the season, it marked the first time a team in that division had been four games over .500. When they went five and six games over on the following two days, they should have been awarded the division championship. In the first 56 days of the season, the division leader was under .500, at .500 or one game over .500 on 43 days.[9]

On June 9, the hot-hitting Tettleton slammed two homers to take over the American League's home-run lead in Baltimore's 7–1 win over the Brewers. The victory over Milwaukee ended the O's first two-game losing streak of the season. By Memorial Day, Tettleton had hit 13 home runs, the most ever by that date by an American League catcher. He had 11 home runs, 23 RBIs, and had scored 24 runs in the last 23 games. His total of 35 RBIs was only two shy of his entire 1988 output.

Baltimore battled the Oakland Athletics, the American League West's leader, eight days later. For the first time since August 23, 1986, Memorial Stadium was the setting for a nationally televised game, indicating the continuing interest in the A's and the growing interest in the O's. Bradley proved to be the TV hero, driving in three runs with two doubles as the Orioles topped the Athletics, 4–2. Jose Bautista, who had suffered with back problems and was pitching for the first time in a month, went six strong innings against the powerful A's.

Baltimore took three of the four games in the matchup with the Western leaders. They received help from all quarters. In the final game of the series, Mickey Weston, who had been recalled from Rochester the previous day, made his major league debut and pitched three scoreless frames in relief to pick up his first save in the Orioles' 4–2 win.

From the time of Toronto's managerial change on May 15 until June 21, the Jays had registered 21 wins and 12 losses. Their only problem was that the Orioles had gone 24–9 over the same period.

The Blue Jays' major areas of improvement since Gaston took over had been hitting and relief pitching. Toronto's batters had a .241 average under Williams; they were hitting at a .291 clip with Cito as the manager. Their top relievers, Tom Henke, Duane Ward, and David Wells, had struggled to a 3–11 record and a 4.58 ERA while Williams was the skipper. They rebounded and went 8–1 with a 2.11 ERA after Gaston took the helm.

Gaston had gotten the club going in the right direction, but they were not yet closing the gap. On June 21, although they had climbed into second place, they were still seven games out of first, which was one more than they had been when Cito took over.

Toronto journeyed to Oakland to take on the A's, who were still on top of the American League West. After winning the first two games of the series, 4–2 and 10–8, the Jays dropped the final two, 7–1 and 6–3. Rickey Henderson was the Athletics' hitting star in their pair of victories. The speedy outfielder had just been traded by the Yankees back to Oakland, where he had begun his major league career in 1976.

Following the series in Oakland, the Blue Jays went to Baltimore for a head-to-head matchup with the division leaders. The Orioles took the first two games, 16–6 and 2–1, but Toronto salvaged the finale, blasting Baltimore, 11–1. Steve Cummings, making his first major league start, held the O's to a single run and six hits in the seven innings he worked. George Bell, Felix, Manny Lee, and Ernie Whitt each banged out three hits in Toronto's 19-hit attack. Twelve of them had come off starter Dave Schmidt during his three-inning appearance.

Baltimore welcomed Detroit to Memorial Stadium the next day. In game one, the cellar-dwelling Tigers scored 16 runs on 18 hits in a 16–5 win. Ballard righted the listing ship the following day and raised his own record to 10–3, in Baltimore's 8–1 victory. Ripken and Worthington hit bases-empty home runs to provide an offensive spark.

Ballard ended his slump in which he had gone 0–2 in four starts since his last win on June 5. His performance was also a hopeful sign for a staff which had surrendered 52 runs and 97 hits in 60 innings for an average of 14.5 hits per game.

The Orioles were in a position which looked promising; after all, as Chass pointed out, "Since the Boston Red Sox of 1978 crumbled ... no American League East team that had a lead of three and a half games or more entering July has failed to win the division championship."[10]

And a number of the young Orioles had already experienced the pressure of a pennant race and the thrill of victory. As Hemond remarked, "The fact that Rochester had won the Governor's Cup the year before helped the younger players on the club. They knew about winning."[11]

Baltimore went to Toronto and began a series on July 3. The Jays had slid into fifth place as the Yankees, Red Sox, and Brewers moved ahead of them. In the opener, Schmidt rebounded from his horrendous outing against Detroit, pitching a perfect game for 6⅓ innings to lead the O's to a 8–0 victory. They followed the next night with a 5–4 decision over the Blue Jays in their 81st game of the campaign. Robinson gave a managerial overview of the win as well as a perspective on the team at the halfway point in the season: "We got the defense, turned the double plays, and our pitchers let them hit the ball to somebody.... Those are the things we have been doing all season."[12]

Rookie reliever Gregg Olson, who had recorded his 13th save in the victory, spoke about his view of the O's success: "We haven't looked back and we don't look any further ahead than the next game. Honestly, I don't think anyone on this club even realized it was 81 games."[13] Olson later added, "In 1989 we had so many rookies that we all didn't understand why we couldn't compete. They turned the whole club over and were set on letting all the young guys play."[14]

With half of the campaign behind them, the Orioles' 47–34 record marked a 23-game improvement over 1988 when they had been 24–57 at the halfway point. After the series of trades of veterans for youngsters, Baltimore made its remarkable comeback with one of the major leagues' lowest payrolls, which totaled less than $8 million. Hemond remarked, "We had diminished our payroll and had improved our team."[15]

On July 14, Ripken and Tettleton represented the Orioles in the All-Star Game, which went to the American Leaguers, 5–3. With the season a little more half finished, Tettleton, Bradley, and Ballard were the only O's listed among the top ten players in the Junior Circuit in a number of offensive and pitching categories. The Baltimore catcher, with 20 home runs, was tied for third place with Toronto's Fred McGriff, and was also third in Slugging Percentage. Bradley was tied for the league lead in triples with the Angels' Devon White. In the lists of pitching accomplishments, Ballard, with 10 wins, was deadlocked for the fourth spot with a number of other American Leaguers. However, he was not among the leaders in

Cal Ripken, Jr., a fixture for the Orioles (Baltimore Orioles).

ERA. The Orioles' success, which had given them a major league–best 5½-game lead over the closest rival, the Yanks, had been a team effort.

Baltimore added two more games to its lead the next couple of days, but, beginning on July 19, the O's suffered through two weeks of horrendous play. Over that span, they won once, lost 13 times, and watched their 7½-game lead almost evaporate.

The O's had been decimated during their trip through the West. The Athletics and Twins swept them, and the Kansas City Royals took two of their three games with the Orioles. Baltimore's 4–3 win over the Royals in their series opener left them a game short of tying the league record for consecutive losses by a first-place team. The 1953 Yankees and the 1970 Twins shared the mark, having each dropped nine in a row.

The Orioles' last stop on the disastrous road trip was in Boston. The Red Sox won the first three against their faltering Eastern Division rivals. In the series finale on August 2, Baltimore beat Boston, 9–8, for only their second win since July 19. After the victory, the O's were just two lengths in front of the Red Sox. The American League East had become a tight race again, and Boston, Toronto, Cleveland, and Milwaukee were all within 3½ games of the lead.

Baltimore's defense, which had been one of its strongest points, had deserted them during the losing streak. In their last 24 games they committed 24 errors; in their first 82 they had 38 miscues. The offense also sputtered, and Tettleton hit only two home runs over a 26-game stretch.

Robinson recounted his club's horrors:

> It's been a matter of concentration.... Most of these errors have come on routine plays, not on difficult ones. A short throw to second base, picking up a ball in the outfield. It's a reaction to being stuck in the streak, you think about a lot of other things, but you don't get out of it unless you get back to doing exactly what the moment on the field calls for. No more, no less.[16]

The Orioles went home to begin a 10-game homestand, hoping to rediscover the magic that had eluded them since mid–July.

Worthington offered a player's thoughts about the situation, saying "A year ago, everything just went into winning a game, just breaking the streak.... The goal now is not to just win a game, but to get back to what we already have done."[17]

On August 4, Baltimore welcomed the Texas Rangers to Memorial Stadium to begin a three-game set. Orioles fans had not deserted the team, as 37,754 were there for the opener, which the O's dropped, 6–4.

While Baltimore was losing to Texas, the Blue Jays were topping the Yankees, 2–1, in Toronto. Jays right-hander Dave Stieb retired the first 26 Yanks to face him. With two gone in the ninth, outfielder Roberto Kelly lined a sharp double to left, breaking up Stieb's perfect game. Stieb would, however, hold on for his 11th victory.

The Orioles and Bob Milacki beat Texas the next night, 5–2, before a crowd of 48,776. One day later, the O's took the finale, 3–2, in 10 innings. Mike Devereaux's bases-empty homer in the 10th made a winner of Mark Williamson, who had pitched 1⅔ scoreless innings in relief of rookie Pete Harnisch. After Texas left town, the Twins and the Red Sox followed them to Memorial Stadium.

The O's split the 10 games in their home park. Two of the wins were recorded by 29-year-old rookie Dave Johnson, who had been recalled from Rochester on August 1. The Baltimore native beat Minnesota, 6–1, in his second major league start. The hot-hitting Devereaux drove in three Baltimore runs. In the final game of the home stand, Johnson handled Boston, also by the score of 6–1. Both of his wins were route-going efforts.

Baltimore left town for a short three-game trip to Detroit, holding a 2½-game lead over the Brewers, Blue Jays, and Red Sox. The O's picked up their eighth victory in 10 extra-inning games with a 4–1, 10-inning decision over the Tigers in the series opener. Worthington's three-run homer sealed the win as Olson registered his 18th save of the season. Baltimore split the remaining pair of games, winning 2–0 and losing 4–0.

The Orioles relief corps had been effective during the season. As Hemond remembered, "Williamson did a good job as a closer until Olson took over. Then he became a very effective set-up man for Olson and played a vital role toward the club's success."[18]

On August 17, the Orioles returned home to meet their two closest rivals—Toronto and Milwaukee. Ballard pitched his club to a 11–6 win over the Jays in the series opener. Stan Jefferson, who was hitting under .200, drove in five runs with a homer and a single. Ripken delivered a two-run shot in the Orioles' eight-run fourth inning. The O's shortstop moved into third place on the consecutive-games played list with 1208.

Rookie hurlers Johnson and Milacki were the losers in games two and three as Toronto won, 9–2 and 5–1. Johnson, for the first time in his major league career, was hit hard during his short three-inning stint. Milacki surrendered only one hit over seven innings but gave up two runs, which were enough to have the loss pinned on him. He was Baltimore's hard-luck pitcher during much of the season.

Harnisch, the third consecutive rookie to start for the Orioles, got his club a split in the series as Baltimore picked up a 7–2 decision over the Jays. Toronto remained 1½ games off the pace.

Tettleton had come upon hard times. He was lost to the club for about a month after a cyst was removed from one of his knees, and he was not back in the lineup until early September. Hemond spoke about what the catcher's time on the D.L. meant to the Orioles: "I feel Mickey's absence from our offensive attack cost us games that would have enabled the team to clinch the Eastern Division prior to the deciding final weekend in Toronto."[19]

Milwaukee came to town trailing Baltimore by one-half game. The Orioles picked up three wins against their closest rival. Ballard [13–6] pitched a 5–0, seven-hit shutout, and he was helped by home runs by Jefferson and Ripken. Johnson followed with his third complete game in August, a 4–2 victory. Milacki [8–11] closed out the Brewers and a 5–2 Oriole home stand with a well-pitched 3–1 victory. Toronto climbed into the runner-up position in the AL East as Milwaukee dropped off the pace.

Perhaps the magic had returned and there was reason for renewed hope for the Orioles. A confident Robinson remarked, "I'm not surprised by this team anymore ... I stopped being surprised around the end of May. I'm not surprised by what they do, by how they do it or by what they have accomplished."[20]

Yankee Stadium was the first stop on a critical Baltimore road trip. On August 24, the Orioles split a doubleheader with the Bronx Bombers, losing game one, 5–1, and capturing the nightcap, 9–2. The struggling Yanks remained 10½ lengths off the pace as a result of the day's action. The rejuvenated O's took the next three from New York and headed to Cleveland.

Following an off day on August 28, Baltimore had a 71–60 record, and the Blue Jays, who had beaten the Brewers, 8–2, while the O's were idle, stood at 69–62.

The last three days of August set the scene for Baltimore's final month of the campaign. The O's won only one of the trio of games they played against the Indians, and Toronto tripped the Chicago White Sox three times. The Cleveland finale was a disaster. Going into the game with a tenuous one-length lead over Toronto, a quartet of Baltimore pitchers gave up 11 runs and 15 hits in the Indians' 11–0 romp. Johnson, Schmidt, Thurmond, and Holton each took his lumps from the Cleveland bats. Joe Carter, who hit two home runs and had three RBIs, and second baseman Jerry Browne, who went 4-for-5, led the surge.

As August drew to a close, Baltimore had company in first place for the first time since May 26. The Orioles and the Blue Jays were in a flat-footed tie on the perch at the top of the American League East with identical 72–62 records.

On September 1, the day that baseball lost its charismatic commissioner, Baltimore lost its hold on first place for the first time in over three months. They had been at the top for 96 consecutive days and for 115 of the season's first 150 days, the latter being the most ever by a club which had finished in the basement the previous year.

While the Blue Jays, who were powered by Glenallen Hill's grand-slam, were beating the Twins, 7–3, for their 10th win in 11 games, the Orioles were absorbing a 10–1 whipping at the hands of the White Sox. Chicago got off to a fast start when Daryl Boston hit a bases-loaded home run off Milacki.

The following day, both of the top teams won their games. The Jays beat the Twins, 4–2, and the O's topped the White Sox, 2–1. Robinson used five pitchers in the game, and Olson picked up his 23rd save, which tied the American League record for rookies.

Toronto maintained its one-game lead until September 6, when Baltimore lost to the Indians, 6–0, and the Blue Jays beat the White Sox, 4–2. The Jays, with the win, extended their lead to two games.

Baltimore captured a doubleheader in Texas the following day, winning the first game, 8–3, and beating Nolan Ryan for the third time in the season. The O's went on to top the Rangers, 9–2, in the nightcap. Baltimore took three-out-of-four from Texas, and the Blue Jays had the same success against the Indians. The final game of each series was an extra-inning thriller. Toronto topped the Cleveland, 7–5, in 16 innings, and Baltimore edged Texas, 4–2, in 10 innings.

On September 15, the Blue Jays held a 1½ game lead over the Orioles.

Gammons, in *Sports Illustrated*, traced the recent happenings in the American League East:

> The Orioles have been America's sentimental favorite this year, just as the Red Sox were in 1967 and the Mets were in '69. But when August turned to

September, the Blue Jays passed Baltimore, and the Red Sox were five games off the lead. For the O's, the impossible dream had become improbable.[21]

The late-season unevenness in the Orioles' pitching was seen on September 19, when Milacki's record reached 12–12 in a 6–2 decision over the Tigers. That was the club's 14th win in the last 17 games started by Milacki and Ballard. The O's were 5–10 in games pitched by others on the staff.

Baltimore continued their brave battle, refusing to surrender:

> Despite their unexpected rise from last season's ashes, the Orioles do not seem unnerved by their station or their status. They are a team composed of young, impressionable players, yet they have not been burdened by the race that stares at them each night.[22]

As the campaign was winding down, Olson, who had gone on to set the rookie record for saves with 26, described his and his teammates' approach: "We kept our mouths shut.... Everybody waited for us to fall, but I knew we wouldn't. We showed that we weren't a fluke. We weathered a slump and bounced back. Now we're still in it."[23]

One game separated the division-leading Blue Jays and the second-place Orioles as the season's final series for the two teams opened in Toronto on September 29. George Vecsey, writing in the *Times*, captured the excitement surrounding the matchup:

> The next three days could be the best weekend of the year in North American sports. Two teams from Baltimore and Toronto will play not once, not twice, but three times, to decide a championship, with the Blue Jays one game ahead when they call attendance tonight.
>
> If the Orioles win twice, they will meet again Monday in a playoff in Babe Ruth's home town. Great stuff. Two teams going at each other, day after day, different pitchers, different substitutes, different lineups, all the little subplots until somebody wins.[24]

Toronto had gone 73–48 since Gaston took over. Would this be their year to win the division, or would it be a repeat of the horrors of 1987 when they lost their last seven games, including the final three of the season in Detroit to drop from the top and hand first place to the Tigers?

Would this be their year to go on to take the American League Championship Series or would it be another 1985, when they held a three-games-to-one lead, only to lose the pennant to Kansas City?

Baltimore had already won 32 more games than in 1988. Three more would provide a fabulous finish to a captivating campaign.

The first game was a thriller. The teams battled to a 1–1 tie into the 11th inning. Bradley's home run as Baltimore's lead-off hitter turned out to be the O's only run of the game as they stranded 11 baserunners. A wild pitch in the eighth by Olson, in relief of Ballard [18–8], enabled Tom Lawless to score the tying run. In the bottom of the 11th inning, Lloyd Moseby's two-out single scored Nelson Liriano from second base to bring the Jays a 2–1 victory. Toronto went two games ahead with two to play.

They captured the division championship the next day. For the second day in a row, Baltimore took a lead into the eighth inning. The Blue Jays came back to trip the Orioles, 4–3, with a dramatic three-run rally in the eighth. Johnson had a 3–1 lead and a two-hitter going into the fatal frame. Walks, a sacrifice bunt, a pair of singles, and a sacrifice fly off Johnson, Kevin Hickey, and Williamson accounted for the winning runs.

Hickey, who had followed Johnson to the mound, remembered the fatal pitch the previous day, his spring training excitement, and the Orioles' fans:

> We were one pitch from beating the Blue Jays, a curve ball that bounced in front of home plate (from Olson)....
>
> I said in spring training ('89) if we could stay healthy and worked hard and believe in each other & get some breaks, why not contend for 1st place. People forget the game is played between the lines....
>
> I want to thank the fans of Baltimore for their courtesy & support. Every player should play for the greatest fans in baseball. They really love their team no matter what. They were great to me and my family.[25]

The Orioles took the final game of the season, 7–5, with McDonald, the season's first draft pick, registering his first major league victory with an inning of perfect relief. That was, at least, a promising sign for the future.

Baltimore had played harder and hungrier than any team in the division and, perhaps, in all of baseball. Harnisch mentioned a couple of other things that also helped bring the O's success: "Amazing, every two-out hit we needed we got. Different heroes every night!... Defense, Defense, Defense! The best D-team in all of baseball history!"[26]

The O's 32½ game improvement surpassed the 1979 Athletics' 29-game rise as the best since divisional play began in 1969. They were a single game shy of tying for the best record in baseball for a team which had a 100-loss season the previous year. The O's were the first team ever with 25 victories and 25 saves from rookies. Bradley became the first Oriole to reach double figures in doubles, triples, home runs, and stolen bases in the same season. Ripken had extended his consecutive game streak, moving into third place on the list. Olson picked up the baseball writers' AL Rookie of the Year Award, and Worthington received the same honor from *The Sporting News*. But the Orioles fell a whisker short of reaching their dream of capturing their division's championship.

A decade later, Hemond thought back and remembered:

> It was too bad that owner Edward Bennett Williams wasn't around to see the club in 1989. He died during the 1988 season. I respected him a great deal. I came to the Orioles prior to the 1988 season, and Williams would call me during the losing streak at the beginning of my first season with the Orioles and give me support.
>
> The 1989 season for any of us, who experienced the unexpected turnaround from 1988 to the next year, will forever be cherished in our memory bank.
>
> As I look back, I remember wondering whether this was real or was I dreaming. When we lost, it was disappointing, but it had been a privilege to have been there and seen it. Frank [Robinson] did a great job. In my view, the managerial job that he did in 1989 should go down as one of the best of all time. Even after the bad streak in July when we could have folded, he brought the team back. Frank was masterful. Every time he put the hit-and-run on the batter hit the ball. Every time he put on a double steal it worked. I believe there were only two comebacks to better 1989. One was the New York Giants in 1903 [34½ games] when John McGraw brought several of his Baltimore Orioles along with him upon becoming manager of the New York club. The other was the Boston Red Sox in 1946 [33 games] with its returning stars from World War II including Ted Williams, Johnny Pesky, Dom DiMaggio, and several others. They made a slightly better comeback than the 1989 Orioles. Our comeback, however, was done strictly in changes of personnel on a normal basis.[27]

Notes

1. From News Release, Major League Baseball, 24 August 1989, 1.
2. Murray Chass, "A Cloud Darkens Opening Day," *New York Times*, 2 April 1989, Sec. 8, 1.
3. Hal Bodley, "Series: 'Modest Little Sports Event,'" *USA Today*, 19 October 1989, sec. C: 3.
4. Murray Chass, "Blue Jays May Be the Strongest of a Weak Bunch," *New York Times*, 2 April 1989. Sec. 8, 15.
5. Roland Hemond, Telephone conversation, 2 November 1998.
6. Peter Gammons, "Inside Baseball," *Sports Illustrated*, 12 June 1989, 78.
7. Mark Thurmond, Letter, November 1998.
8. Hemond, Telephone conversation, 4 January 1999.
9. Murray Chass, "In East, Orioles Gain Catbird Seat and Hope It's Permanent," *New York Times*, 4 June 1989, sec. 8, 3.

10. Murray Chass, "Orioles Gathering Backers in Their Ability to Go All the Way," *New York Times*, 2 July 1989, sec. 8, 3.

11. Hemond, Telephone conversation, 2 November 1998.

12. "Victory Gives Orioles a Midseason Milestone," *New York Times*, 6 July 1989, sec. 2, 11.

13. "Victory Gives Orioles...," sec. 2, 11.

14. Gregg Olson, Letter, 1999.

15. Hemond, Telephone conversation, 2 December 1998.

16. David Faulkner, "Suddenly, No Room at the Top," *New York Times*, 4 August 1989, sec. 2, 11.

17. Faulkner, "Suddenly, No Room...," sec. 2, 12.

18. Hemond, Telephone conversation, 2 November 1998.

19. Hemond, Telephone conversation, 2 November 1998.

20. Michael Martinez, "Orioles Give and Take as Yanks Fall 10½ Out," *New York Times*, 25 August 1989, 19.

21. Peter Gammons, "Inside Baseball," *Sports Illustrated*, 11 September 1989, 148.

22. Michael Martinez, "Orioles: Young Team Heading for an Old-Style Photo Finish," *New York Times*, 22 September 1989, 29.

23. Martinez, "Orioles: Young Team...," 29.

24. George Vescey, "Baseball's Finest Days: The Best," *New York Times*, 29 September 1989, sec. 2, 9.

25. Kevin Hickey, Letter, March 1999.

26. Pete Harnisch, Letter, March 1999.

27. Hemond, Telephone conversation, 2 November 1998.

13. 1991 Atlanta Braves and Minnesota Twins

From the Cellar to First Place for a Pair of Teams

The 1991 World Series, the 88th edition of the Fall Classic, matched two teams which had finished in the cellars of their respective divisions the previous year. The Minnesota Twins had climbed from the basement of the American League West to capture the loop's pennant, and the Atlanta Braves had repeated the rare pattern in the National League. As a conclusion to their exciting seasons, these two "last-to-firsts" battled through five one-run games, with four being decided on the final pitch. Three of the encounters required extra innings, setting a record. The finale was a 1–0, 10-inning masterpiece.

In 1961 the Washington Senators, under the ownership of Calvin Griffith, became the Minnesota Twins as part of the American League's expansion to 10 teams.

The transplanted Senators played in Metropolitan Stadium in Bloomington, Minnesota, which is equidistant from the downtown centers of the Twin Cities, Minneapolis and St. Paul.

The Twins were competitive during their first 10 seasons in Minnesota. They won the American League pennant in 1965, but lost the World Series to the Los Angeles Dodgers in seven games. They finished in second place the next two seasons.

From 1971 until 1984, when Carl Pohlad, a wealthy Minneapolis banker, purchased the franchise, the Twins struggled both on the field and at the gate. They had climbed no higher than third place in the American League West and finished in the lower half of the division in eight of the 13 seasons.

In 1982 the team moved indoors, playing in the new Hubert H. Humphrey Metrodome in downtown Minneapolis, and began to develop a group of young, promising players to improve the club. In 1987 they reached the top, capturing the World Championship with a Fall Classic best-of-seven victory over the St. Louis Cardinals.

The Twins were unable to maintain their lofty perch, dropping to second place the following season. In 1989 they finished in fifth. A year later they fell into the basement with a 74–88 record and were 29 games behind the pennant-winning Oakland Athletics.

Catcher Brian Harper looked back at the 1990 campaign and said, "I really felt that last year we weren't a last-place team.... We just had one of the strangest years I've ever been involved with in pro ball.[1]

Harper was possibly recalling that, on one occasion, his team had turned a pair of triple plays in a game and still lost it to the Boston Red Sox. Or, perhaps, he was remembering the Twins allowing 10 unearned runs in a single game.

In January 1991, general manager Andy MacPhail signed free-agent pitcher Jack Morris to a three-year contract which, including incentives,

would pay him $11.6 million. Morris had been born and raised in St. Paul, and joining the Twins represented a homecoming for him. He was leaving the Detroit Tigers, the only major league club he had been with during an illustrious 13-year career. The powerful right-hander had led the majors in wins during the decade of the '80s but had struggled to a 21–32 record and a 4.65 ERA during his final two seasons with the Tigers. Some suggested that the Twins were gambling on a "has been."

Jack Morris back home in Minnesota (Minnesota Twins).

The Twins also strengthened the club with other free agents, wooing the California

Angels' switch-hitting outfielder Chili Davis and the San Diego Padres' Mike Pagliarulo, each of whom signed with Minnesota. And, with less fanfare, they signed pitcher Carl Willis, a career minor leaguer who had considered retirement after the 1990 season.

Pagliarulo replaced third baseman Gary Gaetti, who had gone to the Angels after being granted "new look" free agency in the collusion ruling. Pitcher Juan Berenguer had taken the same route to the Braves.

Pitcher Steve Bedrosian, who came from the San Francisco Giants in a trade, and rookies Chuck Knoblauch and Scott Leius were expected to play important roles in 1991. Knoblauch and Leius had come up through Minnesota's minor league system.

Eleven games into the 1991 season, Minnesota found themselves back in the cellar, having won only twice. On June 1, the Twins, carrying a 23–25 record and in fifth place, began their climb. That day they beat the Kansas City Royals and started a club-record 15-game winning streak, which stretched until June 17. The skein was the longest in the majors since 1977 when Kansas City had won 16 straight.

A day before Minnesota's first June loss, they climbed into the lead for the first time since October 4, 1987. Minnesota played outstanding baseball during June and were 22–6 for the month.

After the streak ended, skeptics reminded the optimists on the Twins' bandwagon that all of their victories had come against teams playing under .500 baseball. With the exception of their two wins over the division-rival Royals on the first two days of the month, all the other victories had come at the expense of the bottom three teams in the American League East.

One of Minnesota's surprises had been 23-year-old right-hander Scott Erickson. In the middle of June he held a 9–2 record and a major league–leading 1.53 ERA. The veteran Morris commented on the second year sinker-baller's success, saying, "He gives a team a lot of confidence when he's pitching.... You feel that if you catch and hit the ball and get a couple of runs early, you'll win the game."[2]

While the Twins were climbing, the three-time champion Athletics were falling. Besides suffering a number of injuries, pitcher Dave Stewart and outfielder Rickey Henderson were having sub-par seasons. Minnesota also passed the Texas Rangers, whose bats powered the club, but could not make up for the team's weak pitching staff.

By mid–August, Minnesota was 2½ games ahead of Chicago. The White Sox, who were led by pitcher Jack McDowell and power-hitting Frank Thomas, stayed in the race longer than any other of the Twins' challengers.

Through July, the Twins had beaten up on the American League East teams, going 44–20, but they had gone only 17–22 against the clubs in their own division. They began to fare much better against the Western teams, and, after a number of important wins, MacPhail said:

> It was a key period.... We had to get better against the West. California can be particularly troublesome for us. We have to be pleased with what we did, just like that long stretch of road games when we more than held our own.[3]

On August 16, after losing three in a row, Minnesota opened an important home series against Oakland. The Twins took three out of the four games, coming from behind in each victory.

In the opener, Minnesota came back to beat the A's, 5–4, in 12 innings. They scored a pair of runs in the ninth to tie the game before pushing across the winning run three innings later. Oakland jumped on top in the second matchup, but the Twins' offense came to life and they finished with a 10–4 win. In game three, Minnesota rallied for three runs in the eighth to pick up a 6–4 victory. The finale went to the A's, 8–7, although the home club made a valiant effort to add the game to its win column.

On August 31, the day the Twins had to set their roster for postseason play, MacPhail replaced two pitchers with outfielder Jarvis Brown and first baseman Paul Sorrento. If Minnesota got to the American League Championship Series and beyond, they would have nine pitchers rather than their usual 10 or 11. MacPhail recalled that he had done the same thing in 1987, when he added Don Baylor to the roster and removed Steve Carlton. The Twins general manager explained the maneuver:

> If you need 10 [pitchers] in postseason, you have a problem.... Chances are you're not going to win that game. ... You may get back-to-back, prolonged extra-inning affairs, or one real long one might leave you short. But we could hit for Gene Larkin or run for Brian Harper. We'd have Brown to run without using another guy. Those things are more likely to happen.[4]

Minnesota continued to build its lead and finished 95–67, eight games ahead of the second place White Sox. Kirby Puckett (.319), Harper (.311), and Shane Mack (.311) were the Twins' leading hitters. Davis powered 29 round-trippers, and Kent Hrbek contributed 20.

Davis commented on the team's surprising success:

> The Twins put together a bunch of no-names, has-beens and castoffs and we all jelled together.... A lot of us were put in the position where we were told we couldn't play anymore. That we were past our prime. Well, we all migrated here and proved them wrong.[5]

Erickson led the pitchers with a 20–8 record. Morris finished the season at 18–12, and Kevin Tapani chipped in with a 16–9 mark. Minnesota manager Tom Kelly tapped the trio to do the bulk of the Twins' postseason pitching. Rick Aguilera was ready in the bullpen, having picked up 42 saves during the regular season.

The Braves had struggled regularly since their move from Milwaukee to Atlanta in 1966. In 1969 and 1982, Atlanta finished at the top of the National League West, but they lost three straight postseason games on both occasions. Other than those two seasons and 1983, when they finished in second place, they had not been legitimate contenders for the division's crown. A third consecutive basement-finish in 1990, with a 65–97 record, provided little optimism for the near future.

The club strengthened itself for the 1991 campaign, dipping into the free-agent market. Newly-appointed general manager John Schuerholz signed infielders Raphael Belliard, Sid Bream, and Terry Pendleton. Berenguer, a free-agent acquisition from Minnesota, was ticketed for the bullpen. Schuerholz had replaced Bobby Cox, who had left the front office to become the club's manager.

The Braves' path to the National League West title was bumpier than the road taken by the Twins. On May 17, they briefly occupied the division's top spot, and in early June they were 25–19 and one-half game behind the league-leading Los Angeles Dodgers.

Like Minnesota's Erickson, Atlanta's Tom Glavine was having an outstanding season. In mid–June, the 23-year-old left-hander was working on an eight-game winning streak and had a 10–2 record. Leo Mazzone, the team's pitching coach, commented about the talented lefty who was in his fourth season:

> You always try to project what they would be like at the major league level.... When I thought of Tom Glavine, he reminded you of a Whitey Ford type. The way he goes about his business. The style of pitching, being offensive minded. Going out with that cockiness, but it's a good cockiness. He's just confident.[6]

By the All-Star break the Braves had fallen off the pace and were a game under .500 and 9½ lengths out of first place. Even after a strong start, especially for this particular franchise, it was probably expected that their upward movement had ceased, and they would continue a downward slide through the division to their home in the basement.

A glance at the standings on August 17th showed that, surprisingly, they were back nipping at the heels of the Dodgers and only a game behind.

They were in the midst of winning nine of 11 games while Los Angeles was floundering.

On August 27, Atlanta beat the Montreal Expos, 3–2, behind Charlie Leibrandt, while the Chicago Cubs were topping the Dodgers, 2–1. The Braves' victory hoisted them back into first place.

In mid–September, they were 1½ games ahead. One of the Braves' victories had been the Senior Circuit's first three-man no-hitter, by the triumvirate of Kent Mercker, Mark Wohlers and Alejandro Peña.

Cox had to adjust to losing some of the team's outfield during the campaign. On July 31, back-up center fielder Deion Sanders played his final game for the Braves before heading off to the Atlanta Falcons' pre-season football camp. Later, left fielder Otis Nixon entered a drug treatment program.

Atlanta and Los Angeles waged a nip-and-tuck, down-to-the-wire battle. It was a struggle that wasn't decided until the final weekend of the season.

On September 20, Atlanta went to Los Angeles, trailing the Dodgers by one-half game. Following the Braves' 3–0 win in the opener, they pulled ahead. However, they dropped the next two, 2–1 and 3–0, and left town 1½ lengths behind the front-running Dodgers.

The two teams entered the final weekend of the regular season with identical 92–67 records. Atlanta was set to host Houston and the Dodgers were in San Francisco to play the Giants.

There was great excitement in Atlanta. It had also spread to other places as well, as the Braves' late-season contests were broadcast not only throughout the Southeast on the Braves Radio Network or on the TBS cable superstation, but on major network television and ESPN, too.[7]

On Friday, October 4, Atlanta, behind Steve Avery, who picked up his 18th win with relief help from Peña, beat Houston, 5–2. The Giants handled the Dodgers, 4–1. Atlanta had a narrow one-game lead with two to go.

The Braves clinched the division crown the next day with another 5–2 win over the Astros, which was coupled with the Dodgers' 4–0 loss to the Giants. John Smoltz picked up the victory, and Ron Gant, the club's home run leader, powered another one.

In Atlanta, the Southeastern Savoyards Light Opera Company performed "H.M.S. Pinafore" and celebrated the Braves' pennant-clinching win. At the beginning of the concert, the conductor, in white tie and tails, turned to the orchestra and raised not a baton—but a tomahawk.

Since the tomahawk first arrived at the ballpark sometime in early May—possibly in the hands of some Florida State University Seminoles who were in the stands—it had become the rage. Paul Braddy, a 38-year-old Atlanta entrepreneur, had quit his job as sales manager for a urethane company to manufacture tomahawks full-time for Braves fans.

The movements of the chop were something new Braves fans needed help with, and so the *Boston Globe*, with tongue in cheek, published instructions:

1. With a straight back, hold upper arms at a 45 degree angle to body and lower arm vertically.
2. Now, prepare to chop with force and determination.
3. Chop continues with upper arm moving to 90 degree angle to body.
4. Head nods.[8]

In the final games of the regular season, the Braves lost, 8–3, and the Dodgers won, 2–0, but the division had been decided a day earlier. The batting race, however, was still up for grabs. On the last day of the campaign, Pendleton clinched the National League batting title with a .319 average, barely out-pointing Hal Morris of Cincinnati in one of the tightest batting races in either league since Dave Winfield nudged past Don Mattingly seven years earlier. Gant finished with 32 home runs, 105 RBIs, and had his second consecutive 30 homer–30 stolen base season.

Glavine's 20–11 record, 2.53 ERA, and 246⅔ innings pitched led the Braves staff. Avery (18–8), Leibrandt (15–13), and Smoltz (14–13) were the other major contributors. Avery and Smoltz were undefeated after August 1st. Berenguer registered 17 saves out of the bullpen. Peña, who was acquired from the New York Mets during the season, also provided important relief work.

The Twins met Toronto, who had finished 91–71 in the American League East in the League Championship Series. The Blue Jays had also strengthened themselves by a series of off-season acquisitions. They added second baseman Roberto Alomar and outfielders Joe Carter and Devon White. During the campaign, Toronto was never more than two games out of first place, and they finished seven lengths in front of Boston and Detroit.

The Twins' path to the pennant had only one rough spot. Minnesota topped the Blue Jays, 4 games to 1, including three victories in Toronto's SkyDome. Puckett had an outstanding series and received the Lee MacPhail MVP Award for the American League Championship Series. Kirby had eight hits and five RBIs in the last three contests, including the game-winner in the finale.

Minnesota was one step closer to a second World Championship. MacPhail, reflecting on his team's remarkable transition, said, "Never in your wildest dreams do you believe you'll see such things. But it happens again and again and that's what makes the game so special."[9]

The regular season had gone down to the wire for the Braves; the National League Championship Series was no different. Their opponents, the powerful Pittsburgh Pirates, had taken over first place in the National League East on April 29 and breezed to a 14-game romp over the Cardinals. Twenty-game winner John Smiley was the ace of the staff, and Bobby Bonilla, Barry Bonds, and Andy Van Slyke were the most productive Pirate hitters.

Atlanta finally outdistanced the Pittsburgh Pirates in a battle of seven games. Cox's moundsmen tossed three shutouts at the Pirates, including two 1–0 gems.

The World Series opened indoors in the Metrodome in Minneapolis on Saturday, October 19. For the fourth year in a row, the teams represented the Wests of the National and American leagues. For the first time in major league history, two teams had climbed from their division's basement the previous season to reach the Fall Classic.

The Twins picked up a 5–2 victory in game one. Greg Gagne's three-run homer in the fifth inning broke the game open and gave the Twins a 4–0 lead. Hrbek, who had not hit well in his previous World Series appearances in 1987, contributed a double and a home run to the cause. Knoblauch banged out three hits, giving him a total of 10 for the postseason. He also made a sprawling grab of a ground ball in the eighth inning to start an important double play. Morris picked up the win, pitching seven innings and giving up both of the Braves runs. Leibrandt took the loss. "Homer hankies," the special weapon of the Twins fans, were waving in all their glory.

The following day, Davis, the Twins designated hitter, banged a two-run homer off Glavine, continuing the home team's charge. The ball landed 20 rows deep in the left-centerfield stands, 380 feet from home plate. The Braves rebounded, scoring in the second and fifth frames, each time on sacrifice flies.

In game one, it had been Minnesota's number nine hitter, Gagne, who delivered the decisive blow—a three-run homer. The heroics in the second game were provided by Leius, the Twins' eighth man in the lineup. With the score tied, 2–2, the rookie infielder drove Glavine's first delivery in the home half of the eighth inning into the seats, providing the margin of victory.

After a travel day, the Series resumed in the home of the Braves. Inside Atlanta–Fulton County Stadium, 50,878 fans were there to see the first World Series game ever played in their hometown. Their city was 0–83 in combined years of having professional teams fighting unsuccessfully for a world title. What the Braves, Falcons, Hawks and Flames had failed to do in previous seasons, this baseball team was hoping to achieve in 1991.

Avery, the young Atlanta left-hander, was the Brave charged with keeping Minnesota from picking up their third consecutive win. Erickson went to the mound for the Twins, who were playing outside on real grass for the first time in over two weeks.

Avery, perhaps a bit jittery with the weight of the city of Atlanta resting on his shoulders, struggled in the early-going. Dan Gladden tripled to open the game, the ball falling between David Justice and Gant and rolling to the wall. Better communication between the two outfielders might have turned the three-bagger into an out. A Knoblauch sacrifice fly scored Gladden, and Minnesota was first on the scoreboard for the third straight game. The run also broke Avery's 16⅓ consecutive scoreless-inning streak in postseason play.

However, the next run off the Atlanta lefty didn't come until the seventh inning, when Puckett deposited a pitch into the left-field seats. By that time, home runs by Justice and Lonnie Smith had helped the Braves build a 4–2 lead.

Davis, the Twins' powerful designated hitter, was relegated to pinch-hitting duties for the three contests in Atlanta, since National League rules did not allow the designated hitter. He was called to pinch hit in the eighth inning, with Harper on first. He greeted reliever Peña with a two-run homer to left, tying the score, 4–4.

Bedrosian, Willis, and Mark Guthrie held the Braves scoreless from the sixth through the 11th innings. With Kelly and Cox making maximum use of their rosters, the game went into the 12th inning. In the top of that frame with one out and a runner on first base, Mark Lemke, the Braves second sacker, bobbled a routine double-play ball. Mercker saved Lemke from the goat horns, striking out Hrbek with runners at the corners. Kelly sent up his only available pinch-hitter, pitcher Aguilera. Jim Clancy retired him on a line-drive to center.

Lemke, nearly the goat, turned hero a few minutes later when he drove home a sliding Justice, who had singled and stolen second base to move into scoring position.

Game three went to the Braves, 5–4. It was the longest night game in World Series history—four-hours-and-four-minutes with an ending time of 12:42 A.M. Forty-two players made the boxscore, and only two position players failed to see action.

The fourth contest was also a one-run thriller, with the Braves prevailing, 3–2. For the fourth straight game, the Twins struck first, getting on the board in the top of the second inning. A Pagliarulo single off Smoltz scored Harper, who had doubled. Pendleton countered with a homer in the third off Morris to knot the game, 1–1.

In the fifth, the Braves had two baserunners tagged out at home. Smith was gunned out in a bone-crushing collision with Harper. Later in the inning, Pendleton was cut down at the plate, trying to score from third on a wild pitch in the dirt.

Pagliarulo and Smith traded home runs in the seventh and the score remained tied, 2–2.

In the bottom of the ninth, the previous night's hero, Lemke, tripled to center. After an intentional walk to Jeff Blauser, Jerry Willard (one of only two position players to miss action the previous night), came to bat as a pinch-hitter. His sacrifice fly to right scored Lemke with the winning run of game four.

In the fifth matchup, the suspense ended much earlier than it had in any of the games to date. Atlanta scored four times in the fourth and added six in the seventh on their way to a 14–5 romp—the most runs ever scored by a National League team in World Series history.

The Braves pounded their drums, tomahawk-chopped, and banged out 17 hits off five Minnesota hurlers. Justice, Smith, and Brian Hunter cracked home runs. For Smith, it was his third in as many games. Lemke added a pair of triples to continue his magical October and tie a World Series record for three-base hits.

Atlanta had captured the three games in Fulton County Stadium to take a 3–2 lead. Games six and seven would be played back indoors under the Metrodome's cream-colored Teflon ceiling. The tomahawk would take a back seat to the homer hankie.

In the words of Yogi Berra, Minnesota was hoping for "déjà vu all over again." In 1987 they had beaten the St. Louis Cardinals twice in the Metrodome and then had proceeded to drop all three games in Busch Stadium. Returning home, they regained the winning touch and finished off the Cardinals, picking up their first championship.

Erickson, who had been chased by the Braves in the fifth inning of game three, started game six for the Twins. Avery, who had pitched into the eighth in the same contest, took the mound for Atlanta.

Minnesota once again broke on top, restoring the optimism of the home folks by scoring twice in their first at-bat. In the top of the fifth, the Braves rebounded to tie the game, 2–2, only to fall behind again when the Twins added a tally one-half inning later. Atlanta came back to knot it, 3–3, in the visitors' half of the seventh. For the second time, the teams were headed for an extra-inning affair.

The name of the game that night was "Puckett." The Twins 5'8", fire-plug center-fielder got Minnesota to the 11th inning and ended it there. Along the way, he had singled, tripled, driven in a run on a sacrifice fly, and scored a run himself. He had also made a leaping catch against the center-field Plexiglas panel, above Tony Oliva's retired number 6, robbing Gant of extra bases and the Braves of an almost certain run.

As a fitting conclusion to his night, Puckett, the Twins' powder keg, faced Leibrandt, leading off the bottom half of the 11th.

Kirby Puckett, the leader of the Twins (Minnesota Twins).

With a blast beyond the fence, he delivered a 4–3 victory to the hometowners. The clubs were deadlocked at three games apiece.

Morris, starting his third game and with one of the Twins wins, was charged with picking up the most crucial victory of the season. Smoltz, who had been nearly unbeatable during the second half of the season, took the hill in the Metrodome for the Braves. As a youngster growing up in Detroit, he had idolized his mound opponent when Morris pitched for the Tigers.

Innings came and went, with each hurler tossing zeroes at the opposition. Minnesota had baserunners in scoring position with two out in the second and third frames, but Smoltz retired the Twins before any damage could be done. The Braves had men at first and third with one away in the fifth, but Morris also escaped, getting Pendleton on a pop fly to shallow left and striking out Gant.

With the game scoreless, the eighth inning proved to be a tale of missed opportunities for both teams. Atlanta, batting in the top half of the inning, sent Smith to the plate against Morris. He singled to right field, and Pendleton followed with a line-drive hit to left-centerfield. With the crack of the bat and the course of the ball unknown, Lonnie raced toward second base. The Twins middle infielders, Knoblauch at second and Gagne at shortstop, played decoy with an imaginary ball. Knoblauch pretended to field it and made an imaginary feed to Gagne at the bag. The shortstop faked the catch and made the "toss" to first to complete the "double play." What was play-acting for the double-play combo was all too real for the baserunner; at least real enough to cause him to hesitate as he approached the second-base bag.

By the time Smith picked up sight of the ball near the left-centerfield wall, Gladden was about to retrieve it and fire it back to the infield. Smith slowed as he rounded second and could only advance as far as third base. Pendleton arrived at second with a double but no RBI.

Brave runners stood at second and third, with no one out. The first run of the game—and perhaps 1991's most important deciding run—was 90 feet away in the person of a most-embarrassed Smith. With the infield drawn in, Gant hit a weak grounder to first, and the baserunners were unable to advance. The Twins manager called for an intentional walk to the left-hand-hitting Justice, loading the bases. Bream, another left-hander, dug in against Morris.

Instead of driving in the go-ahead run, Bream started one of baseball's rarities, a 3-2-3 double play. This one was painfully real for the Braves. Bream hit a sharp grounder to Hrbek, who threw home to Harper, forcing Smith. The Twins catcher pegged the ball back to first base, nipping Bream for the final out of the inning. For the eighth consecutive inning, Atlanta had not scored.

Some consolation for Atlanta and more frustration for Minnesota followed in the bottom of the eighth. The Twins loaded the bases with one out, and the home team had the go-ahead run only 90 feet away. Hrbek hit a soft liner to Lemke at second base. He stepped on the bag, completing an unassisted double play and keeping Minnesota off the scoreboard.

The Twins had runners at first and second with no one out in the bottom of the ninth and failed to score again. This time reliever Peña induced Mack to hit into a double play, and he ended the inning by striking out Sorrento, a pinch-hitter. Another game had moved into extra innings.

In the last half of the 10th inning, Gladden hit a broken-bat fly ball to left-centerfield and hustled to second with a lead-off double. Knoblauch sacrificed Gladden to third. Peña intentionally walked Puckett and Hrbek, loading the bases. Pinch-hitter Gene Larkin, with four plate appearances in the World Series and 10 in postseason play, was sent to bat for the Twins.

Atlanta brought their outfield in, stationing them about 200 feet from home plate. Their only hope was that a short fly ball would enable them to hold Gladden at third. The infield was positioned so that they could cut the run off at the plate. A repeat of a 3-2-3 twin-killing would be welcomed.

Larkin slapped Peña's pitch to left-center, over the head of Hunter, and Gladden easily scored the first and only run of the game. All he had to do was trot in from third and let the celebration begin. He hesitated on his way to the plate. Later, he commented, "I just wanted to enjoy it for a second.... I knew it was finally over, and that we had won."[10]

The Twins won, 1–0, with Morris pitching a seven-hitter over 10 innings—the Fall Classic's longest seventh game pitching performance.

Smith, the first player in history to appear in four World Series with four different teams (Philadelphia in '80, St. Louis in '82, Kansas City in '85, and Atlanta in '91), contributed three home runs. But he also had to claim his part in the event which may be remembered the longest—a costly hesitation around the second-base bag at a crucial juncture of the final game.

An exultant Pagliarulo commented after game seven:

> This was the greatest game.... They had a chance to win—but they didn't. We had a chance to win—but we didn't. Then we did. I kept thinking of the 1975 Series tonight. This is why baseball is the greatest game there is.[11]

Mike Barnicle, columnist for the *Boston Globe*, reflecting on some of the greatest sporting events of the past, and especially the monumental clash between the Red Sox and the Cincinnati Reds in 1975, echoed Pagliarulo's sentiments: "This World Series, though, was different. It was played out on another level, some high and memorable plane that will be recalled for decades."[12]

The Last-to-First World Series was one of the greatest of all time. It will long be remembered for the hesitation, for the extra innings, for the intrigue, and the suspense. Both the Twins and the Braves will remember it as the time they climbed from the basement to the penthouse in one glorious season.

Notes

1. Jim Caple, "Twins Climb from Bottom to the Top," *1991 World Series Souvenir Scorebook*, 68.

2. Michael Martinez, "Two Young Pitchers Are Making Their Marks," *New York Times*, 13 June 1991, Sec. 2, 15.

3. Murray Chass, "Resurgent Twins Are Hurdling Tests That Count," *New York Times*, 22 August 1991, Sec. 2, 17.

4. Murray Chass, "Twins Toss a To-and-Fro Strategy," *New York Times*, 15 September 1991, Sec. 8. 7.

5. Caple, "Twins Climb...," 68.

6. Malcolm Moran, "Two Young Pitchers Are Making Their Marks," *New York Times*, 13 June 1991, Sec. 2. 15.

7. Richard Sandomir, "A Weekend Schedule of None but the Braves," *New York Times*, 4 October 1991, Sec. 2, 9.

8. Michael Madden, "For Atlanta Fans, the Beat Goes On," *Boston Globe*, 14 October 1991, 51.

9. Claire Smith, "Twins Are In, Jays Fall on Heroics by Puckett," *New York Times*, 14 October 1991, Sec. 3, 1.

10. "Series Provides Lasting Images," *Springfield* (MA) *Union-News*, 29 October 1991, 31.

11. Steve Rushin, "A Series to Savor," *Sports Illustrated*, 4 November 1991, 27.

12. Mike Barnicle, "The Game to Remember," *Boston Globe*, 30 October 1991.

14. 1998 Florida Marlins

A Meteoric Fall from the
Pinnacle to the Basement

One of the most precipitous comedowns in major league history occurred in 1998 when the Florida Marlins, who had been the world champions the previous season, plummeted to the basement of the National League East, finishing with a 54–108 record and 52 games behind the division-winning Atlanta Braves.

The Marlins had won the 1997 Fall Classic after only five years in existence. That was the shortest time that any expansion team had needed to make it to the top of baseball. Their 1998 comedown was more a fall for the franchise than for the team. Few of the players who had celebrated the 1997 championship were wearing Marlins' uniforms a year later.

The 1985 Basic Agreement between the players and the owners permitted the National League to add a pair of teams. In 1990 the wheels began to roll toward adding two more teams to the Senior Circuit. The expansion clubs would bring the National League to 14 teams, matching the American League in number.

On September 18, 1990, the league's expansion committee heard presentations from four South Florida groups and from representatives from other parts of the country trying to land one of the new franchises for their area.

The National League announced the finalists on December 18. The areas still in the running were Buffalo, Denver, Orlando, South Florida, Tampa–St. Petersburg, and Washington, D.C.

The group headed by H. Wayne Huizenga was chosen to represent

203

South Florida. With a background in a number of diverse businesses, Huizenga was most prominently recognized as the head of Blockbuster Entertainment Corporation.

Earlier in the year, he had made his first foray into South Florida sports when he spent $30 million to purchase 15 percent of the Miami Dolphins football team and a 50 percent interest in Joe Robbie Stadium, where the Dolphins played their home games.

Huizenga's plan was to have a National League club play in the Miami stadium. On January 26, 1991, renovations began in an effort to convince the expansion committee that the Florida city was one of the two best sites for new franchises. A month later the committee toured Joe Robbie to see if it would meet the standards for a major league park.

At the end of March, a pair of exhibition games between the New York Yankees and the Baltimore Orioles were played there, and they drew over 125,000 fans.

On June 10, 1991, baseball commissioner Fay Vincent announced that Denver and South Florida were the recipients of the two new National League franchises. Two days later, all of the club owners, meeting in Santa Monica, California, unanimously approved the plan.

The Florida club had moved from hope to reality, and they would begin play in 1993. When that day arrived, they would be known as the Marlins. The name was Huizenga's choice:

> When H. Wayne Huizenga made his decision on a nickname for Florida's first Major League Baseball team, he turned to one of his favorite forms of recreation. A long-time sport fisherman, Huizenga dubbed his team the Marlins because the fish is "a fierce fighter and an adversary that tests your mettle." But the selection also has historical basis. From 1956–70 and 1982–88, various minor league clubs in Miami carried the Marlins name.[1]

The playing facility was progressing; the administrative structure was being put in place. In July 1991, Carl Barger, the president of the Pittsburgh Pirates since 1987, took the same post with the Marlins. Later that year, Montreal Expos' general manager Dave Dombrowski joined the Florida club as their first general manager. On November 7, the team hired Fredi Gonzalez to be the Marlins' first minor league manager. He would be the skipper of the Erie Sailors of the New York–Penn League in 1992. The Marlins also planned to operate a team in the Gulf Coast League's Central Division that summer. Carlos Tosca was signed to manage them.

All the new club needed was players. On December 16, 1991, they signed their first Marlin hopeful. Clemente Nuñez, a 16-year-old, right-handed pitcher from the Dominican Republic was inked to a minor league contract.

In February the new franchise held its first-ever tryout camp at Bucky Dent's Baseball School in Delray, Florida. Over 600 hopefuls showed up. Ryan Whitman, a 20-year-old right-hander, was signed at the close of the camp. Southpaw pitcher Mark Stephens became the first Marlins signee to appear in a professional game. His contract had been optioned to the Salinas Spurs of the California League.

Florida had the final pick in the first round of the June 1992 amateur draft, and they chose University of Miami catcher Charles Johnson.

On June 15, Erie played its first game of the season. The last names of some of the players were Clem, Donahue, Lynch, Lucca, Pettit, Roman, Samuels, and Whitman. The Sailors opener was a game of firsts for the Marlins' organization. John Lynch threw the first pitch, Brad Clem had the first at-bat and later collected the first hit, and Lou Lucca drove in Scott Samuels with the Florida franchise's first run.

The Marlins' minor league operation was successful in their initial year of competition. Erie made it to the New York–Penn League finals, before losing to the Geneva Cubs, 6–3 and 7–4. The Gulf Coast Marlins won 14 games in a row, which was tops for any minor league club that season.

In order to provide another stepping stone to the majors, the Marlins signed a two-year agreement, beginning in 1993, with the Triple-A Edmonton Trappers of the Pacific Coast League. Matt Turner, a right-handed pitcher, was the first player signed for the Edmonton roster.

Rene Lachemann was named Florida's first manager on October 23, 1992. He had been a major league coach and manager since May 6, 1981, when he became the skipper of the Seattle Mariners, replacing Maury Wills. Rene selected his older brother, Marcel, to serve as the Marlins pitching coach. Marcel would be joined by coaches Vada Pinson, Doug Rader, Frank Reberger, and Cookie Rojas.

On November 17, major league baseball held its expansion draft to help stock the two new teams which would begin play the following spring.

Scouting Director Gary Hughes spoke about why the Marlins scouts had spent tens of thousands of hours preparing for the draft:

> First of all we wanted to be sure that we had reports on every professional player that was available for the draft. We were looking for long term success rather than immediate success. We were looking for players that would be productive major league players for years to come. As we do with any draft, we were looking for the best athletes available.[2]

After the Colorado Rockies, who had won the first pick by a flip of a coin, selected pitcher David Nied, Florida took Toronto farmhand Nigel Wilson. Wilson, a left-handed hitting outfielder, had played with the Class-AA Knoxville club the previous summer. The Marlins selected 36 players from the other 26 major league rosters during the three rounds of the draft. They also made four trades using some of the players they had acquired in the draft. One of them brought shortstop Walt Weiss from the Oakland Athletics.

Three weeks later, the Marlins participated in their first Rule V draft, adding pitchers Mike Myers and Stanley Spencer as well as outfielder Scott Pose.

In the Rule V draft, which takes place each December, clubs are allowed to take players who are not protected by being placed on another team's 40-man winter roster. (Such a draft doesn't apply to first or second-year players.) When a club takes a player in this draft, it pays $50,000 and agrees to keep him on its 25-man roster for the full season. If they decide not to keep him, he must be offered back for $25,000 to the club which lost him in the draft.

The day after the draft the Marlins signed their first free agents, infielder Dave Magadan, who had been with the New York Mets, and pitcher Charlie Hough, formerly with the Chicago White Sox. Before the month was over the Marlins added first baseman Orestes Destrade, who had played in Japan for four years, and catcher Benito Santiago, who came via the free-agent route from the San Diego Padres.

Tragedy struck the organization on December 9 when Barger collapsed while attending baseball's Winter Meetings in Louisville, Kentucky. The club's first president, who had been instrumental in getting the franchise off the ground during his 17 months on the job, died a few hours later.

After Florida's first spring training, when they went 14–17, they were ready to begin the regular season. Their opening day roster was filled with players who had come through free agency and trades, as well as 12 players who had been selected in the expansion draft. Bret Barbarie, Chuck Carr, Jeff Conine, Bryan Harvey, and Trevor Hoffman had been taken in the first round of the November draft. Jack Armstrong, Ryan Bowen, Cris Carpenter, Steve Decker, Monty Fariss, Junior Felix, and Richie Lewis had been selected in the final two rounds.

On April 5, the Marlins played their inaugural game at Joe Robbie Stadium before a sellout crowd of 42,334. The glitsy pre-game activities were capped off by Joe DiMaggio, Barger's childhood idol, who threw out the first ball.

The home team picked up their first win on a very special day:

After eight decades of watching major league teams head north at the end of spring training, Florida got its first taste of regular-season play today and found the result to their liking as the expansion Florida Marlins defeated the Los Angeles Dodgers, 6–3.[3]

Hough pitched six innings for the win, with Harvey working the ninth and registering his first save. Conine had a perfect day at-bat, going 4-for-4 and scoring a pair of runs.

Each member of the team was wearing a specially designed patch on the right sleeve of his uniform. The name "Carl" appeared at the bottom of the patch as a remembrance of the club's deceased president.

As the season progressed, there were other players who made debuts with the club. Henry Cotto, Robb Nen, Rich Rodriquez, and Gary Sheffield joined the Marlins through trades. Carpenter, Hoffman, and Magadan went to other clubs, although Magadan was reacquired from Seattle in November.

On July 13, Harvey and Sheffield had the honor of representing the Marlins in the All-Star Game. Sheffield responded by homering in his first at-bat.

Florida finished the season in sixth place with a 64–98 record, which was the fifth highest mark of any expansion team in its first year. The Mets were a spot below them in the National League East. The Marlins were big winners at the gate as over 3 million spectators passed through Joe Robbie's turnstiles.

None of the Marlin regulars finished over .300, with Cotto's .296 and Sheffield's .292 leading the way. Destrade powered 20 home runs and had 87 RBIs. Chris Hammond, who had come from Cincinnati in a pre-season trade, was the club's big winner with an 11–12 mark. Harvey racked up 45 saves, which was third best in the league.

On February 21, 1994, Donald A. Smiley became the Marlins' second president, after serving as the club's vice president of sales and marketing. Prior to joining the Florida organization in 1991, Smiley had held a variety of positions with Blockbuster Entertainment Corporation.

The home games during the Marlins' second spring training were played in the new Space Coast Stadium at the Carl F. Barger Complex in Viera, Florida. Their pre-season record was 13–18.

Florida's opening day lineup looked wholly different from the one which had taken the field the previous April. Carr was in center field, and newcomer Jerry Browne was at third base. Former Oakland infielder Kurt Abbott had replaced Weiss, who had gone to Colorado.

In the strike-shortened 1994 season, the Marlins finished in fifth with a 51–64 record. Since both leagues had been divided into three divisions, fifth place was as far as you could fall in the East. Conine's .319 average was the club's high-water mark to that point. Sheffield led the team with 27 homers, and David Weathers' eight wins topped the pitching staff.

The owners opened the gates for the 1995 spring training at the scheduled time, but the players they hoped to see were not there. Since a new Basic Agreement had not been agreed upon, the Players Association had asked players on the major league clubs' 40-man rosters to stay away from the camps. Replacement players went through the exhibition schedule and prepared to wear the uniforms of the major league clubs at the start of the regular season.

On March 31, 1995, the longest strike in sports history ended when U.S. District Court judge Sonya Sontomayer in Manhattan, New York, blocked the owners from implementing new financial working conditions for the players. As a result of the ruling, major league baseball reverted to the rules which had been in operation at the time of the strike. The striking players voted to report to work while the negotiations between the two sides continued.

Soon after the ruling, the Marlins, who were committed to spending the money to build a contender, went into the free-agent market, signing four key players. Pitchers John Burkett and Bobby Witt were added to the roster along with outfielder Andre Dawson and infielder Terry Pendleton.

Johnson, who had caught the attention of Florida scouts with his defensive prowess behind the plate, his rifle-arm, and his power, was ready to take over as the Marlins regular catcher. He had been a Class-A Midwest League All-Star in 1993 and received the same honor in the Class-AA Eastern League in 1994.

He continued to display his defensive skills, but he struggled at the plate early in the 1995 campaign. After hitting only .143 through June 23, he went on a streak and raised his average 93 points before going on the disabled list in August.

Based on Johnson's rookie showing, Dombrowski said:

> There are very few catchers who have more offensive potential. He has the total package as a defensive catcher and is the type of player who you could see on the All-Star team for years to come.[4]

Because of the late start of the regular season, the schedule for each team was shortened by 18 games. Despite painful labor struggles early in the year, baseball fans witnessed a historic event near the end of the campaign. On September 6, Cal Ripken, Jr., broke Lou Gehrig's consecutive-game streak by playing in his 2,131st straight game, and then celebrated with all of baseball during his joyful, ceremonial jaunt around Camden Yards.

In September Smiley expressed optimism about Florida's future:

> After a slow start ... the club turned it up a few notches and delivered exciting baseball to all our fans. We will continue to ... develop and improve. Following the conclusion of the season on October 1 here at Joe Robbie Stadium, the entire organization will be hard at work to make sure the 1996 campaign is the best season yet.[5]

Florida ended 67–76 in 1995, and both their fourth-place finish and their 22½ lengths behind the division winner represented their most competitive showing to date. Sheffield led the hitters at .324, and Conine, who had made his second All-Star appearance and was the game's MVP, hit .302 with 25 home runs. Greg Colbrunn had 23 homers. Rookie second baseman Quilvio Veras, who had come in a trade with the Mets, led the majors with 56 steals. Pat Rapp, taken from the San Francisco Giants in the expansion draft, had an impressive season with a 14–7 record and a 3.44 ERA. Burkett matched him in wins at 14–14.

In 1996 the Marlins struggled through their poorest spring training, going 9–22 with one tie. It wasn't because the organization had been unwilling to spend the money to strengthen the club. During the off-season, Florida added five players from the group of free agents. They signed pitchers Kevin Brown and Al Leiter. Outfielders Joe Orsulak and Devon White and infielder Craig Grebeck also joined the fold. In January the Marlins signed right-handed pitcher Livan Hernandez, who was a Cuban defector. After hearing offers from a number of teams, Hernandez agreed to a 4-year, $4.5 million contract with Florida. All but Grebeck and Hernandez were key contributors during the '96 season.

Through June, the Marlins went 39–41. Their hoped-for improvement wasn't taking shape. On July 7, Lachemann was relieved as the team's manager, and John Boles took over as field general on an interim basis. Boles came down from the front office, where he had served as vice president of player development.

Under Boles, Florida put together a 40–35 record, finishing the campaign 80–82, in third place, and 16 games from the top of the National League East.

On August 26, Joe Robbie Stadium became Pro Player Stadium. Fruit of the Loom, whose sports apparel brand is "Pro Player," had become the facility's corporate sponsor.

Sheffield had a banner year. He hit .314, stroked 42 homers, knocked in 120 runs, and scored 118 times. Edgar Renteria was the only other regular over .300, at .309. Brown, a right-hander, went 17–11 with a major league-leading 1.89 ERA. Leiter, the left-handed part of the tandem, was 16–12 with 200 strikeouts. Nen added 35 saves out of the bullpen.

On October 4, 1996, Jim Leyland was named Florida's third manager. Leyland, who had piloted Pittsburgh for the past 11 years, was considered one of the best managers in the game. He brought over 800 major league wins with him to the Marlins. From 1990 to 1992, his Pirates had finished in first place in the National League East, but they were defeated all three times in the League Championship Series.

After 1992 the Pirates began to cut costs and stayed out of the free-agent market. Leyland continued to do a good job with his club even after some of the most talented players departed for other teams.

With the manager in place, Huizenga, the Marlins' billionaire owner, went deep into his pockets to acquire more free agents. During the spending spree, he committed over $89 million for six players, including Moises Alou, Bobby Bonilla, John Cangelosi, Dennis Cook, Jim Eisenreich, and Alex Fernandez. Three of the new Marlins were franchise players and received substantial packages to sign with Florida.

Bonilla, who had left the Pirates to go to the Orioles during Leyland's tenure, signed a four-year contract worth $23.3 million. Alou, who had been with the Expos, inked a five-year, $25 million agreement. Fernandez, who had gone 16–10 for the White Sox in 1996, agreed to a five-year, $35 million deal.

Suddenly, on paper, Florida was one of the best teams in baseball. They also had one of the highest payrolls for 1997. It was estimated to be in the range of $54 million.

The Marlins got a jump start on the regular season by putting together a remarkable 26–5 spring training record, by far the best in the franchise's history.

It was an exciting summer. Baseball celebrated the 50th anniversary of Jackie Robinson's arrival in Brooklyn, and major league stadiums added his number 42 to the other retired numbers hanging in places of honor. All 28 clubs engaged in interleague play for the first time, enraging some baseball purists.

Florida got off to a fast start in April against the Chicago Cubs and Cincinnati Reds, but soon went on the road where they dropped a total of five straight against San Francisco and Colorado. Nevertheless, the month was a successful one for the club, and they finished 15–10. It was only the second time in the team's history that they won five more games in a month than they lost. The best was yet to come. During May, the Marlins were also plus five, and in June they were plus six. They were dominating in August, going 19–10. As well as Florida was doing, especially at Pro Player Stadium, Atlanta was playing even better and kept the Marlins in their wake.

Early in the season, Brown, Fernandez, and Leiter gave Florida quality work on the mound. Brown, who had held the Cubs to one hit in seven innings on opening day, tossed a no-hitter at the Giants in 3Com Park on June 10. He hit Marvin Bernard with a pitch in the bottom of the eighth to ruin his perfect game, but he was otherwise flawless in the Marlins' 9–0 romp.

Although Florida struggled on the road, especially early in the campaign, they excelled in two critical areas. They went 12–3 against American League clubs, beating Baltimore and Toronto all three times they played, and topping Boston, Detroit and the defending world champion Yankees in two of their three meetings.

Their second important accomplishment was going 8–4 against Atlanta. Rookie left-hander Tony Saunders feasted on the Braves, going 3–0. He was 1–6 against other clubs.

On June 27, Hernandez was recalled from the minors, and the rookie right-hander pitched five innings for his first major league win in Florida's 4–2 victory over Montreal. He went on to win nine in a row before dropping three at the close of the campaign. He became only the second National League pitcher to begin his big league career with nine consecutive victories.

At the All-Star break, the Marlins were 50–36, in second place, 6½ games behind Atlanta. Alou, Brown, and Johnson were chosen to be on the National League squad for the game in Cleveland.

Florida sent second-year outfielder Billy McMillan to the Philadelphia Phillies on July 20 for Darren Daulton, a postseason-tested veteran, to add strength to Leyland's bench. Six days later, Mark Hutton was traded to Colorado for Craig Counsell, who, before the end of the season, became the Marlins' regular second baseman.

Brown continued his masterful pitching and, in mid–July, tossed a one-hitter at the Los Angeles Dodgers in Florida's 5–1 win. A fifth-inning single by Raul Mondesi kept Kevin from getting his second gem of the summer.

After a terrific August, the Marlins entered September with a head of steam. Smiley was eagerly looking ahead:

> With the Marlins tough five starters—Kevin Brown, Al Leiter, and Alex Fernandez, and rookie sensations Livan Hernandez and Tony Saunders—along with one of the top bullpens in the league, and a host of big bats in the lineup, there is no doubt in my mind that Jim Leyland will make this team a contender to the very end.[6]

Early in the month, the Marlins drew to within 2½ games of the Braves, but that was as close as they would come to overtaking them. On September 23, in Montreal, Florida won, 6–3, to clinch a wild-card berth and their first date for the postseason. Appropriately, Brown was on the mound as he won his seventh straight game.

Florida finished the regular season 92–70 and nine lengths behind the Braves.

Although Marlin players were not among the leaders in several offensive categories, many had solid years. Bonilla, who was playing third base for his new team, led the hitters with a .297 average. Alou banged out 23 homers and drove in 115 runs, both career highs for him. Sheffield's average dropped to .250, but he hit 21 home runs.

Fernandez finished at 17–12, and Brown followed with a 16–8 record and a 2.69 ERA. Leiter, who missed some time with a bone bruise on his right knee, was 11–9.

There was a new record holder on the club. Over two years, Johnson caught 171 consecutive games without an error. That accomplishment broke the long-standing major league mark of 147 which had been set in 1947 by Buddy Rosar of the Philadelphia Athletics.

On September 30, Florida met San Francisco in Pro Player Stadium to open the best-of-five-game National League Division Series. The Giants had battled the Dodgers down the stretch to capture the National League West.

Leyland had Brown ready to face the Giants, who he had no-hit in June. Kevin retired the first 14 batters before Stan Javier singled with two outs in the fifth. When Javier attempted to steal second to get into scoring position, he became the victim of Johnson's rifle arm.

San Francisco took the lead in the top of the seventh on Bill Mueller's home run. In the bottom half of inning, Johnson tied the game, 1–1, with a solo shot into the left-field stands off Kirk Rueter.

Cook relieved Brown in the eighth and held San Francisco scoreless in the left-hander's two innings of work. In the bottom of the ninth the Marlins loaded the bases and Renteria singled home Johnson for the winning run in the 2–1 victory.

Leiter, another lefty, was on the mound for game two the next night. He did not fare as well as Cook had in the opener. Al surrendered singletons in the first four innings. Fortunately, Florida was also putting runs on the board, and they were ahead, 5–4, after four. Bonilla's two-run blast in the first and his run-scoring single in the third had accounted for three of the Marlins' tallies.

Hernandez came out of the bullpen to start the fifth. This was a new role for the 22 year old, but he adjusted well, giving up only one run in four innings.

After eight innings, Florida held a slim 6–5 lead. Two errors by the normally steady-fielding Marlins allowed the Giants to score off Nen and tie the game, 6–6. In the bottom of the inning, Florida was the benefactor of a huge break which allowed them to win the game, 7–6. After Sheffield singled and Bonilla walked, Alou shot a sharp single to center. Dante Powell charged the ball and rifled a throw home in an attempt to get Sheffield. The ball was on line and it appeared that it would be in time to nail Sheffield at the plate. However, the ball hit the mound and bounced erratically, allowing Sheffield to score the winning run.

After a day for travel, the two teams were in 3Com Park for the third matchup. The game was not as close as the first two had been. In the top of the sixth, White's eye-popping grand slam gave the Marlins a 4–1 lead. San Francisco countered with a single in the bottom of the frame, making the score, 4–2. Fernandez held the Giants to two runs, both on homers by Jeff Kent, in his seven innings on the hill.

Florida added a pair in the eighth, and Cook and Nen each threw a hitless and scoreless inning to nail down the 6–2 victory and the National League Division Series.

The Marlins were in the National League Championship Series. They traveled to Turner Field, Atlanta, to meet the other National League Division Series winner. The Braves had swept the Houston Astros in three games.

The Marlins brought a season of dominance over the Braves into the League Championship Series. Only a few clubs during Atlanta's decade of dominance had taken the regular season series from the Braves, and the Marlins stood 8–4 in 1997. But, as Florida realized, this was a new season. Pitching usually dominates in a short season like the National League Championship Series, and the Braves were dominating in that phase of the game.

On October 7, Greg Maddux was Atlanta's starter in the opener of the seven-game set. The four-time Cy Young winner had gone 19–4 in 1997. The Marlins got to the crafty right-hander early. With two down in the first, Alou chopped a bases-loaded bouncer down the third-base line which eluded Chipper Jones' outstretched glove. Three runs crossed the plate and Florida was off and running. A key error earlier in the inning by Atlanta's Fred McGriff made the trio of runs unearned. McGriff's single in the bottom of the frame off Brown scored Keith Lockhart to make the score, 3–1.

The Marlins added to their lead in the third by scoring twice. Alou drove in his fourth run of the game and Johnson plated the fifth tally with a double. Maddux, who was used to near flawless fielding behind him, didn't get it that night. For the second time in the game, a critical error helped Florida's cause and the two runs were unearned.

Bases-empty-homers off Brown by Jones and Ryan Klesko accounted for a pair of Braves runs. Kevin lasted six innings and the bullpen came through again. Cook, Jay Powell, and Nen each tossed a hitless and scoreless inning. Florida had a 5–3 victory in its column.

Game two went to Atlanta, 7–1, behind lefty Tom Glavine who worked 7⅔ innings.

Kenny Lofton laid down a bunt to open the bottom of the first. Johnson pounced on it and fired the ball past first base for his first error in 175 games. With Lofton on second, Lockhart tripled to bring home the first run. Atlanta added two more on Jones' homer before Fernandez could get out of the first inning. Klesko stroked a two-run four-bagger in the third.

Florida's Fernandez lasted only 2⅔ frames, and he left the game complaining of the same discomfort in his shoulder that he had felt during the third game of the division series against the Giants. During his short outing, he gave up five runs.

While Glavine, who was 14–7 during the regular season, kept the Marlins' bats quiet, his club added two runs in the seventh to cement the victory. Mark Wohlers and his 100-MPH fastball closed the door on Florida in the ninth.

The next day, the Marlins received news that Fernandez' discomfort was caused by a torn rotator cuff and he was through for the season and, probably, longer.

The series moved to Pro Player Stadium for game three. John Smoltz, who had been the Cy Young winner in 1996 and was 15–12 in '97, went to the mound for the visitors. Leyland gave Saunders the assignment to repeat his magic against the Braves. However, the stakes were much higher this time.

The young left-hander, pitching in front of 53,857 fans, surrendered two runs in 5⅓ innings and left the game trailing 2–1. Hernandez came out of the bullpen again, and he finished out the sixth and pitched the seventh, giving up a pair of hits.

In the bottom of the sixth, Florida added four runs to take a 5–2 lead. Johnson was the main man in the Marlins rally. Renteria doubled with one out and Sheffield walked. Bonilla drove a shot to the warning track in left which Klesko tracked down for the second out. Daulton doubled to right, scoring Renteria and tying the game, 2–2. Smoltz walked White intentionally to load the bases.

That appeared to be a good strategy on the Braves' part. Johnson, who was the next batter, had yet to get a hit in 12 appearances in his career against Smoltz. Also, the Florida catcher had been up with the bases jammed on 13 occasions during the season and was still looking for his first hit. The Braves' tactic backfired when Johnson blasted a three-run double into the gap in left-centerfield.

Florida's bullpen went into action for the final two innings, trying to protect the home club's 5–2 lead. Cook and Nen were perfect, holding the Braves without a hit or a run.

Game four was another pitching masterpiece by an Atlanta hurler. Denny Neagle, the club's fourth starter, took a regular season mark of 20–5 into the game. He went the distance, surrendering only four singles. Leiter, who gave up all four Atlanta runs in six innings, took the loss.

The fifth game was played in Miami, and it was a pitching matchup between Maddux, a seasoned veteran, and Hernandez, an up-and-coming youngster.

Hernandez opened the game by giving up a triple to Lofton and walking Lockhart. With runners at first and third, he proceeded to strikeout the heart of the Braves order—Jones, McGriff, and Klesko.

Florida scored in the bottom of the first when Maddux, who is one of baseball's most-accomplished control pitchers, hit White with a pitch and then threw one away, moving the Marlins' lead-off batter to second. With one out, Bonilla drove a pitch the opposite way for a single, and White scored. In the top of the second, Michael Tucker blasted one of Hernandez's deliveries to dead center field for a game-tying homer.

During the rest of the evening, most of the attention was on Hernandez. With some help from home-plate umpire Eric Gregg's expanded strike zone, the right-hander chalked up 15 strikeouts, which was a National League Championship Series record. The Braves touched him for only three hits in his route-going performance.

Florida scored the go-ahead run in the bottom of the seventh. Bonilla drove a ball deep to right-field and Tucker appeared to have it in his glove, but it was dislodged when he collided with the wall. With Bobby on second, Conine singled to give Florida a 2–1 lead, which was all Hernandez needed. The Marlins took a 3–2 lead in the series.

Leland had been hoping to bring Brown back for his second start in either game four or five, but an ongoing bout with a viral infection kept Florida's ace on the sidelines. When the series was resumed in Atlanta on October 14, Brown was ready to go against Glavine. He struggled early but ended up going the distance.

Florida broke on top with four in the first, one better than they had done in the opener against Maddux. Glavine, another control pitcher, walked the bases loaded, and Bonilla's two-run single gave the Marlins a lead they would not relinquish in their 7–4, League Championship Series–clinching win.

The major league's Cinderella team had gone 8–4 against Atlanta during the regular season. In the postseason, they were 4–2. That was a pattern very few had expected.

The Marlins' wild-card ticket to the postseason was taking them to one more stop—Cleveland. The Indians won the American League Central Division with an 86–75 record and finished six games in front of the White Sox. They topped the Yankees, 3–2, in the American League Division Series and beat the Orioles, 4–2, in the League Championship Series.

The Fall Classic opened on October 18, in Miami. Pro Player Stadium was jammed with 67,245 excited and hopeful fans.

Leyland, who was in his first World Series, chose Hernandez to start for Florida in their historic first Fall Classic game. Orel Hershiser, who the Marlins had beaten in the franchise's first game in 1993, was on the hill for Cleveland. Hershiser had a 14–6 record during the 1997 regular season.

With the score tied, 1–1, in the fourth inning, Alou hit a three-run homer, and Johnson followed with a titanic 438-foot shot into the upper deck in left field. That was the 11th time that players had hit back-to-back home runs in the long history of the World Series.

Conine, who had gone 4-for-4 against the Dodgers ace in the club's inaugural game and was the only Marlin left from that team, drove Hershiser from the mound in the fifth with a run-scoring single.

Hernandez, who went 5⅔ innings, Cook, Powell, and Nen spaced out four Indians runs, two of which came on homers off the bats of Jim Thome and Manny Ramirez. The Marlins and Hernandez picked up a 7–4 victory in the opener.

In the second game, Brown was matched up against Chad Ojea who had gone 8–9 in '97. Kevin, still not feeling up to par, struggled for six innings, giving up six runs and 10 hits. Cleveland scored in the top of the first and then a series of singles in the fifth led to three more runs. Sandy Alomar sent one out of the park for one of the two tallies off Brown in the next inning. Cleveland won, 6–1, and the Marlins ace suffered his first loss since July 27.

With the Series tied, 1–1, the scene shifted to Jacobs Field, Cleveland. The third game was far from a masterpiece. The four-hour-and-12-minute affair was played in temperatures which were a few degrees above freezing. Each team committed three errors, and the pitchers combined to issue 17 bases on balls. Leiter and the Indians' Charles Nagy [15–11] were both ineffective, giving up 12 runs between them in a combined 10⅔ innings on the mound.

When Leiter left the game with two outs in the fifth, Cleveland held a 7–5 lead. The Marlins battled back and had tied the game, 7–7, going into the top of the ninth. That set the stage for one of the strangest innings in the Fall Classic's history.

Bonilla scored the go-ahead run when center fielder Marquis Grissom overthrew third base as Bobby was hustling from first to third on a single. Six more runs crossed the plate before Jose Mesa retired the Marlins, who had built a 14–7 advantage.

Nen, who had given up only one run in five postseason appearances, surrendered four more in Cleveland's at-bat in the bottom of the ninth. He finally got Omar Vizquel to ground out to end the 14–11 slugfest.

Sheffield, who was battling a windchill factor in the 20s, singled, doubled, homered, and drove in five runs during the uncomfortable night for baseball. Eisenreich, the designated hitter, and Daulton, who was playing first base, also contributed key hits in the Marlins' win.

The following night, the shoe was on the other foot as the Indians and rookie right-hander Jaret Wright [8–3] beat Saunders, one of Florida's rookie hurlers. Saunders, who had been the master of the Braves but not any other team, struggled during his two-inning stint, giving up six runs.

Wright, on the other hand, went six innings and held a 7–3 lead when he departed. The Indians continued to build from there for their 10–3 victory.

Alou's two-run homer in the sixth couldn't counterbalance home runs by Matt Williams and Ramirez and eight other Cleveland hits.

With the Series deadlocked, 2–2, game five was a high scoring, back-and-forth, 8–7 encounter. Florida scored twice in the top of the second to take the lead, but the Indians put one on the scoreboard in the bottom of the inning. Alomar homered with two on in the third to put Cleveland ahead, 4–2. Alou responded with a three-run blast to center in the sixth to give the advantage back to the Marlins, 5–4. Florida added another run in the same inning and then scored in the eighth and ninth to stretch the lead to 8–4.

After throwing 134 pitches, Hernandez struggled in the bottom of the ninth, and the Indians scored twice before he could retire a batter. Nen came into the game in relief and gave up Cleveland's seventh run before Alomar flied out to end the game. Florida was ahead in the Series, 3–2.

On October 25, the Fall Classic resumed in 80-degree weather in Miami. The Marlins needed one win to claim the crown as World Champions.

It did not happen that night as Ojea and three Cleveland relievers sent Brown, who lasted five innings, to his second loss, 2–1. Before leaving the game in the fifth, the offensive-minded Ojea had driven in a pair of runs with a single in the second inning and scored another in the fifth. Alou was the only Marlin to cross the plate.

The season had been reduced to a single game. Leiter and Wright were the starters, but five other pitchers for each club went to the mound before the Marlins captured the hard-fought contest, 3–2, in 11 innings.

Second baseman Tony Fernandez's two-run single in the top of the third gave Cleveland a 2–0 start. Bonilla, who had been suffering with hamstring problems during the Series, homered in the bottom of the seventh to narrow the gap to 2–1.

In the bottom of the ninth, Alou started what might have been the Marlins' final at-bat with a single. After Mesa struck out Bonilla, Johnson singled to right and Alou raced to third. Counsell scored Moises with a sacrifice fly, knotting the game, 2–2, and sending it into extra innings.

Neither team scored in the 10th inning of the season's most important matchup. Cleveland also failed to add a run in the top of the eleventh. Bonilla open the bottom half of the inning by touching Nagy for a single. The Cleveland starter-turned-reliever retired Greg Zaun, who had run for Johnson in the ninth and had taken his place behind the plate.

Counsell bounced a tailor-made double-play ball toward Fernandez, but the sure-fielding second baseman didn't make the play. Bonilla dashed to third on the miscue which kept the inning alive. Eisenreich was walked intentionally to load the bases. White, the next batter, chopped a ball toward second and the hard-charging Fernandez fired it home to force Bonilla.

With two outs, Renteria brought the Series to a glorious end for the home team and their fans by singling to score a jubilant Counsell.

The Marlins were World Champions. Hernandez picked up the Fall Classic's Most Valuable Player Award. Florida had made it to the pinnacle of baseball in their fifth season of major league play—three less than it had taken the 1969 Mets to get there. In amazing fashion, the Marlins had accomplished it from the wild-card spot in the postseason's starting gate.

Before the celebrating had died down, a new sound was heard in Marlinland. Huizenga was talking about all the money the championship season had cost him. He spoke about the huge financial losses he had suffered while the club was capturing the crown.

Huizenga began to dismantle the club, player by player, in a cost-cutting measure. By the end of the following May, the club's 1997 payroll of just under $54 million had been reduced by nearly $42 million.

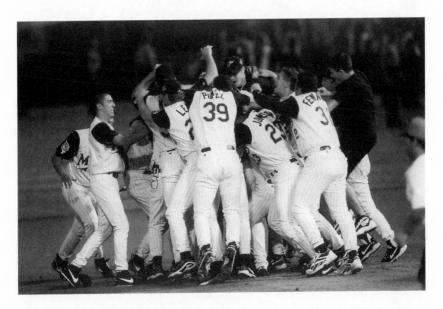

The Florida Marlins celebrate their 1997 World Championship (Florida Marlins).

Florida's demolition derby began on October 31 when Daulton became a free agent after the Marlins did not pick up the 1998 option on his contract.

Eleven days later, Alou, a member of the 1997 All-Star team, was traded to Houston. Florida received Oscar Henriquez, Manuel Barrios, and a player to be named later to replace Moises' .292 batting average, 23 home runs, 115 RBIs, and the remaining four years of his five-year, $25 million contract.

November 18 was a decisive day in the Marlins' restructuring. Atlanta-killer Saunders, along with minor leaguers Mike Duvall and Randy Winn, were taken by the Tampa Bay Devil Rays in the expansion draft. Right-handed pitcher Kurt Miller was sent to the Cubs for a player to be named later. White was dealt to the Arizona Diamondbacks, the other expansion team, for Jesus Martinez. The final move sent Nen, the Marlins' top closer, to San Francisco for three players without major league experience.

Two days later, left-hander Ed Vosberg was traded to San Diego in exchange for Chris Clark. Conine, the last of the original Marlins, left the club, going to Kansas City for Blaine Mull.

On December 12 the Marlins released Alex Arias, and three days later Brown and his large contract became the property of the Padres, and Derrek Lee, Steve Hoff, and Rafael Medina became Marlins. Cook, who had been effective out of the bullpen during the postseason, was traded to the Mets on December 18 for a pair of minor leaguers. Abbott became a member of the A's the following day as Eric Ludwick came east.

After Leiter went to the Mets, along with infielder Ralph Milliard, in a trade on February 6, Florida's pitching staff had been decimated. None of the Marlins' new hurlers held the promise of replacing Brown, Leiter, and Nen in 1998. Fernandez, who had rotator-cuff surgery, was expected to be on the disabled list for the entire season.

Opening day was a day for celebrating. On March 31, the World Championship banner was raised in Pro Player Stadium. After the festivities, the new edition of the Marlins defeated the Cubs, 11–6, with Hernandez registering the win.

On April 5, in pre-game ceremonies, World Series rings were given to the remaining members of the previous year's club. Most of the heroes of the championship season were not there for the presentation, which was followed by a 5–2 loss to the Milwaukee Brewers, the new team in the National League.

Florida was in the midst of an 11-game losing streak which began the second day of the season. During late May and early June, the Marlins suffered through 11 straight losses again. On the positive side, they put together one four-game winning streak from July 10 to 13.

On May 15, Barrios, Bonilla, Eisenreich, Johnson, and Sheffield were packaged in a blockbuster deal with the Dodgers. The Marlins received Mike Piazza and Todd Zeile from Los Angeles. Piazza, who would be eligible for free agency following the 1998 season, had not been able to make a deal with Los Angeles. Before the trade, the All-Star catcher had turned down a potentially record-setting $85 million, seven-year offer from the Dodgers.

One week later, on May 22, Piazza was traded to the New York Mets in exchange for outfielder Preston White, left-handed pitcher Ed Yarnall, and the ever-popular player to be named later. After Piazza's trade, Florida's payroll had shrunk to $12 million. The Marlins had dealt away most of the players who had delivered the 1997 championship. Of the 25 players who had appeared in the World Series, 15 were gone. Florida was retooling with young prospects and a much smaller payroll.

At the time of the mammoth trade with the Dodgers, Florida was sitting in the basement of the National League East. They had fallen there on April 10 after a 4–1 loss to Pittsburgh. From that point on, with the exception of eight days in late April and early May when they were in fourth place or tied for fourth, the Marlins spent the rest of the season in the cellar.

Some of the day-to-day players were Cangelosi, Counsell, Todd Dunwoody, Cliff Floyd, Ryan Jackson, Mark Kotsay, Lee, Renteria, and Zaun. Jackson was in the majors for the first time, and Dunwoody, Kotsay, and Lee had each played fewer than 25 games in 1997, which was their first year in the big leagues.

The club's "big-three" in the starting rotation were Hernandez, along with rookies Brian Meadows and Jesus Sanchez. Antonio Alfonseca, rookie Vic Darensbourg, Matt Mantei, and Rob Stanifer were Leyland's first pitchers out of the bullpen.

On June 22, two major league teams from Florida met during the regular season for the first time. The opening interleague matchup between the expansion Devil Rays and the Marlins took place in Tropicana Field in St. Petersburg. The Marlins won, 3–2, in 11 innings. The following night, Tampa Bay was victorious, 6–4. The series moved to Pro Player for the third and fourth games. They went to Florida by the scores of 8–4 and 5–1. The Marlins would at least be the 1998 Florida champions.

As the season progressed they fell deeper into the hole as the distance between the division leader and themselves increased. On July 4, the Marlins were 31–55 and 26½ games behind Atlanta, who had led most of the way. On September 11, Florida lost its 100th game and fell to 46 lengths behind the Braves. The champs finished 54–108 and 54 games below Atlanta.

The Marlins continued to clean house throughout the summer. On July 5, Powell was traded to the Astros, and Felix Heredia, also a pitcher, went to the Cubs on the final day of the month.

Team and individual statistics illustrated the Marlins' long struggle. Their .248 batting average placed them just above the Diamondbacks, who had the weakest offensive performance in the majors at .246. Floyd's .282 average, 22 home runs, and 90 RBIs led the club's regulars. Renteria was also at .282 and Kotsay finished with a .279 average.

Florida's combined 5.18 ERA was the highest in the National League. Meadows, with an 11–13 record and a 5.21 ERA, had the most wins and most losses on the staff. Hernandez worked a team-high 234⅓ innings on his way to a 10–12 record and 4.7 earned runs per game. Joe Fontenot, who had come to the Marlins in the trade with the Giants for Nen, had eight starts, went 0–7, and posted a 6.33 ERA.

Mantei, the Marlins' most effective reliever, had nine saves in 42 appearances and posted the club's only sub–3.00 ERA, at 2.96. Alfonseca followed with eight saves and Powell contributed seven. By comparison, Nen had racked up 35 in 1997.

Florida also stumbled at the box office. Pro Player welcomed 1,750,395 spectators, which was almost 614,000 fewer that in 1997.

By the end of the campaign, only Alfonseca, Cangelosi, Counsell, Floyd, Hernandez, Renteria, and Zaun remained from the 1997 World Championship team. Cangelosi, Renteria, and Zaun would join the list of the departed before the start of the 1999 season.

Shortly after managing his final game of 1998, Leyland stepped down as Florida's skipper. The following day, October 2, Boles began his second term as the Marlins manager.

Besides cutting the budget, Huizenga had been actively trying to sell the franchise. On January 19, 1999, John W. Henry, who was in the investment business, closed the deal to purchase the Marlins. Henry also brought a baseball background to the franchise. He had been an owner of the Pacific Coast League team in Tucson as well as the West Palm Beach Tropics of the defunct Senior Professional League.

The people of South Florida had experienced the thrill of climbing to the heights of baseball and, one year later, had watched their club plummet to the worst record in the National League since 1969.

Notes

1. *Florida Marlins 1998 Media Guide*, 6.
2. Adolfo Salgueiro, "Birth of the Marlins," *Marlins Opening Day Magazine*, 5 April 1993, 12.
3. Larry Rohter, "It's All Sunshine in Florida Debut," *New York Times*, 6 April 1993, Sec. 2, 12.
4. Chase Campen, "Top Gun," *Marlins Magazine*, 1995, Vol. 3, Edition 5, 20.
5. "President's Message, *Marlins Magazine*, 1995, Vol. 3, Edition 5, 6.
6. Don Smiley, *Marlins Magazine*, September 1997, Vol. 5, Issue 6, 6.

15. 1999 New York Mets

An Amazing Comedown and
an Amazing Comeback

The final regular season of the 20th century witnessed another memorable collapse. The New York Mets stunned their loyal fans by performing a freefall which appeared to have eliminated any hope they had of appearing in the postseason for the first time since 1986. In 1998 and now in 1999 it was almost as if Flatbush's familiar fate of the 40s and 50s had been transported on the wings of disappointment to Flushing. Yet, just when it appeared as if a much-too-early end to a season of heightened expectation would bring the recurrent pain of what could have been, the Mets made a miraculous climb back into contention for the final spot in the National League Division Series.

In 1969, the "Amazin" Mets thrilled their fans, awakened the baseball world, and seized the major-league crown. A late-season rush propelled them past the Chicago Cubs in the National League East. The Mets followed the surge by taking three straight from the Atlanta Braves in the National League Championship Series, and then completed their amazin' mission by defeating the heavily-favored Baltimore Orioles in five games to win the World Series.

Thirty years later, in 1999, the Mets were amazing again. Two weeks before the end of the regular season, manager Bobby Valentine's New Yorkers, who were trailing the Braves by one game, went into Atlanta's Turner Field to face the division-leaders, who were in a dogfight with the New York Yankees for the title "Best Team of the 90s."

In 1990 Atlanta had finished in the cellar of the National League West,

223

but since that time they had been in the postseason seven of the eight years. Their only non-postseason year was 1994 because, simply put, baseball, shut down by the strike, did not have a postseason. The Braves beat the Cleveland Indians in 1995 to win the World Series, and battled to the Fall Classic three other times.

The 1999 Mets, who appeared to have a lock on no less than a wild-card ticket to the postseason, had dreams of upending the Braves in Atlanta in the three-game set beginning September 21. A winning series in Atlanta would set the stage for a monumental matchup against the Braves the following week in Shea Stadium. That series would be for the division championship.

The Mets had struggled early in the 1999 campaign and in June, after the team's first 55 games, things were going so poorly that three of the club's coaches were unceremoniously dismissed. Valentine predicted that he too would be fired after the next 55 games if his club didn't straighten itself out. Bobby, who was in his 12th season as a major league manager, the last three with the Mets, had yet to take a team to the postseason. It looked as if he would not get there in 1999 either.

During the next 55 games the team played amazing baseball, compiling the best record in the majors over that stretch by winning 40 games and losing only 15 times.

New York trailed the Braves by only one game at the start of series in Atlanta. The Mets also held a four-length lead for the wild-card spot over the low-budget Cincinnati Reds, who were the surprise club in the National League Central Division and stood in second place behind the Houston Astros.

The opener in Atlanta was the first of the Mets' final 14 games of the season. During that span, the National League East's top two clubs would face each other six times.

Braves third baseman Chipper Jones' two home runs powered Atlanta to a 2–1 victory in game one. In the bottom of the first inning he hit a solo shot off Rick Reed to give his club a 1–0 lead. The Mets tied the game, 1–1, in the third, but Jones hit another four-bagger in the eighth to provide the margin of victory.

The next night Jones homered again in the first inning, but this time with a man on base, and Atlanta jumped out to a 2–0 lead. They were on their way to a 5–2 win.

A 6–3 loss in the series finale left the mesmerized Mets four games behind the Braves. An outspoken Jones, who was soon to incur the wrath of the Mets' fans in Shea, suggested that New Yorkers "drag their Yankee gear out of the closet because the Mets were finished."[1]

While the Mets were losing, the Reds were taking two-out-of-three from the Padres in San Diego. Cincinnati was now just two games behind the Mets in the wild-card race.

For the second year in a row, New York stood on the verge of a colossal collapse that would cost them an appearance in the postseason. In 1998 they had lost the final five games of the season, including the last three to the Braves in Atlanta, and that had cost them a wild-card berth. Had they won but one of those five games, they would have at least been part of the playoff between the Cubs and the San Francisco Giants for the final postseason spot.

But the 1999 Mets were a different team from the one which had ignominiously faded the previous season. Third baseman Robin Ventura was hitting .308 at the start of the Atlanta series, and outfielders Benny Agbayani [.292], Roger Cedeño [.320], Shawon Dunston [.320], Darryl Hamilton [.317], and Rickey Henderson [.326] had also added punch to the New York lineup. Pitchers Armando Benitez, Octavio Dotel, Orel Hershiser, Pat Mahomes, Chuck McElroy, Kenny Rogers, and Billy Taylor were all new to the Mets' 1999 roster. Rogers had gone 5–0 since being acquired from the Oakland Athletics and pitching his first game for his new club on July 28. Hershiser, who had been with the Giants in 1998, was the club's top winner with a 13–10 record.

After their disappointing stop in Atlanta, the Mets could find some solace in the fact that they were heading to Veterans Stadium, Philadelphia, to face the floundering Phillies. Philadelphia sat in third place in the National League East, 25 games behind the front-running Braves. The Phils had dropped 23 of their last 27 games.

Philadelphia pulled out a come-from-behind, 3–2 victory in the opener on September 24. With the Mets' Masato Yoshii holding a 2–1 lead after seven innings, Valentine went to his bullpen in the bottom of the eighth. Lefty Dennis Cook walked pinch-hitter Kevin Sefcik, the Phils' lead-off batter. The Mets manager summoned Turk Wendell to the mound, and the right-hander retired the next two Phillies. Valentine called the bullpen again and brought in Benitez, the team's fire-balling closer, to get the final out of the game. However, Bobby Abreu greeted Benitez with a run-scoring double to tie the game, 2–2, and Mike Lieberthal followed with a single to drive in the winning run.

The following afternoon, former Met Robert Person, who had been traded to the Toronto Blue Jays before the 1987 season for first baseman John Olerud, took the hill for Philadelphia. The Phillies faced Rogers, who, coming off a hamstring injury, was unusually wild. The Phils' first two runs crossed the plate on back-to-back home runs in the second inning by Lieberthal and Rico Brogna, also a former Met. Person went six strong innings and left with a 4–0 lead. Philadelphia eventually took the second game, 4–2.

Following the Mets' fifth consecutive loss, Valentine made a pronouncement. Perhaps this would produce the same results as his stunning words after the first 55 games had done. The frustrated New York skipper said:

> As crazy as it gets, I probably shouldn't come back next year but that's not my decision.... If we don't get into the playoffs I shouldn't. But that would be an easy decision if we don't get to the playoffs. I'm not making anybody's decision.[2]

Paul Byrd, another ex–Met, was the Phillies pitcher on the next-to-last Sunday afternoon of the regular season. Brogna powered another home run, Byrd had a strong outing, and the Mets dropped the game 3–2.

During the Mets' six-game losing streak, their stone-cold offense had produced only 12 runs. By and large, the batters had been unable to get the key hits to drive home the baserunners—and the Mets had their share of baserunners.

While the Mets were dropping the series finale in Philadelphia, the red-hot Reds were beating the St. Louis Cardinals, 7–5, in 12 innings. With the win, Cincinnati vaulted one game ahead of New York in the wild-card race. The Reds were also closing in on the division-leading Astros.

New York had a day off to ponder their deteriorating situation and to prepare to welcome the Braves to Shea Stadium for three games. On September 27, while the Mets rested, the Reds were winning. They beat the Cardinals again and moved into a tie with Houston for the Central Division lead.

The change of venue didn't help the Mets in the opener, and their freefall continued. Atlanta thumped New York, 9–3, and chased Hershiser from the mound after just 24 pitches and one-third of an inning of work. It was the veteran right-hander's shortest outing in 459 career starts. Hershiser left trailing, 3–0, and the Mets never challenged the Braves and Tom Glavine, who gave up only one run and six hits in seven innings.

That same day, Cincinnati continued its blistering pace by beating Houston, 4–1, and taking a one-game division lead. The Mets were now chasing the Astros for the wild-card ticket, and they stood 1½ lengths behind.

The Mets saw a ray of hope in Shea Stadium the next night. Greg Maddux, seeking his 20th victory of the season, was the victim of a Mets seven-run uprising in the fourth inning. Olerud's grand slam was the big blow as New York got eight straight hits off Maddux. The Mets beat the Braves,

9–2, and ended their seven-game losing streak. Meanwhile, in Houston the Astros topped the Reds, and the two clubs were tied again for the lead in the Central Division with 95–64 records. Suddenly, there was also a wild-card race again.

With Cincinnati and Houston idle the next night, the Mets had a disheartening outing in the finale against the Braves. After coming from behind and tying the game, 3–3, on Edgardo Alfonso's 26th home run of the season in the bottom of the eighth inning, the game went into extra innings. In the top of the 11th, Brian Jordan tripled and came home on Ozzie Guillen's sacrifice fly to put Atlanta ahead, 4–3. New York failed to score in the bottom of the inning, suffering their eighth loss in nine games.

The Mets, now two full lengths behind in the wild-card derby, stumbled into the final series of the regular season against the Pittsburgh Pirates. While the Mets and Pirates were doing battle in Flushing, the Astros were finishing at home against the Los Angeles Dodgers, and the Reds were in Milwaukee to meet the Brewers.

David Waldstein, writing in the *New York Post*, set the scene for New York's October 1 opener against Pittsburgh. He wrote of the Mets,

> They had lost eight of the previous nine games and were in need of a small miracle to get them in the playoffs....
> If three different games ended in a certain way, the Mets would be eliminated by the end of the night.[3]

A small Mets miracle did in fact happen that night, keeping them alive for the postseason. They topped the Pirates, 3–2, in 11 innings. Dunston, pinch-hitting for Mahomes, led off the final frame with a single. Dramatically, with two outs, Ventura drove him home with a double to end the game. Earlier, New York had relied on home runs with Ventura slamming one in the fourth and Mike Piazza, who had been mired in a horrible batting slump, powering a four-bagger in the bottom of the sixth. Mahomes, with two innings of effective relief, raised his record to 8–0.

The same day in Houston, the struggling Astros dropped their ninth game in 13 outings, losing to the Dodgers, 5–1. Cincinnati followed suit, falling to the Brewers in County Stadium, 4–3, in 10 innings. The two National League Central clubs remained tied, leaving the Mets a single game behind in the race for the National League's wild card.

The Mets' comeback continued on Saturday night, October 2, as they blanked Pittsburgh, 7–0. Reed went the distance to register the shutout, giving up three hits and posting a career-high 12 strikeouts. Piazza homered for the second straight day.

The Mets had taken the field knowing the outcomes of the two matchups that affected them. Cincinnati had dropped another game, losing to Milwaukee in a 10–6 slugfest. That meant that a win by New York would create a tie for the wild card. Houston had taken a one-game lead over the Reds in the Central Division by shutting out Los Angeles, 3–0, behind Jose Lima who won his 21st game to go with 10 losses.

As New York prepared to meet Pittsburgh on the final day of the regular season, the Mets knew that their season had been reduced to three options: they would either be the wild-card entrant in the National League Division Series; they would need to win a sudden-death game to earn their ticket to the postseason; or their season would unceremoniously end.

That fateful Sunday afternoon in the final game of the regular season, the Mets' Hershiser, trying to rebound from his shortest career start, surrendered a run in the top of the first to provide Pittsburgh a 1–0 lead. After that, however, he held the Pirates to a pair of hits during his 5⅓ innings on the mound. Olerud scored the tying run in the fifth, and the game remained knotted until the bottom of the ninth.

New York rookie reserve outfielder Melvin Mora, who was 4-for-30 in his brief major league career, slapped a one-out single to give the Mets a baserunner. Alfonso followed with a single to right, sending Mora to third. Flushing's favorites were 90 feet away from victory. The Mets and their fans, who thought they had seen the end in sight a few days earlier, now were hopeful again.

The Pirates intentionally walked Olerud to load the bases and bring up Piazza, who was the 1999 league leader in hitting into double plays. Piazza didn't have to swing the bat as reliever Brad Clontz, who had pitched briefly for the Mets in 1998, uncorked a wild pitch on his first delivery to the New York catcher. Mora made the 90-foot dash to the plate for the winning run.

Ralph Branca, who 48 years earlier to the day had delivered the unforgettable pitch to Bobby Thomson in the Polo Grounds in uptown Manhattan, was in the stands from the sixth inning on, watching and cheering for the Mets in their exciting comeback. He had a special rooting interest: Valentine is his son-in-law.

Branca had arrived late because he had a commitment to be at a card show in South Jersey earlier in the day. The game was tied, 1–1, as Branca was moving to his seat. Valentine had just gone to the bullpen to replace the 41-year-old Hershiser with Cook.

Branca knew about trips from the bullpen to the mound in the heat of a critical late-season game. He remembered Burt Shotton's call for him, rather than Carl Erskine, to replace Don Newcombe and face Thomson. He remembered too well his second pitch to the New York Giants outfielder, and the fly ball that sailed into history as "The Shot Heard Round the World."

Following the game, Ralph was in a good mood. He said, "Oct. 3 owed one to the Branca family.... This takes away 80 percent. But it still owes us."[4]

With the Mets now one-half game ahead of Cincinnati, their agonizing wait began. Houston, who could have ended the day tied for the division lead, beat Los Angeles, 9–4, and nailed down the Central Division crown by two games over the Reds.

The Reds and the Brewers, whose game was scheduled to start at 4:00 P.M. EST, were in a lengthy rain delay in County Stadium. The game did not get under way until 5 hours, 47 minutes later. When it did, approximately 500 chilled fans were left to greet the action. In the third inning, Cincinnati left fielder Greg Vaughn's three-run homer highlighted the Reds' five-run rally. They went on to win, 7–1, with Pete Harnisch and Ron Villone combining for the six-hit shutout. There would be a playoff showdown.

After losing five of six crucial games to the Braves, a three-game set in Philadelphia to the going-nowhere Phillies, and being virtually buried by the New York media, the Mets had miraculously comeback to gain one more chance to make it to the postseason.

The Mets and the Reds met in Cincinnati's Cinergy Field on Monday, October 4. The winner would fly to Phoenix to face the Arizona Diamondbacks, the champions of the National League West, in the Division Series. The loser would go home.

New York took charge of the game from the opening pitch and, after six pitches, led, 2–0. Henderson, the Mets lead-off hitter, delivered a sharp single to left. Alfonso followed with a home run to deep center field, and the Mets had two runs on the board. Later in the game, Alfonso added an RBI double and Henderson banged a home run down the left-field line.

Left-hander Al Leiter, who had pitched in the postseason for the 1997 World Champion Florida Marlins, was at the top of his game against the Reds. He went the distance for the first time in 1999, shutting out Cincinnati, 5–0, while striking out seven and allowing only two hits.

Following the victory, Hershiser spoke about the season's difficulties:

> We've come back from devastating things twice. There was the devastation of the coaches [being fired] and the devastation of all the losses in a row at Atlanta that left us with only the chance at the wild card.[5]

The usually hard-hitting Mets were showing signs of recovering from their lean times. One of New York's strong suits throughout the season was their defense. The team set the major league record for the fewest errors [68] and were the only National League club to have less than 100 boots in 1999. Rey Ordóñez, the Mets' talented shortstop, ended the season with a best-ever, 100-consecutive-errorless-games streak intact. The club's stellar fielding also led to the Mets' allowing only 30 unearned runs, also a record.

The Mets starting pitching had been another matter. At times during the season, it was their Achilles' heel. Now the starters were driving the comeback.

New York, which had not been to the postseason since 1988, had made it after being two games down with three to go. The 1962 San Francisco Giants had been the last team to accomplish the feat.

Valentine would be there for the first time after 12 years and 1,407 games as a major-league manager. Reliever John Franco, the Brooklyn kid, would be playing after the regular season, which was something he hadn't done during his 16 years in the majors.

Some questioned whether the Mets, who had gone through the draining collapse followed by the exciting comeback, would have enough left to challenge Arizona in the upcoming series.

The expansion Diamondbacks were another 1999 comeback team, having put together the greatest one-year turnaround in major-league history. In 1998 their record had been 65–97. A year later, they won 35 more games than the previous season. The 1903 Giants had improved by 34½ games from the year before and had held the mark until Arizona bettered them.

Arizona won the division title in their second season of play, which was also a record. The previous record-holders, the 1969 Mets and the 1976 Royals, had taken eight seasons to capture their first division flag. The Diamondbacks' first trip to the postseason took one year less than it had taken the 1997 Marlins, who had made it as a wild-card team and eventually won the World Series.

In the opener, New York had the monumental and unenviable task of facing 6'10" left-hander Randy Johnson. Johnson was 17–9 for the season with a 2.48 ERA. He was one of the most overpowering pitchers in the game and had racked up 364 strikeouts during the campaign, one of the highest totals in baseball history. The challenge did not deter the red-hot Mets.

In the top of the first inning, Alfonso, the second batter, homered to give New York a 1–0 lead. They went ahead 3–0 in the top of the third before Arizona scored once in the bottom of the inning off Yoshii, the Mets starter. Ventura led off the fourth for New York with a double and later scored to make it 4–1. In the bottom half of the frame, Erubiel Durazo,

Arizona's first baseman who had begun the season with Double-A El Paso and had come to the majors in July, homered to make the score 4–2.

In the bottom of the sixth, Diamondback left fielder Luis Gonzalez hit a two-run, 452-foot blast into the right-field seats which tied the game and drove Yoshii from the mound. The game remained 4–4 until the top of the ninth when Ventura led off with a single and, with one out, Ordonez followed suit. After Johnson walked Mora to load the bases, manager Buck Showalter replaced him with Bobby Chouinard. On a 3-and-1 count, Alfonso homered just inside the left-field foul pole. Four runs crossed the plate and New York led 8–4, the final score. Strong relief by Cook, Wendell, and Benitez had kept Arizona off the board after Yoshii's departure. Along with batting stars Alfonso and Ventura, Olerud delivered three hits which produced a pair of runs.

The first game was in the book and, surprisingly, Johnson had suffered his sixth successive postseason defeat.

Rogers and Todd Stottlemyre matched up in game two. Once again, the Mets got on the board first, scoring in the top of the third. Arizona came right back in the bottom of the inning and took a 3–1 lead. Steve Finley, who was the game's hitting star, singled in two of the three runs. In the fifth, he doubled in two more and, two innings later, he walked to force in another run, which was his fifth RBI of the evening. Matt Williams contributed three hits to the offense and scores three times. Stottlemyre went 6⅓ innings and gave up the Mets' only run. The final score was 7–1 and the series was tied.

After a day off to rest, travel, and regroup, and with Piazza sitting on the bench with a sprained left thumb, the Mets took the field in Shea Stadium for game three. Reed took the hill and backup catcher Todd Pratt went behind the plate. New York scored first for the third time in the series, and took a 3–2 lead into the bottom of the sixth. At that point, the resurgent Mets scored six times and took a commanding 9–2 lead. Neither team scored again. Alfonso's double was the club's only extra-base hit. Henderson, with three singles, and Olerud, with two, led the 11-hit attack. Reed went six innings for the Mets, and Wendell, Franco, and Hershiser split the remaining three innings. The Mets were one win away from going to the league's championship series.

New York continued to amaze by winning on Saturday, October 9, and acquiring a spot in the NLCS against the Braves.

The Mets' Alfonso homered in the fourth inning, his third four-bagger of the series, to give New York a 1–0 lead. Greg Colbrunn's home run in the top of the fifth knotted the game, 1–1. The Mets took a 2–1 lead in the next inning when Agbayani's double scored Henderson.

Leiter, who had won big games for New York throughout the season, took the one-run lead and a two-hitter into the eighth inning. On June 6, the left-hander beat Roger Clemens and the Yankees in Yankee Stadium to end an eight-game losing streak. He also stopped the seven-game September slide, and had put his club into the division series with a 5–0, route-going shutout over Cincinnati in the wild-card playoff. Leiter walked pinch hitter Turner Ward with two outs in the top of the eighth. Tony Womack reached base on a grounder that Alfonso could not field.

Valentine brought in Benitez to face Jay Bell, and the Diamondbacks second baseman lashed a two-run double which gave Arizona a 3–2 lead. During the bottom of the eighth, Womack misjudged Olerud's routine fly ball to right field that turned a potentially easy out into a baserunner. Alfonso, who was running from first base on the play, reached third. Cedeño's sacrifice fly scored Alfonso, and the back-and-forth game was tied again, 3–3.

Game four went into the bottom of the 10th, and the magic of another memorable moment was witnessed in Shea Stadium by over 56,000 fans. Ventura led off the inning against Matt Mantei, Arizona's premier reliever, who was pitching his third inning. The Mets third sacker flied out to Womack in right.

Pratt provided the memory. With one away, he delivered a long drive to center field that just eluded a leaping Finley's glove as the ball snuck over the eight-foot wall at the 410-foot sign and gave New York a momentous 4–3 win. It was baseball's fourth series-ending home run. The Mets were in the League Championship Series against the Braves, and Pratt and his accomplishment joined a very special list including Bill Mazeroski and the 1960 World Series, Chris Chambliss and the 1976 American League Championship Series, and Joe Carter and the 1993 World Series.

Pratt had brought an interesting history to the Mets. He had been a career backup catcher for the Red Sox, Cubs, and Phillies. When the Seattle Mariners told him they couldn't afford to sign him during the 1996 spring training, he packed his bags and headed home. He went to work for Bucky Dent at his baseball school in Delray Beach, Florida, and spent time managing a Domino's Pizza. The Mets invited him to spring training in 1997, and after some ups and downs between (the club's Triple-A club in) Norfolk and Flushing, he stuck with the parent team. Now he was the newest hero in Mets history.

It took three agonizing seconds for Pratt and the crowd of 56,177 to react to the homer, because many—Pratt included—thought leaping center fielder Steve Finley pulled the ball back into the park. When Finley slumped against the wall, Pratt—who froze around first expecting Finley to flash the ball—broke into a trot as confetti flew and fireworks exploded high over center field....[6]

The win was also a big one for Franco, who was participating in his first postseason. He picked up his first victory after dropping 10 straight decisions since September 13, 1997.

And the win, which put the Mets in the NLCS, was especially exciting for Leiter, since Sandy Koufax, his mentor, was watching his performance from the Mets' VIP box.

In the American League, the wild-card Boston Red Sox had put together a scintillating comeback to beat Cleveland in the division series and capture a place in the League Championship Series against the World Champion New York Yankees. Cleveland had taken the first two games, 3–2 and 11–1. Boston, with their backs to the wall, stunned the Indians, winning the next three by football-like scores of 9–3, 23–7, and 12–8.

As the Mets prepared to head for Atlanta to continue their miraculous comeback, the magic of the fourth game remained:

> It was a ball off Todd Pratt's bat that maybe was over the center-field fence and maybe was not. In that moment between knowing and not knowing, time stood still at old Shea, right before old times came crashing into the place with a roar the Braves could hear in Houston, mostly out of an October Saturday in 1986 when we first found out that anything can happen in the bottom of the 10th.[7]

New York's woes returned when they traveled to Turner Field for the NLCS. Two weeks earlier, the Braves had swept the high-flying Mets in a three-game set. On October 13 and 14, Atlanta swept New York again and sent the Mets back to Shea, trailing 2–0.

The Braves took the opening NLCS game, 4–2, with Maddux picking up the win and Yoshii absorbing the loss. Atlanta scored in the first inning and New York never held the lead. Catcher Eddie Perez, who had taken over for Javy Lopez in July after the All-Star receiver suffered a season-ending knee injury, hit a home run and a double to power Atlanta's attack. Light-hitting shortstop Walt Weiss contributed a double and two singles to the Braves offense. Alfonso was the only Met with two hits and both of them were doubles.

New York's loss the following day was much more disappointing. The Mets jumped out to a 2–0 lead but, in the bottom the sixth, Atlanta score four times on two-run homers by Jordan and Perez off Rogers. The Mets scored in the top of the eighth to make it 4–3. Atlanta manager Bobby

Cox summoned ailing starter John Smoltz from the bullpen to protect the narrow lead, which he did with a perfect inning of relief. It was Smoltz's first relief appearance in a major league career that dated back to 1988.

Alas, the Mets' bats had gone cold again. Olerud, Piazza, and Ventura were 1-for-21 in the series.

During the off-day back in New York, Fred Wilpon, the Mets co-owner, visited with his players as they were working out at Shea. Wilpon was trying to encourage his troops as they prepared for game three the following evening. William C. Rhoden, writing in the *New York Times*, described the club's situation and Wilpon's outlook:

> The Mets have been yanked back to earth, once again, by Atlanta. But when someone asked Wilpon if he was ready to cash in the chips and begin thinking of what a great season this had been, he cut in. "No way, I'm not even going to let you finish. We're in it for this series. We're going to win some games here."[8]

When the NLCS was resumed on Saturday, October 16, Leiter took the mound for the Mets, attempting to end another slide. The Braves sent out Glavine, who was 3–0 against the Mets in 1999.

Leiter walked Atlanta's lead-off hitter Gerald Williams, and Brett Boone followed with a dribbler back to the box. Leiter looked to second base for a possible force on Williams but decided to go to first. His throw was wide and pulled Olerud off the base for an error. Atlanta had runners on first and second with no one out.

Leiter retired Mets killer Chipper Jones on a pop to second. The fans, who were upset because of Jones' early burial of their team, mocked him, chanting, "Lar-ry, Lar-ry, Lar-ry," his given name—and one he didn't like to use.

With one out, Williams and Boone took off on an attempted double steal. Piazza tried to get Boone at second, but his errant throw sailed into center field, enabling Bret to take third. Williams scored on the miscue, and the Braves had taken a 1–0 lead on a walk and a pair of errors. It was the first time all season that New York had committed two errors in one inning.

Mora, starting in center field for the first time in the majors, saved another run when he gunned down Boone after catching Jordan's short fly ball. The bang-bang play, which had Boone barreling into Piazza, left the Mets catcher woozy and suffering from a slight concussion. The collision followed by the out ended the inning, leaving Piazza with time to recover and enabling him to take his spot behind the plate in the top of the second.

The unearned run off Leiter turned out to be the only run of the game as the Mets dropped to 0–3 in the series. Both starting pitchers did masterful jobs. Leiter went seven innings and gave up only three hits. Glavine also went seven, surrendering seven hits while striking out eight Mets. New York's Franco and Benitez handled the Braves in relief, hurling two hitless innings. Left-handers Mike Remlinger worked the eighth inning for Atlanta and John Rocker closed out the game in the ninth to pick up his third series save.

A situation in the ninth inning raised questions in the minds of those who believed that some of Valentine's decisions had not been for the best. With the Mets trailing, 1–0, none out, and Agbayani on first as the result of a base on balls, Valentine sent up Pratt to hit for Ventura. Instead of trying to bunt the tying run to second, Pratt got the hit sign and struck out. Mora flied out and Ordoñez's grounder forced Agbayani at second. Three outs and the game was over.

Reed and Smoltz faced each other in game four. The two teams were scoreless until the bottom of the sixth when Olerud hit a solo home run. Reed entered the top of the eighth having given the Braves only one hit and having faced the minimum 21 batters. He was greeted at that point by successive home runs by Jordan and Ryan Klesko which put Atlanta ahead, 2–1. After Reed retired Andruw Jones, Valentine called Wendell from the bullpen, and the reliever ended the inning without further damage.

Cedeño led off the bottom of the inning for the Mets with a single, his third hit of the game. Smoltz then retired Ordoñez on a popped up sacrifice attempt. Remlinger replaced Smoltz and struck out Agbayani. With two outs, the Braves pitcher walked Mora. Cox then brought in Rocker, who, throughout the series had expressed a deep disdain for the New York fans. The lefty reliever was greeted by a thrown baseball, a cup of beer, other hurled objects, and a lusty round of hisses and boos.

Olerud, who was 0-for-9 against Rocker with five strikeouts for the season, was the first Met to face the lefty reliever with the high-nineties fastball. The two Mets baserunners surprised Rocker and the Braves and executed a double steal to put the tying run at third and the go-ahead run at second. On a 2-and-2 pitch, Olerud got his bat on a low-and-away fastball and hit a three-hopper back up the middle. The high bouncer just eluded Rocker, tipped off shortstop Guillen's glove, and rolled into short center field. Before the ball could be thrown home, two runs had crossed the plate and the Mets had regained the lead, 3–2.

After the Mets were retired, Benitez strolled to the mound to face Atlanta. He had handled them all season, and he did the same that evening: a three-up, three-down inning nailed down the Mets' first win of the series.

It was the third one-run victory in the first four games of the series and, for the second straight day, New York pitchers had held the Braves to only three hits.

On Sunday, October 17, the Mets faced the Braves for what could be the final game in Shea that season. The stadium in Flushing was full with 55,723 fans hoping to see one more miracle. To get it, they would have to sit through the rain and the longest game in postseason history.

Olerud got New York off to a fast start with a two-run homer off Maddux in the bottom of the first. The score remained 2–0 until the top of the fourth when Boone and Chipper Jones hit back-to-back doubles off Yoshii, the Mets starter. Boone scored on Jones' hit to bring the Braves to within one. Jordan's single to left field scored Jones, and it was a 2–2 game. After Yoshii walked Klesko, Hershiser replaced the struggling right-hander and retired Atlanta.

It was 11 innings before another run would cross the plate, During the run drought, both teams had a number of opportunities to score. Both halves of the sixth and the top of the seventh were strange at-bats for the Braves and the Mets.

In the top of the sixth, Atlanta loaded the bases without benefit of a hit. With one away, and two strikes on Maddux, the Braves pitcher attempted a bunt on a surprise suicide squeeze. He failed to make contact, and Klesko, who had broken from third, was hung up in the baseline and eventually tagged out at the plate by Hershiser to end the threat.

Piazza led off the bottom of the sixth for the Mets and hit a chopper toward third. After fielding the ball, Chipper Jones threw low to first, and Klesko dropped it for an error on the first baseman. Ventura, who at the point was 0-for-the-series, was a strikeout victim. Mora blooped a single to right and Piazza stopped at second. Hamilton, who had a pair of hits in his previous at-bats, hit a hard grounder to Klesko, who thought about stepping on first base but threw to second to try to force Mora. The throw was wide of the bag, and Klesko had his second error of the inning. However, with one out and the bases loaded, Ordoñez grounded into a double play on Maddux's first pitch.

In the top of the seventh, the Braves loaded the bases again without the benefit of a hit. With one out, Hershiser's pitch grazed Boone's uniform jersey. Otis Nixon came into the game to run for Boone. Wendell replaced Hershiser and struck out Chipper Jones, with Nixon stealing second on the third strike. After Wendell went 2-and-0 on Jordan, Valentine called Cook from the bullpen to finish an intentional walk to the Braves right fielder. Cox sent up Brian Hunter to hit for Klesko, and Valentine brought in Mahomes to face the pinch hitter. Mahomes walked Hunter on four pitches and the bases were loaded again. Andruw Jones flied out to left to end the inning.

Valentine went to his bullpen regularly during that part of the game. In the seventh and eighth innings he used five pitchers to face 10 Atlanta hitters. Maddux worked seven innings for the Braves, giving up two runs and seven hits. Terry Mulholland followed him to the mound and pitched a pair of scoreless innings. Remlinger, Russ Springer—who issued Atlanta's first walk of the game in the 12th—Rocker, and rookie right-hander Kevin McGlinchy saw action in the game for the Braves.

The game remained tied, 2–2, and went into extra innings. The rain, which had started falling in the fifth inning, was steadier now. In the 13th, Atlanta's Keith Lockhart, who had replaced Boone at second base, slapped a two-out single to right field. Chipper Jones followed with a double to right, and Lockhart, who was off and running on the hit, tried to score from first base to give the Braves the lead. Mora fielded the ball in right, hit Alfonso with a perfect relay throw, and the second baseman pegged the ball to Piazza to nail Lockhart by more than 10 feet. The subsequent collision strained the right forearm of the battered and bruised New York catcher, and Pratt replaced him in the top of the 14th.

In the top of the 15th, the Braves, who had set a postseason record by stranding 17 baserunners, got another opportunity when Weiss led off with a line-drive single to left field. Since both clubs were almost out of pinch hitters, Cox sent McGlinchy, who had pitched the 14th, to try to sacrifice Weiss to second. Dotel, another rookie who was in his third inning of work for the Mets, was wild high to McGlinchy and the count went to 3-and-2. McGlinchy had the take sign on the next pitch, which was a strike, and Weiss stole second base as the hitter was called out. Williams followed with a fly ball to left for the second out. Lockhart delivered again, slamming a triple to right center to put Atlanta ahead, 3–2. After Chipper Jones was intentionally walked, Dotel struck out Jordan to end the rally.

With the Mets possibly facing their final outs of the season, Dunston challenged McGlinchy with one of the most exciting at-bats of 1999 or any other campaign. The veteran right-handed hitter worked the count to 3-and-2 and then fouled off six tough pitches, sending them into the stands along the right-field line. On McGlinchy's next delivery, Dunston singled up the middle. Valentine sent up Dotel, but changed his mind and replaced him with pinch-hitter Matt Franco. Dunston used his speed on a slippery field and stole second to get the tying run into scoring position. McGlinchy walked Franco, putting runners at first and second with no one out.

Out in the Mets bullpen, Reed began throwing in case the game went into the 16th inning. It was the same Reed who had pitched seven innings the day before. Valentine choices were limited to him or Leiter since he had gone through the other nine members of the staff. Cox had decided to stay with McGlinchy to open the 15th since he had gone through his bullpen and did not want to use Kevin Millwood, who was penciled in to start game six—if there was one.

Alfonso dropped a bunt and moved Dunston and Franco up a base. Valentine called Cedeño to run for Franco at second base. Olerud was given an intentional pass to load the bases with one out. Pratt, who had replaced Piazza in the 14th, drew a walk and Dunston was forced home with the tying run. As Dunston crossed the plate, television analyst Joe Morgan uttered, "The Mets will not die!"[9]

Ventura, who had been 0-for-16 before hitting a single in the 11th, came to the plate. He was hoping to lift the ball to the outfield to allow Cedeño to score from third with the winning run. With one swing of the bat, Ventura ended the game in dramatic fashion, blasting McGlinchy's pitch over the right-field wall for a grand-slam home run to bring the Mets a 7–3 win. With Ventura mobbed by teammates between first and second base, and unable to touch any more bases, he had banged one of the most important and exciting singles in baseball postseason history. The Mets had won, 4–3, and were headed back to Atlanta after getting their heart-pounding victory and second win in the NLCS.

Bob Costas, announcing the game on NBC-TV, caught the glory and the confusion of the moment. "I looked at the umpires, but they'd left the scene, but as we were going off the air, we got it from Red Foley," Costas said afterward, referring to the game's official scorer. "For a long time, the scoreboard said 3–3, then 7–3, and as I was leaving, it said 4–3."[10]

It was strange and ironic that "5 hours, 47 minutes" had again become part of the Mets' late-season story. That was the exact length of time that the Reds—and vicariously the Mets—had to wait for the all-important final game of the season to get underway in Milwaukee's rainy County Stadium.

The Braves fans were also getting excited. They had not filled their ballpark for some of the earlier postseason games, but on Tuesday evening, October 19, a record crowd of 52,335 was at Turner Field. In front of the throng, the Mets relived the calamity, exhilaration, exhaustion, and disappointment of the past four weeks all in one game. While New Yorkers were beginning to buzz again about the possibility of the first Subway Series since 1956, the Mets had their minds on winning the sixth game of the NLCS and becoming the first team ever to come back from an 0–3 deficit to take a postseason series to the seventh game. Then they would begin to worry about game seven and what might come after that. On the clubhouse blackboard an optimistic Valentine had written, "Why Not?"

The question was the same as the one that an optimistic Mets team had carried with them to Atlanta for the September 21 series opener against the Braves. The first inning of game six of the NLCS produced the same level of discouragement as the earlier trip to Turner Field.

After Millwood held New York scoreless in the top of the first, Leiter took the mound for the bottom of the inning, starting with three days' rest for only the second time in his career. The left-hander hit Williams, walked Boone, and plunked Chipper Jones to load the bases. Jordan singled through the left side and Atlanta had the lead. Andruw Jones hit a tapper back to the mound, and Leiter's throw to second in an attempt to force Jordan was late. Perez followed with a single, and Leiter was gone after facing six hitters. Five of those six would score, and the Braves held a 5–0 lead after one inning. Disappointment reigned in the New York dugout, and in the hearts of their hopeful fans.

As had been the case recently for the Mets, they would be back, attempting to turn the bad times around. In the top of the sixth, Piazza's sacrifice fly and Hamilton's two-run single brought New York to within two of the Braves, 5–3. Before the resurgent Mets could catch their breath, Jose Hernandez delivered a pinch hit, two-run single off Cook in the bottom of the frame to send Atlanta out to a 7–3 advantage.

But the Mets, once again, refused to die. Before they were finished with their at-bat in the seventh, Piazza capped off a four-run rally with a two-run homer off Smoltz, and the game was deadlocked, 7–7. It looked like it might be the previous night's struggle revisited, but with higher numbers on the board.

An inning later, excitement grew in the New York dugout after the Mets scored to take an 8–7 lead. A key to the run was a successful sacrifice bunt by Ordoñez, who had attempted to sacrifice three times earlier in the series and had popped out on each occasion. An omen, perhaps. Mora's single scored the go-ahead run. Now the Mets had the taste of victory back in their mouths, whereas earlier they were smelling one final defeat.

But the Braves rebounded when pinch-runner Nixon stole second base and went to third on Piazza's errant throw on the steal. He would later score to knot the struggle, 8–8.

Both teams scored in the 10th, and it was 9–9. Outfielders' throws played a big part in both halves of the inning. During the Mets' at-bat, with Agbayani on third base with one out, Pratt hit a short fly to Andruw Jones in center. Agbayani tagged after the catch and made a dash for home. Jones' throw was in time but up the line, and the Met runner slid around Greg Myers to give New York the lead. In the bottom of the 10th, Andruw Jones singled up the middle on a 3–2 pitch from Benitez. After Myers flied out to left, Klesko walked. With runners at first and second, Guillen, pinch-hitting for Weiss, singled to right field scoring Jones. An alert Mora gunned a throw to third base that never touched the ground, nabbing a sliding Klesko for the rookie outfielder's third assist of the series. Instead of runners at first and third with one out, the Braves had Guillen at first with two away. Benitez got out of the inning, and the game went into the 11th.

The Mets went quietly against Springer, and the Braves came to bat facing Rogers. Williams greeted the New York starter-turned-reliever with a double into the left-field corner. Boone dropped a sacrifice toward first base, and Williams scampered over to third. Rogers walked Chipper Jones and Jordan intentionally to load the bases and set up a force out at home. Rogers' first two pitches to Andruw Jones were low. The Braves hitter tapped the next pitch toward third base, but it rolled foul. Ball three followed, and Rogers' fifth pitch was a called strike two. Tension gripped everyone as Rogers stared in at Jones and took the sign for the next pitch. The full-count delivery sailed high and outside for the fatal ball four. Williams sprinted across the plate, the Braves were ticketed to the World Series, and the Mets' season, which was highlighted by an "amazin" final four weeks, was over.

A disappointed Valentine spoke after the game about his heroic team, saying, "I told them they played like champions.... We don't have a trophy, but they did everything they had to."[11]

As the century drew to a close, there had been one more reminder of how powerful the excitement of the comeback and the disappointment of the comedown continue to be for fans of the game.

Notes

1. Judy Battista, "Bats, Balls and Barbs: Mets and Braves Are Ready," *New York Times*, 12 October 1999, Sec. 4, 1.

2. *USA Today Baseball Weekly*, 29 Sept.–5 October 1999, 22.

3. David Waldstein, "Mets Are Zombies on Night of Living Dead," *New York Post*, 2 October 1999, 52.

4. George Vecsey, "Once Again, an October 3 for Baseball History," *New York Times*, 4 October 1999, Sec. 4, 3.

5. Joe Kay and Kit Stier, "Leiter's Gem Crowns Mets' Comeback," *USA Today Baseball Weekly*, 6–12 October 1999, 20.

6. Pat Borzi, "Pratt's 10th-Inning Home Run Clinches One More Trip to Atlanta," *Newark* [NJ] *The Star-Ledger*, 12 October 1999, 60.

7. Mike Lupica, "Another New York Classic Sprints to Destiny's Door," *New York Daily News*, 10 October 1999, 70.

8. William C. Rhoden, "For the Mets, a Dream Deferred," *New York Times*, 16 October 1999, Sec. 4, 1.

9. Joe Morgan while reporting on the game on television, 17 October 1999.

10. Richard Sandomir, "Only Extra Thrills," *New York Times*, 18 October 1999, Sec. 4, 7.

11. "Braves Return to the World Series with 11-Inning Win Over Mets," Major-LeagueBaseball.com, Posted 19 October 1999.

Index